# Pastoral Supervision

# Pastoral Supervision

*A Handbook*

Second Edition

Jane Leach
and
Michael Paterson

scm press

Published in 2015 by SCM Press
Editorial office
3rd Floor
Invicta House
108-114 Golden Lane,
London
EC1Y 0TG

SCM Press is an imprint of Hymns Ancient & Modern Ltd
(a registered charity)
13A Hellesdon Park Road
Norwich NR6 5DR, UK
www.scmpress.co.uk

British Library Cataloguing in Publication data

A catalogue record for this book is available
from the British Library

978 0 334 05344 6

Typeset by Regent Typesetting, London
Printed and bound by
CPI Group (UK) Ltd, Croydon

# Contents

*For Iain who oversees from heaven.*
*For my parents who watch over me with love,*
*and for Mario who knows more than anyone*
*just how much I need supervision.*

Michael Paterson


*For those with whom and from whom I have*
*learnt the value and the practice of supervision: my*
*theological students; my supervisees; my colleagues;*
*and my teachers.*

Jane Leach

# Acknowledgements

This book could not have been written without the many supervision relationships we have been engaged in during the course of our ministries. We are indebted to those who have supervised us, those we have supervised and those we have taught, alongside all of whom we have learnt what it is to be disciples, ministers and pastoral supervisors. We are particularly grateful to those who have given us permission to use their stories as the basis for examples in this book. Without their generosity many of the processes of supervision outlined here would have lacked the vitality and realism their stories offer.

Our thanks are still due to those who helped us in the process of drafting and editing the first edition: Linda Dunbar, the late Robin McGlashan and Jessica Rose for their comments on the text, and David Lyall for his encouragement and the Foreword to that edition.

We are grateful, as ever, to Natalie Watson and the editorial team at SCM for their guidance and careful attention to detail in the production of this second edition. Of course, any remaining errors are our own.

Jane and Michael
*The Feast of the Epiphany 2015*

# Preface to the Second Edition

In the five years since 2010, when this book was first published, significant changes have happened in the world of pastoral supervision.

The work of APSE (Association of Pastoral Supervisors and Educators) continues as a professional body promoting supervision among people of faith and offering accreditation routes for supervisors. Its annual conferences continue to gather people from across a spectrum of ministerial and supervisory approaches. In 2014 APSE entered into a reciprocal partnership with the Australian-based association Transforming Practices.[1] That ongoing work has been supplemented by the establishment of the Institute for Pastoral Supervision and Reflective Practice, whose primary focus is to promote training, publication and research into pastoral supervision.[2] It is a delight to report that, at the time of writing, several people within the UK are now engaged in doctoral research in the field of pastoral supervision.

Recent publications bear witness to the transformative and soulful dimensions of supervision. Shohet's 2011 collection of essays, *Supervision as Transformation*, brings to the fore supervision's inherent invitation to reconnect the practitioner with their own core values and motivation.[3] Thus Weld writes of supervision as 'a base camp where batteries are recharged' and challenges supervisees 'to reach deeply into themselves and connect with the wider human consciousness that supports them in the work they do'.[4] Similarly, Creaner describes supervisory practice as 'an inside-out rediscovery of what I always knew to be true for myself',[5] while Coombe underlines 'supervision's capacity to uncover that which has been inwardly sequestered, abandoned or oppressed and then return its knowledge, energy and value to the individual or the group'.[6] Supervision as an invitation to vocational regeneration underpins Paterson and Rose, *Enriching Ministry: Pastoral Supervision in Context*, which forms a sequel to this book.[7]

In the field of training for pastoral supervision, in 2010 the only course available was a two-day intensive skills workshop that Jane and Michael had established at Wesley House, Cambridge. While this continues to flourish, there are also regular short courses at Sarum College, Salisbury, a one-year certificate course in Nottingham, a similar extended course in Belfast and a professional diploma in pastoral supervision and reflective practice held in Glasgow.[8] In addition, a diploma in cross-professional creative supervision with an emphasis on the soulful dimensions of practice has been established in Edinburgh.[9]

At the level of *praxis*, the three levels of seeing based on John's account of the resurrection recorded in the fourth Gospel (see page 70) has been widely adopted within a model of Values-based Reflective Practice promoted by the Scottish Government for use in the Scottish NHS. Two consecutive independent research projects have shown its value in making difficult conversations possible. Uses include debriefing after critical incidents and responding to complaints. In practice it is complemented by the adaptation of a hermeneutic tool drawn from feminist and liberation theology, which asks five questions of any given situation: Whose needs were met? What does the situation have to say about our abilities and capabilities? Whose voice was heard and who was silenced? What was valued, overvalued or undervalued? And what does the situation reveal about you (the practitioner or the team)? Those five questions translate the APSE definition of pastoral supervision as theologically/spiritually rich, psychologically informed, contextually sensitive and praxis based into a practical method used to aid reflection in every health board in Scotland.[10]

Meanwhile within the churches more serious attention has started to be paid to the need for training for those exercising supervisory roles. The Methodist Church and the Church of Scotland now require those supervising its probationer ministers to have received some training, and various dioceses of the Church of England have established regular supervision groups for training incumbents. There is also increasing recognition of some of the complexity of the work in which clergy are involved – often without adequate contexts for reflection and the disentanglement of difficult issues. The Methodist Church's forthcoming report on its handling of past cases of abuse and neglect, for example, will recommend the systematic development of pastoral supervision for its ministers.

Finally, this book, while substantially an update of the 2010 edition, contains several new elements:

- A new chapter outlining a generic approach to pastoral supervision written for those who do not share the dominant therapeutic paradigms underpinning most of the extant supervisory literature (Chapter 2).
- A new chapter on attending to the body (Chapter 6), which introduces some of the literature of creative supervision and relates this to a theology of incarnation.
- An expansion of the three levels of seeing with prompts to root this in practice (Chapter 3).
- An outline of Values-based Reflective Practice, which marries the three levels of seeing with five core questions drawn from theological reflection (Appendix 4).
- A list of professional bodies and associations that promote pastoral supervision (Appendix 6).
- A new list of suggested reading.
- Eleven new diagrams outlining the structure of a supervision session (Figures 2.1; 2.2; 2.3); an expansion of the three levels of seeing (Figures 3.1; 3.2; 3.3); the empowerment triangle (Figure 4.5); Hawkins and Shohet's seven modes (Figure 5.1); an aide for choosing how best to work in any given supervision context (Figure 5.2); four kinds of power (Figure 8.3) and a structure for group supervision (Figure 9.2).

Pastoral supervision draws upon a wide range of resources, which it harnesses to support the well-being of God's people. While it borrows much from other disciplines, we remain convinced, with Karl, that 'in a time of spiritual hunger and institutional deterioration' pastoral supervisors 'have an important mission to demonstrate that the "rejected stone" of spirituality may indeed be the "cornerstone" of environments that sustain practitioners and serve people well'.[11] It is for that purpose that this book is offered.

## Notes

1 See www.transformingpractices.com.au.

2 See www.ipsrp.org.uk.

3 Robin Shohet (ed.), 2011, *Supervision as Transformation: A Passion for Learning*, London and Philadelphia: Jessica Kingsley.

4 Nicki Weld, 2012, *A Practical Guide to Transformative Supervision for the Helping Professions: Amplifying Insight*, London: Jessica Kingsley, p. 115.

5 Mary Creaner, 2011, 'Reflections on learning and transformation in supervision: a crucible of my experience', in Shohet, *Supervision as Transformation*, p. 147.

6 Nicola Coombe, 2011, 'Fear and stepping forward anyway', in Shohet, *Supervision as Transformation*, p. 182.

7 Michael Paterson and Jessica Rose (eds), 2014, *Enriching Ministry: Pastoral Supervision in Context*, London: SCM Press.

8 These courses are run by members of the Institute of Pastoral Supervision and Reflective Practice. Further details may be found at www.ipsrp.org.uk.

9 This course is run by Michael Paterson and Jessica Rose. Further details may be found at www.creativesupervisiontraining.org.uk.

10 Values-based Reflective Practice is outlined in Appendix 4.

11 J. C. Karl, 1998, 'Discovering spiritual patterns: Including spirituality in staff development and the delivery of psychotherapy services', *American Journal of Pastoral Counseling* 1:4, pp. 1–23.

# Introduction

This book is a practical guide to the ministry of pastoral supervision. It is intended to be useful to chaplains, ministers, spiritual directors and pastoral counsellors who supervise the work of others, and to anyone seeking supervision for their own ministry. It provides an approach to supervision that begins in prayer and Scripture yet which is open to insights from other supervision disciplines. It offers examples of pastoral supervision in practice and tools for use in self-supervision and when supervising others.

## What is Pastoral Supervision?

In a nutshell, **pastoral supervision**[1] is a relationship between two or more disciples who meet to consider the ministry of one or more of them in an intentional and disciplined way. Such an arrangement allows each person being supervised to give an account of their work, to explore their responses, review their aims and develop their strategies and skills. Pastoral supervision is practised for the sake of the supervisee, providing a space in which their well-being, growth and development are taken seriously, and for the sake of those among whom the supervisee works, providing a realistic point of accountability within the body of Christ for their work as chaplains, local church ministers, spiritual directors, pastoral counsellors or youth workers.

Although the term 'pastoral supervision' may be new to some readers, the practice of disciplined reflection on the work of ministry with a colleague may well be familiar, perhaps from a training context or staff team. In some contexts this may be referred to as consultancy or mentoring or coaching. Although each of these terms may have nuances of meaning according to setting, our choice of the term 'pastoral supervision' is intended to place the practice of disciplined reflection with another as an act of accountability within the body of Christ, while also acknowledging that there is much for the churches to learn about effective reflection on ministry from other supervision disciplines.

In this sense, although 'pastoral supervision' may be new terminology,[2] practices of Christian accountability and oversight are as old as the Church itself. In Chapter 1 we explore, for example, the relationship between Jesus and his disciples as he sends them out to minister, and afterwards listens to their account of all they have done and taught.

## Why Pastoral Supervision?

The book arises from our shared commitment to developing the practice of pastoral supervision within the churches – a commitment that was forged through our experiences of local ministry, healthcare chaplaincy and theological education.

As a Methodist presbyter working in rural Norfolk, Jane found that, beyond the structures of training, ministry was an isolating way of life that could easily lose focus and direction. Although there was a staff team, this did not provide a context for her growth as a practitioner through reflection with others or a realistic means of being accountable for the sometimes sensitive work she was doing with individuals and the demanding work of helping churches re-imagine mission amid cultural change and numerical decline.

While working at the London Lighthouse with those affected by HIV and AIDS, Michael found himself needing to rethink his theology if it was to be relevant to those among whom he was ministering. Ironically, it was not within the chaplaincy team that he found the means of making a bridge between his theology and his practice, but in the context of psychotherapeutic supervision with an Anglican priest. The need to bring to bear both the insights of secular disciplines and the perspectives of theology has been a passion of his ever since.

This commitment underpins the way each chapter of this book begins by reflecting on the Scriptures before bringing these into conversation with the tools from other supervision disciplines that we have found helpful. This is not to suggest that there is always a neat coincidence between what the Christian narrative is saying and what other disciplines are bringing. Rather, we find such dialogue fruitful in enriching our understanding of the Scriptures as well as improving our practice of pastoral supervision.[3]

That joint practice began to develop in 2000, when we were both appointed to work within the Cambridge Theological Federation as directors of pastoral studies for ordinands. While we had both already discovered the need for supervision for our own practice, it was as we began to supervise others that we realized the importance of systematically thinking through what effective pastoral supervision might be. It was in peer supervision with one another and in supervising student ministers that we first began to develop the approaches and tools offered here. Latterly these have been refined as we have trained senior ministers and chaplains in pastoral supervision.

The generosity of those with whom we have worked in giving their permission for their stories to be told has meant that this book is full of concrete examples of supervision practice. Names have been changed in the text to prevent identification, but we hope that the examples explored provide a window into the processes of pastoral supervision and also into our own ongoing learning process.

In the five years since this book was first published we have both continued to learn about the practice and theory of pastoral supervision. Michael is currently engaged in doctoral research exploring the intentional use of the self in pastoral ministry and supervision. Both Jane and Michael have undertaken a diploma in creative supervision at the London School of Psychodrama and some of our learning from that context is contained in the new Chapter 6: Attending to the Body.

## How to Use This Book

For those who are already acting as pastoral supervisors we hope this book will function as a useful **reflective** companion to help you think about your work and the support you receive for it. It may offer you new tools as it brings together **creative, narrative** and **action methods** and develop your awareness of some new dimensions of pastoral supervision.

For those new to supervising the work of others or who would like to offer supervision as part of their own ministry, this book should provide a useful orientation to key concepts and practices within the emerging discipline. You may find it helpful to reflect on your own learning needs as a supervisor before you embark on reading the book, or as you come to the end. For this purpose a learning needs analysis is provided at Appendix 5.

For those seeking supervision the book should help you refine what you are looking for in a supervisor and provide both a flavour of pastoral supervision and some techniques of self-supervision that can help you work out, month by month, what you want to take to a supervisor. The exercises will help you to develop the **reflexive** ability that is necessary to make good use of pastoral supervision.

Although the book takes a practical approach and is designed to support the development of good practice in supervision, we do not believe that this is best learnt solely from reading. If pastoral supervision is a **Christian practice,**[4] then it needs to be learnt within the Christian community. This is not least because accountability within Christian ministry has a certain mutuality about it, whether it is expressed through a cathedral chapter, ministerial synod or local ministry team. It is certainly not a good idea to offer to supervise others without being in a supervision relationship with a more experienced practitioner yourself. To sit with someone as their supervisor is to be in a position of power, whether this is done by personal arrangement or happens as part of your institutional role. Awareness of the power you have and how to use it for the good of those you work with is an essential dimension of all Christian practices, and is best monitored by

4

being in supervision yourself. This dimension of pastoral supervision is explored in more detail in Chapter 8. However, because pastoral supervision is an emerging discipline, finding a supervisor is not necessarily easy. Help with locating a pastoral supervisor or pastoral supervision group can be found through the Association of Pastoral Supervisors and Educators (**APSE**).[5] Help in finding training in supervision can be found via the website of the Institute of Pastoral Supervision and Reflective Practice.[6] Whether you are engaged in pastoral supervision as part of your work or are exploring the possibility of finding a supervisor or starting a peer supervision group, we encourage you to see this book as a work book and therefore to keep a journal as you read it. In this you can do the reflective exercises and keep a record of what is happening in those relationships where you act as supervisor. These records will function not just as an aide-memoire, but to offer you some self-supervision and provide material to take to your own supervision sessions.

## Notes

1 Terms in bold type can be checked in the Glossary at the back of this book.

2 For example, in the UK the Association of Pastoral Supervisors and Educators (APSE) was launched only in 2009.

3 We take our lead from Clodovis Boff: 'We need not look for formulas to "copy" from or techniques to "apply" from Scripture. What Scripture will offer us is rather something like orientations, models, types, directives, principles, inspirations – elements permitting us to acquire, on our own initiative, a "hermeneutic competency" and thus the capacity to judge – on our own initiative, in our own right – "according to the mind of Christ", or "according to the Spirit" the new, unpredictable situations with which we are continually confronted. The Christian writings offer us not a *what* but a *how*, a manner, a style, a spirit.' Clodovis Boff, 1987, *Theology and Praxis: Epistemological Foundations*, Maryknoll, NY: Orbis, ch. 8, 'Hermeneutics: constitution of theological pertinency', p. 149, emphasis in original.

4 Craig Dykstra and Dorothy C. Bass, 2002, 'A theological understanding of Christian Practices', in Miroslav Volf and Dorothy C. Bass (eds), *Practicing Theology: Beliefs and Practices in Christian Life*, Grand Rapids:

Eerdmans, p. 18, define Christian practices in the following way: 'things Christian people need to do together over time to address fundamental human needs in response to the light of God's active presence for the life of the world'.

5 For further information about APSE see www.pastoralsupervision. org.uk. It aims to promote good practice in pastoral supervision through (i) providing a system of accreditation for pastoral supervisors and educators in pastoral supervision; (ii) supporting initiatives in the training of pastoral supervisors; (iii) fostering groups for the support, accountability and continuing development of pastoral supervisors; (iv) encouraging conversation among the various traditions and contexts of pastoral supervision and pastoral supervision education.

6 See www.ipsrp.org.uk.

# I

# Attending to Vision

**Summary**

In this chapter we argue that supervision is a core practice of the Christian Church. Because any authentic ministry is a share in Christ's ministry, it is shared with others in Christ. Although this is an ideal espoused widely in the churches, in practice ministry can be an isolated and isolating experience. Here we argue that mutual accountability in Christian ministry is essential and that it is rooted in the God who calls us into covenant relationship in the body of Christ. While supervision is also practised in other communities and professions, part of the distinctiveness of pastoral supervision is its attention to the vision and vocation into which God is calling us. Towards the end of the chapter, readers are invited to consider how they are accountable in practice and how they might establish a covenantal mode of supervision that is grounded in God's covenant with the Church in Jesus Christ.

He called the twelve and began to send them out two by two ... The apostles gathered around Jesus, and told him all that they had done and taught. He said to them, 'Come away to a deserted place all by yourselves and rest a while.' For many were coming and going, and they had no leisure even to eat. And they went away in the boat to a deserted place by themselves.

Mark 6.7, 30–32

7

## A Vision for Pastoral Supervision

Reading this text with those engaged in ministry often results in the laughter of recognition. Those who have struggled to find time to come away from their responsibilities know what it means to have no leisure even to eat. They know too well that there are always more needs than can be met, and that success breeds work. Just as the disciples are spotted leaving and are met by hungry crowds when they land, so those in ministry who establish a reputation for being effective will struggle to outrun those who seek them out.

If there is no time to eat in such a life, then there is similarly no time to reflect, but Jesus here underlines the importance of rest, food and opportunity to reflect on ministry in his company and in the company of others sent out in his name. Moreover, the gathering of the apostles around Jesus mirrors the sending out of the apostles earlier in the chapter. Both emphasize the point that the ministry the disciples exercise – proclaiming repentance, casting out demons, anointing the sick – is the ministry of Jesus himself: they are sent as his representatives; they are gathered back to share with him what they have done. It is not just in theory that the disciples are Christ's apostles (those sent by him); their accountability is made concrete in their willingness to discuss with Jesus what has been going on.

Although no one in the churches today would want to deny that authentic ministry is a share in Christ's ministry and is accountable to Christ, it can be tempting to spiritualize and individualize what this means. We can argue that while Jesus of Nazareth was on earth the disciples were able to report to him directly; now Christ is ascended into heaven, we are accountable to Christ through prayer. This, of course, is right. Prayer should include us laying open to God what is happening in the ministries we exercise and listening for what the Holy Spirit is saying to us. Yet prayer is a hard discipline; most of us need help to keep us faithful and honest in prayer, and in order to discern what the Holy Spirit is saying to us we need to be part of the Christian community. If

8

we are tempted to think that we do not need supervision because we are people of prayer, this can be an attempt to avoid telling the truth about our ministries. Often it is the courage of others in a group that can help us to find the truths that we ourselves have buried.

Jane remembers being part of a group of Methodist ministers who had been working for five years since leaving initial training. They had all been invited to write a paper outlining what the first five years of ministry had been like for them. The first couple of papers presented were quite upbeat, telling the success stories. The third contribution was more honest about the pain and struggle that ministry also involves. Gradually those who had presented earlier started to amend their stories, admitting to doubts, to exhaustion, to a panic attack while conducting a funeral, to relationship difficulties. Partly the group were learning to trust each other; partly the honesty of one enabled the rest to be more truthful to themselves. Everyone's prayers and stories became more honest as people became more willing to open more of their lives to Christ's judgement and healing.

The Church – the body of Christ – is the community we are given in which to discern together who Christ is and what Christ is saying. Just like those who in the time of Jesus were sent out in pairs, so too those sent in his name today need partners in ministry; we also need time for retreat with others engaged in ministry: time in which we help one another to open up what is really going on and to listen to what the Holy Spirit is saying to us. Yet when we get together we can also need help to deepen our conversation to a level beyond the superficial. Too often if gatherings of those in ministry are not characterized by the telling of success stories and trying to outdo each other with tales of how many hours we have worked without a break, then they are dominated by moaning about the structures and systems within which we work, or about those who seem to have power over our lives. If the community of the Church is to help us honestly to reflect on our ministries, in our experience there needs to be some structure, some skill, some agreement or someone appointed to help us to be intentional in doing this.

In Mark 6 it is Jesus who is intentional and focused. Intentionally he makes space to listen to the apostles and to provide time for them to rest. In the post-resurrection Church – in a manner akin to what we do in order to worship – we need to set aside particular times when we will relate in particular ways and appoint particular people who can help us to keep to our intentions. This is the role of a pastoral supervisor. Whether he or she is working with a group or with an individual, with someone she or he manages or someone who has chosen him or her as an external supervisor, with an experienced practitioner or someone new to ministry, the task of the pastoral supervisor is to be intentional and help others to be intentional about the time spent together. In other words, if supervision is to be effective, supervisors need to have a clear sense of what supervision is (and is not).

## A Definition of Pastoral Supervision

In October 2008, the Association of Pastoral Supervisors and Educators (APSE) was formed around an agreed definition of pastoral supervision.[1] The full text is printed at Appendix 1 but the opening statements set down useful markers in helping pastoral supervisors identify what it is they are offering. APSE suggests that pastoral supervision is:

1. a 'regular, planned, intentional and boundaried *space* in which a practitioner skilled in supervision (the supervisor) meets with one or more other practitioners (the supervisees) to look together at the supervisees' practice'.
2. 'a *relationship* characterized by trust, confidentiality, support and openness that gives the supervisee freedom and safety to explore the issues arising in their work'.

So far these statements might be common to any practice of supervision. Distinctive in the definition of *pastoral* supervision, however, is the third point of the APSE definition, that pastoral supervision is 'spiritually/theologically rich' and 'works within a framework of spiritual/theological understanding in dialogue with the supervisee's world view and work'. *Pastoral* supervision, then, presupposes the spiritual or religious orientation of the supervisor and declares its interest in the belief systems and faith commitments of those who come for supervision. Although – for example, in the healthcare context – not everyone who comes for pastoral supervision may necessarily be Christian, a pastoral supervisor is going to be interested in and motivated by the world view, sense of vocation and vision of their supervisees, and informed by their own.

Extracting the word 'vision' from the word 'supervision' suggests that the term lends itself to word play. 'Supervision' may be seen as a kind of super-seeing – or seeing over; getting an overview; seeing things in the perspective of a broader vision. The word 'supervision' is the Latin version of the Greek word ***episcope***, literally, 'oversight', and is most readily associated with forms of governance in the Church, particularly bishops who exercise personal episcopal oversight.

Pointing this out perhaps suggests that supervision is a kind of watching over – with the unpleasant connotations of being watched to make sure there are no 'oversights'. However, the Methodist ordination service uses the phrase 'watching over' in rather a different tone: 'These things are your common duty and delight. In them you are to watch over one another in love.'[2] This restores the sense of mutuality in collegial oversight and has echoes of the language of covenant. In addition, 'watching over in love' is a reminder of the way Luke's Gospel uses the word *episkeptomai* (from the same route as *episcope*) to speak of God visiting and redeeming his people. This visiting is not understood as popping in to check up on things, but as God coming into the life of the people of Israel as a steady and reliable presence. Supervisors who are not constantly checking up on those they supervise, but are able to be a steady, reliable presence, are worth their weight in gold for they enable those with whom they sit in supervision to see their ministry both in its detail and in the perspective of the kingdom. The metaphors of sight buried in the word 'supervision' suggest that ministry which does not attend to its vision is short-sighted.

This implication of the word 'oversight' came home to Jane on holiday in Corfu. As she drove over the mountain range which forms the backbone of Corfu she passed signposts for a town called Episkopii. Hearing the echoes of *episkopos*, the New Testament word for bishop, she expected, perhaps, an ancient monastery. To her surprise, what she encountered was a place with a view. Rounding a corner the vista opened out from the mountains right down to the sea. Here what was close up could be seen in the perspective of the broader vision.

In this light supervision becomes a practice that can help us see our ministry in broader perspective and in particular can help us attend to the horizon of our vision.

## Attending to Vision

For Christians, in broad terms, our vision is a vision of the kingdom of God, rooted in Christ; yet the way each person in ministry holds that vision and understands their role within it is unique. In this sense, Rowan Williams might have supervision in mind when he asks:

> 'Are you looking *into* your vision? Are you letting yourself be shaped and changed by what you see?' I'm asking, in fact, about the precise degree to which your vision is for you what you live by from day to day, a matter of life and death, sense and nonsense. Are you attending to your vision? Are you stripping yourself in prayer before the terrible and searching Word of God? Are you being refined in that fire? And am I? Is my vision doing that to me, breaking and remaking my thoughts and words, my heart and mind? I have no right to destroy your vision, nor you mine. I have no business to devalue your understanding or make light of your struggles, nor you mine. But we have the right – and perhaps the duty – to put the questions to each other and hear them from each other.[3]

The way Rowan Williams uses the word 'vision' here is similar to the way Christian people often use the word 'vocation'. Both ask the question, 'What is God calling you to?', not just in the sense of what God is calling us to do in a particular situation, but who God is calling us to be – as individuals, as communities and as the whole human race. If supervision is to be faithfully Christian, it needs to attend to these dimensions as well as to the particulars of the actual situations in which ministers find themselves: what is in the foreground needs to be seen in the perspective of the broader vision.

Supervision is an active process of seeking clarity where things are unclear, of recovering vision where it is enveloped in mist and of bringing unseen practice to the loving eye of someone (a supervisor) who wants nothing less than the very best for supervisees and for those to whom they minister. Two mantras underpin the supervisory process and reveal its missiological thrust:

- We reflect on the past in the present in order to improve the future.[4]
- Reflection turns history into learning.[5]

It is that future-facing, other-centred (as opposed to pastor or practitioner-centred) character of supervision that distinguishes it from personal therapy or spiritual accompaniment. Effective pastoral supervision recognizes that the gifts of ministry are treasures held in earthenware jars – jars that can be broken, chipped or cracked. As such, it helps those who minister to ensure that the gifts they have received are not kept for themselves but are shared as generously and effectively as possible with others. Supervision therefore invites a lively and active dialogue between past, present and future. This may be committed to memory using the acronym MAP, in which:

M is for motivation,
A for actual practice,
P for potential practice.

Using MAP helps practitioners reconnect the 'why' of personal vocation with the 'what' of everyday activity. It has been our experience that when practitioners are asked to bring their hidden motivational drivers to the ears of their supervisor, their answers provide a highly personal form of self-audit in which the gaps between vision and reality, espoused practice and actual practice are identified and become the catalyst for change. In the context of a demoralized NHS, Michael regularly asks healthcare practitioners what brought them into the profession (Motivation). Their answers invariably reveal a set of values about dignity, care and compassion. He then asks them to think about how those motivational values played out in their most recent working day. Was dignity to the fore in what they were doing? Was compassion compromised (Actual practice)? Finally, he asks them how they want to express their vocational values when they return to work after supervision (Potential practice).

This MAP, as well as encapsulating the core purposes of pastoral supervision, is being suggested as conversation to begin a supervision relationship because it enables supervisees to express something about their vocation to their supervisor, which enables the supervisor to help them evaluate their current practice in the light of their animating vision.

In an ecclesial context an example of how having established a sense of this motivational vision early on can be helpful in a supervision session is provided by Dave's story. On the first occasion on which an ecumenical group of six ministers met for supervision, each was asked to think about their vocation and their vision for ministry in their context. The words of Rowan Williams quoted above were read out and each person in the group was asked to choose a passage from the Bible that articulated the sense of the vision to which he or she, as a minister, was called. Having written the passage out on a blank postcard, they were then asked to ring those words or phrases they felt were key. In turn, each person shared their words with the group and questions of clarification were asked. Dave, an Anglican priest, shared the following verses from the opening of Romans 12. He placed particular emphasis on the words italicized here:

I appeal to you therefore, brothers and sisters, by the mercies of God, to present your bodies as a *living sacrifice, holy* and acceptable to God, which is your spiritual worship. Do *not* be *conformed* to this world, but be *transformed* by the renewing of your minds, so that you may discern what is the will of God – what is good and acceptable and *perfect*.

At the opening of the group this provided an opportunity for us to get to know each other better as ministers and disciples by gaining a glimpse of what shaped and motivated each of us. In a subsequent session, however, the worth of having done this was demonstrated when Dave presented a problem he was having. The story started off being about his curate who, in Dave's view, had been badly treated by the archdeacon. Although the issue was ostensibly about the curate, it quickly became apparent that the energy in the story surrounded Dave's fury with the archdeacon, and also why Dave was having such difficulty articulating it. Having already heard that what was important in Dave's vision of his ministry was his call to holiness, it was possible to see why the situation was so intolerable. Dave felt that the archdeacon's actions had been unholy, but what was harder for him to handle was the fact that his own sense of holiness censored and suppressed his ability to feel anger towards the archdeacon in the first place. The fruit of the session was in the combination of the foreground – the particular incident involving Dave's archdeacon – and his wider vision of a call to holiness. Without trying to alter Dave's vision for his ministry, the group were able to help him own up to his anger and to express it. In the process, Dave's understanding of the place of anger within a holy life shifted – he experienced the fact that there were holy ways of expressing anger within a group willing to bear it with him. This enabled him to see himself, the archdeacon and his curate more clearly and offered him some perspective in which to make decisions about how to proceed.

This is an example of how pastoral supervision can help those engaged in ministry attend to their vision. Tools for distilling and articulating the vision we have for our ministry are not limited to this one exercise, but finding ways to do this is important for a number of reasons. First, it helps the supervisor or the supervision group understand the kind of minister the person presenting feels called to be and to help them realize their particular calling rather than working on the basis of an inarticulate, generalized and perhaps illusory sense of a shared vision of Christian ministry; this helps to prevent supervisors unwittingly trying to make their supervisees in their own image as sometimes conflicting visions of ministry can be articulated and differences explored rather than suppressed.

Second, it helps the practitioner and those being supervised pinpoint discrepancies between their vision and the practice of their ministry in day-to-day life. These discrepancies are often the source of tension, or feelings or guilt, failure or resentment, or the unwitting cause of conflict with others.

Third, it helps bring assumptions about the aims and direction of ministry into the supervision space as one of those things which might need attention. More will be said in Chapter 7 about the way the supervisor will listen for those aims and values that are not just explicitly named but embedded in the stories the minister tells about their work. In his book *Pastoral Care and Counselling*,[6] Gordon Lynch suggests that all practitioners of pastoral care have a vision of what they do and a vision of what makes for a good life. If this remains unexamined, it can be unhelpfully imposed on others yet never internalized or embodied in the life and ministry of the pastoral carer.

It is not very easy to practise what we preach. Gordon Lynch suggests that there are disciplines, however, that can help us put our practice alongside our best vision of ourselves so that we can ask questions about the relationship between the two. Sometimes we need to repent our inattention to our vision; sometimes we need to listen to our practice, which is better than our ideas about what we think we are supposed to be doing, and to amend our vision; sometimes we need to dig deeper into the reasons why we find our vision impossible to put into practice.

To create a relationship in which attention to vision is possible demands high levels of safety and trust. Both supervisors and supervisees need a clear sense of what the time is for, and discussing this at the outset of a supervision relationship is essential for the creation of a boundaried and intentional space in which God can work. For Kenneth Pohly, an American Methodist minister and founder of the Pohly Institute for Pastoral Supervision, it is the notion of covenant that helps him stay focused in this way: 'When I sit with another person either as supervisor or supervisee to reflect upon our mutual ministry, it occurs within a covenant which not only defines what our ministry is, but who we are as ministers.'[7]

## Pastoral Supervision as Covenant[8] Relationship

For Kenneth Pohly, supervision occurs within the covenant established by God. We belong to one another because of Christ and in and through Christ. This means there is no room for judgementalism – nor for trying to mould another's ministry in our own image. It also means that when we come to another person as supervisor we trust that their intention is to help us see our ministry clearly; to help us tell the truth about ourselves as ministers and to open ourselves to what the Holy Spirit is saying. Although within a supervision relationship one person acts as supervisor, this is done within the context of the body of Christ in which it is understood that the supervisor stands before the same God and is in need of similar contexts for reflection. In any given supervision relationship, supervisor and supervisee(s) will have differentiated roles.

In some contexts where supervision is practised, there is a hierarchical relationship between the parties. A healthcare chaplain may be supervised by a line manager; a training incumbent may need to write a report on a curate; a college tutor can influence whether or not an ordinand is ordained. To pretend otherwise is an illusion and always leads to problems later on – either hard things cannot be said or they are left to appraisals or written reports and the supervisee then feels that trust has been betrayed. In less formal contexts where supervision is arranged between individuals or groups, the facilitator still needs to be aware of their power and their role if the time is to have structure and purpose and meet the needs of the supervisee. The difference that context makes will be explored in much greater detail in Chapter 8, but important in all situations is the production and monitoring of a supervision covenant.

In secular or educational supervision contexts such a document is likely to be called a supervision contract or a learning agreement. In many respects its purpose is the same: to make clear what the aims and boundaries of the arrangement are and to clarify the roles and responsibilities of the various participants. Whatever we call them we should take them seriously since:

> Care and detail over contracts is a form of love towards those we don't know very well. It's a recognition that life is full of unexpected pitfalls, and contracts are a way of holding one another to honesty and honour in the face of temptation and distraction. Contracts can give us security and trust. We should always aspire for every relationship to become a covenant, but we should never let any relationship fall below the level of a contract.[9]

Calling the agreement a covenant is not, however, incidental. It recalls the triadic structure[10] of any relationship within the body of Christ, which not only recalls us to our common humanity and discipleship before the one who calls and sends us, but allows us to let the other be Christ's representative to us in this time and for this purpose. It also recalls us to the central point of Mark 6: that supervision should enable us better to tell the stories of our ministries to God in Christ and to listen to what the Holy Spirit is saying to us; in other words, that we should remember that we represent Christ for each other and should expect the Holy Spirit to be an active participant in pastoral supervision.

If pastoral supervision is understood as a way of attending to vision, it will explicitly want to engage with the supervisee's sense of vocation. If supervision is understood as covenant, it will affect the way the relationship is shaped by prayer and a shared sense of discipleship.

Establishing a Christian framework and ethos for supervision will influence the whole way it is carried out: the venue; the structure; the way the room is laid out; what happens within the session. More attention is paid to these dimensions of supervision practice in Chapter 2.

## The Focus of Pastoral Supervision

In establishing what pastoral supervision is, however, it is perhaps important to explore what it is not. Although some elements such as prayer and reading Scripture together may feature, it is important to be clear about the topics that are particular to pastoral supervision. These are different, for example, from those that belong to **pastoral counselling** or **spiritual direction**.

The definition of pastoral supervision offered by APSE places the emphasis on the work of the practitioner and the supervisee as minister. Although a minister's discipleship and personal life are intimately intertwined with the kind of minister they are and can be, and it is important that a supervisee should be able to bring anything that has a bearing on their working life to supervision, nevertheless the supervisor needs to be clear that their role is to work on spiritual and personal matters with their supervisee only in so far as they impact upon those with whom they work as ministers.

So, for example, if in supervision a personal bereavement is repeatedly what takes the time, but there is no opportunity to explore how this is affecting the practitioner's work, it is likely that in order to be available for pastoral supervision the supervisee needs some additional pastoral care or counselling. While it would be unrealistic to expect that a significant bereavement should not affect someone's work and to preclude it from conversation or enquiry in supervision, it is a question of balance and focus and shared expectations. This includes the expectation that, if a supervisor thinks the supervisee needs more support in a particular area, they should say so in order to free up the supervision space for ministry-focused work.

Discussing expectations of pastoral supervision is an important dimension of establishing a working supervision relationship. This may well involve discussing the supervisee's prior experience of being supervised; it may also involve clarifying the differences between pastoral supervision and mentoring or consultancy.

## The Tasks of Pastoral Supervision

Another way to think about a definition of pastoral supervision is to consider its tasks. Writing in the field of counselling supervision, Francesca Inskipp and Brigid Proctor, with their **functional model of supervision**, suggest that supervision has three generic functions: the normative, the formative and the restorative[11] (see Figure 1.1).

Inskipp and Proctor's model of supervision may be conceptualized as a three-legged stool. Although the context and stage of development of the supervisee will influence the relative prominence of the three functions, they argue that the stool will topple over if one of the functions is missing. They also suggest that each supervisor has preferences between the functions and is likely to emphasize one at the expense of the others. Holding the three tasks of supervision in one's mind can help the supervisor make sure they do not neglect their least favoured mode of working when it is the one most needed.

The **restorative function** is about supporting the supervisee. The work of many ministers, priests and chaplains is exhausting and isolating. Simply being held and heard is part of this function. If the supervisor can listen to the supervisee's feelings about their work and contain them, this is not only an important part of building a supervision relationship but an important part of the supervision itself. This function relates to our discussion about helping the supervisee to connect with their vision and sense of vocation and to gather back to themselves those parts of them that get lost in the work: their sense of humour; their ability to get angry; their ability to ask for help; their ability to preserve some space for themselves; their ability to think straight; their ability to

## Figure 1.1 The three-legged stool of supervision

### Restorative

Supports the supervisee through:

- Active listening.
- Encouragement.
- Feedback.
- Opportunity for discharging feelings.
- Helping them connect with their vision/sense of vocation.
- Helping them recover parts of the self that have got lost in the work.
- Recharging energies.
- Sharing ideas and creative play.

### Normative

Deals with managerial issues and boundaries within the supervision session and beyond it:

- Is the supervisee safe to work with others or do I need to intervene?
- Are there issues of competency to address?
- What policies and procedures does this supervisee need to work to?
- What codes of ethics are relevant and are they being adhered to?
- Are the boundaries of our work clearly set out?
- Am I sticking to them?
- Am I able to challenge my supervisees if they stray from them?

### Formative

Forming the supervisee's work through:

- Guidance on how to interpret or handle situations.
- Teaching about aspects of the work.
- Developing their skills.
- Helping them develop self-awareness.
- Introducing new areas of knowledge/suggesting reading.
- Suggesting different perspectives or ways of tackling things.
- Encouraging growth and change.
- Rehearsing new strategies or roles.

Adapted for the pastoral context from Francesca Inskipp and Brigid Proctor (1993) 1995, *Making the Most of Supervision Part 1: The Art, Craft and Tasks of Counselling Supervision*, Bend, OR: Cascade Publications.

connect with their own feelings. If ministers are to function well, they need the whole of themselves available for their work; one of the tasks of pastoral supervision is to help to restore them to themselves.

The **formative function** is about helping the supervisee to grow. It can involve teaching – although this will never be didactic but will arise out of the work that the supervisee brings. What is appropriate will depend on the stage of development of the supervisee (see Chapter 5). At early stages there may be key skills or areas of understanding that need developing; often it will involve looking in detail at a particular area of the supervisee's work and helping them to interpret it, think through their own impact in the situation and develop new ways of working. This relates to our discussion earlier about the way the vision of the supervisee connects with what they do in a practical sense, helping them to investigate the gaps between their theology and their practice and to grow more nearly into the minister God is calling them to be.

The **normative function**, dealing with ethical, managerial and boundary issues, is perhaps the least favourite of many ministers and yet without attention to these dimensions supervision is likely to fail. In the first instance it is about attending to the boundaries of the supervision. It is about establishing expectations, making an agreement and reviewing it regularly. It is about being clear about roles and making sure, for example, that if a report needs to be written on the supervisee this is understood from the beginning and is done in accordance with transparent procedures. If the supervisor allows the supervisee to break the terms of the agreement without challenge, it is unlikely that any significant work will take place. Similarly, if a supervisor fails to stick to the agreed times and purpose for meeting, this will undermine the supervisee's trust in the reliability of the relationship.

An important dimension of the normative function of the supervision relationship is the establishment of appropriate boundaries for confidentiality. It is crucially important from the outset to discuss the kind of confidentiality that is relevant to the supervision relationship. Absolute confidentiality can rarely be guaranteed and in some organizations there are clear rules about what must be reported to social services or to superiors. Although the reporting of the suspected abuse of children or vulnerable adults is not mandatory by law in the UK (except in Northern Ireland), many organizations have clear rules about this. It is the duty of a supervisor to know their obligations in this respect, and to alert their supervisee to their need to know the relevant codes of conduct for their work, remembering that the law varies in different contexts. This is particularly important when working cross-culturally or supervising someone from a different discipline or work environment.

More generally, the normative function is also about helping the supervisee attend to the normative issues in their own work in other ways: their aims in relation to the aims of the organization within which they work; appropriate codes of ethics for their working environment; their physical, mental and ministerial fitness to work; their ability to set boundaries and expectations and to challenge inappropriate behaviours or expectations.

## Conclusions

Inskipp and Proctor's three-legged stool provides a memorable model of broad application.[12] Held together with a sense of the distinctive nature of pastoral supervision as a practice of accountability within the body of Christ, rooted in the covenant love of God and attentive to the Christian vocation, it provides a useful framework for the tasks to which the pastoral supervisor needs to attend. What follow now are some exercises to help you reflect further on the nature of pastoral supervision and some ideas for getting started in supervision relationships.

# Exercises

## Exercise 1.1 Accountability in the Body of Christ

*For reflection*

Effective pastoral supervision provides space for those in ministry:

* to be ourselves,
* to dream dreams and reconnect with our calling,
* to admit tiredness; weakness; failure; disillusion; ambition; hope; confusion,
* to be heard and have our work valued,
* to be challenged,
* to examine the gap between our conscious intentions and our practice;
* to allow God to work with us through honest interaction with another.

Review the structures of accountability in which your ministry is embedded.
   Ask yourself:

➢ Who values what I do enough to listen to me regularly and without interruptions?
➢ Who gives me space to be truthful about what is happening in my ministry?
➢ Who do I trust enough to be challenged by what they say?
➢ In what context(s) am I attending to my vision and reconnecting with my sense of call?

Looking at Mark 6 it is perhaps possible to argue that the apostles are in training and for this reason need to be under supervision. Supervised practice is an important part of training, but although the kind of supervision needed by those in ministry changes as we grow and develop, being part of an embodied structure of accountability is essential to the authentic exercise of Christian ministry. It is particularly important if you are supervising others that you have the kind of supervision yourself that is able to help you reflect honestly on the impact you have on their lives.

Ask yourself:

> Do I have enough of the right kind of supervision for the work that I do and the influence I have on the lives of others?
> Is there anything I need to do about this?

## Exercise 1.2 What Kind of Supervision?

*For reflection*

Often people are reluctant to find a supervisor for fear of being judged or 'found out' or because of a bad experience in the past.

> What reasons have you heard others – or yourself – give for not being in an effective supervision relationship?
> How might you counter those arguments?

To help you think about the kind of supervision you want to give and receive, take a piece of paper and divide it in half. On the left, write 'Supervisor from Hell'; on the right, 'Supervisor from Heaven'. Write down whatever comes to mind and then discuss with someone else, your supervisor or your supervision group:

> What kind of supervision have you experienced?
> What kind of supervision would you like?
> What kind of supervisor would you like to be?

Look again at Figure 1.1.

> Which of these tasks are you confident in, and which are you in danger of neglecting as a supervisor?
> How would you summarize the tasks of pastoral supervision?

## Exercise 1.3 Making a Supervision Covenant

*To try*

To do this one to one, you will need paper and writing tools. A formatted piece of paper might provide you with the right prompts. An example is provided at Appendix 2. In educational contexts a form will often be provided, but check it through before you use it in a supervision session. Does it cover everything you want to discuss and agree? Make sure at the end that all the relevant parties have a signed copy, especially the supervisee.

To do this in a group, you will need a flip chart and pens and a means of displaying or recording what is agreed for distribution to the group. It is important to have a record so that breaches can be referred to the agreement and review can take place effectively.

The notion of covenant is helpful in reminding us that supervision happens within the body of Christ and needs to be open to God, who initiates the covenant relationship with the Church. At the beginning of any supervision relationship, however, it is also important to make an explicit agreement with the others involved. This should arise from a conversation about expectations. You might start by asking what kind of supervision people have had before and what they valued in it or found difficult. You might ask people to do the 'Supervisor from Heaven/Hell' exercise. Any agreement should cover the following areas:

### 1 The Aim of the Supervision Sessions

The supervisor needs to be clear what they think pastoral supervision is and what they can and cannot offer; the needs of the supervisee(s) must be taken into account. Someone new to ministry may not have experienced this kind of supervision before and will need help to make use of it; on the other hand, they may have been supervised or been a supervisor within another profession with different aims and expectations, which will need clarifying; an experienced practitioner should have more to contribute and more awareness of their own supervision needs. More will be said about this kind of differentiation in Chapter 5.

## 2 The Times, Dates and Venues for the Sessions and the Importance of Reliability

If effective supervision values the work someone does, it needs to take place at a time and place that is sustainable. Find somewhere to meet where you will not be interrupted by phone calls or the doorbell. Think about the kind of room it is – what symbols are visible? How is the furniture arranged? Arrange to meet at a time of day when you will be fresh and able to concentrate. Arrange dates at least two sessions in advance so that if one has to be cancelled at short notice there is a fallback date. Diaries get very full; arrangements can easily drift. A drifting relationship does not inspire trust, so that when you do meet it is harder to do work that really matters. How often you meet will depend on the stage of development of a supervisee (see Chapter 5). For those in training, a weekly arrangement may be necessary; for experienced ministers, monthly may be sufficient, but if you have a heavy pastoral or supervision load a reasonable guide is to receive one hour's supervision for each eight hours supervising others. A one-to-one supervision session would normally last an hour – or an hour and a half if you meet less frequently. Group supervision is usually longer, lasting two hours or more.

## 3 The Structure of the Sessions and Any Preparation Needed

Supervisors and supervisees need to have common expectations of what will happen during the supervision session. Like a typical act of worship in any given congregation, there are predictable stages through which the supervision needs to move in order to fulfil its functions – from rituals of arrival, identifying how to use the time effectively, exploration of the issues presented, to focusing on future practice. Specific attention is given to these processes of supervision in Chapter 2.

In this book you will find a range of tools for supervision that should give you lots of ideas about how to help supervisees present their work and explore it with you. It is important to agree with your supervisee the kind of activities they are expecting and willing to be engaged with. Again, this is about building trust. This is not to say that working patterns need be set in stone as negotiation is always possible in the moment. Preparation for a supervision session is always important. Unless your supervisee knows what they want to get out of a supervision session, it is difficult for them to use it well, so encouraging them to do some thinking beforehand about what they want to bring is important. Often a good way to achieve this is to ask for a specific piece of preparation, but in any case, set aside some time at the start of the supervision to work out how the time should be spent (see Chapter 2). As will become clear in Chapter 6, when a supervisee does not know what to bring to supervision, using objects or cards may be very helpful in eliciting a focus for the session.

## 4 The Boundaries of the Supervision and the Kind of Confidentiality that is Relevant

This involves clarifying both the kind of issue that belongs in supervision and the kind of questions that might be asked. The clearer you are able to be about this, the better able you will be to negotiate an effective agreement with a supervisee or group.

➢ Look at the APSE definition of Pastoral Supervision at Appendix 1.
➢ Try writing out your own definition of pastoral supervision for the context in which you are working.
➢ What do you consider to be its main focus?
➢ What are its tasks?

The importance of establishing the contextually appropriate boundaries of confidentiality in the work of the supervisee was established above (page 18). There also needs to be an agreement between the parties to the supervision relationship about material shared in that context. If the supervisor is working within the same organizational structure, the organization's rules may apply. In some contexts the supervisor has responsibility for the ministry or the development of their supervisee and will be expected to write reports for their own organization or for a training programme. This should be made explicit from the start of the supervision relationship. In both of these cases the kind of confidentiality is determined from outside the supervision relationship.

Where groups or individuals covenant together for supervision but have discretion over arrangements regarding confidentiality, it is important that everyone has confidence that personal stories are not going to be repeated. Even with changed names and place names, many organizations, including the Church, are small enough communities for situations to be recognized. If groups work in smaller units at times, for example in pairs, different levels of confidentiality often work. Good practice suggests that personal stories belong to those who told them and should not be repeated outside that context without explicit permission.

Finally, supervisors need to consider their own code of practice – if you came to believe that your supervisee was unfit to practise, would you want to report this to someone with responsibility for their ministry if they were unwilling to face this? If so, this needs stating from the outset.

## 5 Arrangements for Review

Agreements of this kind are only useful if they are audited. It is helpful to build opportunities for review into the pattern of the supervision – each time you meet at first, then periodically. Good practice for established supervision relationships suggests planning for six sessions at a time and reviewing how it has been in the penultimate session before deciding whether and how to proceed with more sessions.

If you are engaged in a supervision relationship, make some notes in your reflective journal about the kind of agreement you have for working together.

- Do you have a written agreement?
- What are your aims for this work? Are they shared with the others involved?
- What kind of confidentiality are you operating? Is this explicit between you?

- What is the pattern of the sessions? How regular and boundaried are they?
- How effective is the work? What is the view of others involved?
- When was the last time you discussed together how the work is going?
- What arrangements for review do you have?

The practice of making a written supervision agreement may seem rather cumbersome. Our experience suggests, however, that often when supervision relationships break down or cease to serve a useful purpose, it is because expectations have not been clarified and no provision has been made for review, making it very difficult for either side to discuss how the supervision is going or to bring the arrangement to an end. Establishing expectations, boundaries and processes for review are crucial, therefore, in beginning and maintaining a successful supervision relationship.

It is important to note, however, that even with the best supervision covenant in place, supervision relationships do not always work well. Although arrangements for review make it possible for both parties to raise issues and make adjustments that may help, some supervision relationships are best ended. This may be because the supervisor does not have the expertise or experience to supervise this particular supervisee, or it may be that the supervisee simply does not have the capacity for insight, the freedom to take on new ways of working or the level of trust required in effective supervision relationships. Being in supervision for the supervising you do offers a context to help discern which relationships can be improved and which need to end. Further discussion about how to end a supervision relationship is provided in Chapter 10.

## Exercise 1.4 MAP

*To try*

Figure 1.2 Naming your vision

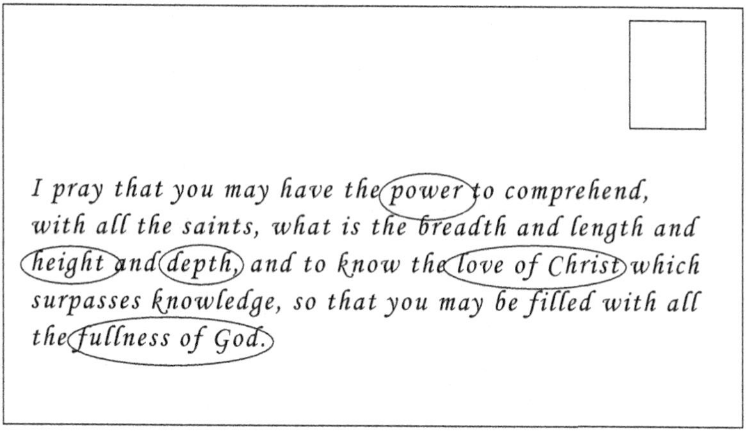

*I pray that you may have the power to comprehend, with all the saints, what is the breadth and length and height and depth, and to know the love of Christ which surpasses knowledge, so that you may be filled with all the fullness of God.*

You will need pens, plain postcards, Bibles and sheets of A3 paper.

This is a good exercise to engage in early on in a supervision arrangement as a way of getting to know people and providing insight into what matters to them. In later sessions it may be appropriate to invite a supervisee to examine or challenge their sense of vocation or vision, but at the moment what matters is to enter into the world of your supervisee(s) and seek to understand it. Items in italics are relevant to groups only. Please consult Chapter 9 about the dynamics of working with a group rather than with individuals.

1. Invite your supervisee(s) to think about their vision of ministry.
2. What biblical passage would they choose as being key to their vision of ministry?
3. Invite them to write this on a postcard and then to circle the words that seem to them to be most significant (Figure 1.2).
4. What do you/*the group* notice or wonder?

5. Suggest that our visions of ministry need ever deeper embedding in our practice.
6. Invite your supervisee(s) to place their postcard in the centre of a piece of A3 paper and around it to map their work (Figure 1.3). Where do their vision and actual practice seem in sympathy with each other? Where are there tensions? Where do they feel they have embodied the vision and seen it flourish; where do they feel disappointed?

## Figure 1.3 Mapping your work

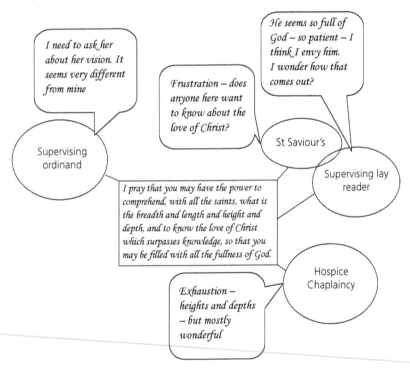

7. Invite each person to focus on one area of their ministry to present to the group in terms of its relationship to their vision.
8. What do you/*the group* notice or wonder?
9. Invite your supervisee(s) to name a concrete step towards their vision of ministry that they want to take, or a way they

want to reframe their vision in the light of their reflection – even to choose another text.

10. Decide together whether it is most useful for your supervisee(s) to retain their postcards and bring them to each session or for the supervisor to hand them out each week.

The postcards can be usefully referred to at the end of any session to help the presenter think about their aims in the encounter/ situation; how these relate to their vision of their ministry; how they might move nearer their vision; or how they now understand their ministry differently. The option to choose a new passage should always be retained – vision is dynamic and contextual and may change through the course of the supervision work.

## Notes

1 See www.pastoralsupervision.org.uk/pastoral-supervision.

2 *Methodist Worship Book*, 1999, Peterborough: Methodist Publishing House, p. 302. © TMCP.

3 Rowan Williams, 2002, *Open to Judgement*, London: Darton, Longman & Todd, p. 110, emphasis in original.

4 Donald Schön, 1983, *The Reflective Practitioner: How Professionals Think in Action*, New York: Basic Books.

5 See David Boud, Rosemary Keogh and David Walker (eds), 1985, *Reflection: Turning Experience into Learning*, Abingdon: Routledge.

6 Gordon Lynch, 2001, *Pastoral Care and Counselling*, London: Sage.

7 K. Pohly, 1988, 'The Purpose and Function of Supervision in Ministry', *Journal of Supervision and Training in Ministry* 10, p. 8.

8 For some the use of the word covenant to describe such a relationship is a misuse of a biblical concept that emphasizes the asymmetrical relationship between God and God's people. The use of the term covenantal is here related to what H. R. Niebuhr calls the fiduciary structure of relationships. For an explanation, see J. W. Fowler, 1981, *Stages of Faith*, San Francisco: Harper & Row, chapter 1.

9 Sam Wells, 2013, *Learning to Dream Again: Rediscovering the Heart of God*, Norwich: Canterbury Press, p. 44.

10 Within the covenant established by God in Christ and in which the Holy Spirit is active.

11 Francesca Inskipp and Brigid Proctor (1993) 1995, *Making the Most of Supervision Part 1: The Art, Craft and Tasks of Counselling Supervision*, Bend, OR: Cascade Publications.

12 Michael Carroll offers a way of characterizing supervision that involves seven tasks. We find the three-legged model more intuitive and memorable. See Michael Carroll, 1996, *Counselling Supervision: Theory, Skills and Practice*, London: Cassell.

# 2

# Attending to the Process

## Summary

In common with other forms of reflective practice, pastoral supervision invites a dialogue in the *present* upon the *past* with an eye to the *future*. Having, in the last chapter, established pastoral supervision as a potentially transformative conversation between motivation, actual practice and potential practice, this chapter outlines six processes that ensure supervision is hospitable, focused, exploratory, monitored, forward-facing and effective.

Now on that same day two of them were going to a village called Emmaus, about seven miles from Jerusalem, and talking with each other about all these things that had happened. While they were talking and discussing, Jesus himself came near and went with them, but their eyes were kept from recognizing him. And he said to them, 'What are you discussing with each other while you walk along?' They stood still, looking sad. Then one of them, whose name was Cleopas, answered him, 'Are you the only stranger in Jerusalem who does not know the things that have taken place there in these days?' He asked them, 'What things?' They replied, 'The things about Jesus of Nazareth, who was a prophet mighty in deed and word before God and all the people, and how our chief priests and leaders handed him over to be condemned to death and crucified him. But we had hoped that he was the one to redeem Israel. Yes, and besides all this, it is now the third day since these things took place. Moreover, some women of our group astounded us. They were at the tomb early this morning, and when they did not find his body there, they came back and told us that they had indeed seen a vision of angels who said that he was alive. Some of those who were with us went to the tomb and found it just as the women had said; but they did not see him.' Then he said to them, 'Oh, how foolish you are, and how slow of heart to believe all that the prophets have declared! Was it not necessary that the Messiah should suffer these things and then enter into his glory?' Then beginning with Moses and all the prophets, he interpreted to them the things about himself in all the scriptures.

Luke 24.13–27

Luke's story opens with two long-faced disciples, bewildered by all they have seen and heard, meeting a stranger who shows interest in them. What is notable as a pastoral encounter is that Jesus does not call the disciples over to join him on his track, nor does he begin by lecturing them as to what they should think or feel, but simply meets them on the road, puts them rather than himself centre stage, asks about things that matter to them and establishes sufficient trust for them to unburden their heavy hearts to him.

What Jesus teaches here is that ministry is expressed in the commitment to walk beside people on the road they are on, in establishing relationships and points of exchange with them and in discovering what makes them tick. Beyond the commitment to the relationship, however, is the commitment to make the events of life transparent. The encounter in this story is made possible not only because Jesus is fully present and attentive to the disciples, but because the disciples are willing to tell their story. They are willing to offer not just the bare facts, but all the spiritual and emotional dimensions of the last few days that are summed up in those poignant words, 'we had hoped' (v. 21).

In pastoral supervision, one of the big questions is how to get the supervisee's work into the room in sufficient depth and detail to be able to work realistically with it. One of the problems many supervision-type conversations face within the churches is that

36

they are often too general and unfocused to be helpful. The supervisee has not thought in a focused way about what to bring to supervision and consequently may either have very little to say or be overflowing with stories about their work that seem to have little thread. Although this can be useful in restorative terms, it can leave little room for the formative task of learning. Part of the job of the supervisor is to help the supervisee bring significant work to supervision, but this is only the beginning, for having helped the disciples tell their story, Jesus attends to assisting them interpret its meaning. The story they have told in human terms he brings into dialogue with the Hebrew Scriptures, broadening the focus of their interpretation of events and redefining the situation they are describing.

Although Jesus' words, 'Oh, how foolish you are' (v. 25) may not normally seem appropriate to pastoral supervision, it is striking that, despite the rebuke, the disciples are moved to invite the stranger to stay with them. Something about his presence with them on the journey has convinced them to listen to him and to invite him more deeply into their reality. When his challenge comes, the disciples are ready to hear it. There is an important lesson here for pastoral supervision: hospitality is required not only from the supervisor in making space for the supervisee to be heard, but also from the supervisee. If truly significant work is to be done, the supervisee needs to take the leap of inviting the supervisor into their home reality where focuses can be broadened and interpretations challenged.

Our attention in this chapter therefore focuses on how to make supervision an intentional and hospitable space. Six processes of supervision will be introduced. These operate both as dimensions of supervision practice of which supervisors need to be aware, but also as stages by which a pastoral supervision session can reliably be structured to achieve its goals.

The six processes or stages of a supervision session are outlined in Figure 2.1:

Figure 2.1 The process of a supervision session

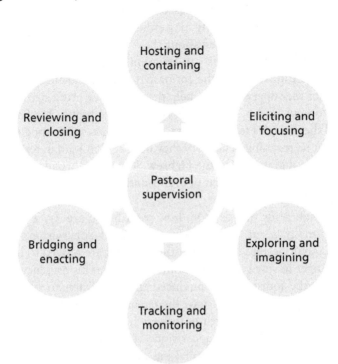

- *Hosting and containing* focuses on the kind of hospitality that enables transformative learning. This includes attention to the ethical framework, organization culture, immediate environment and quality of interpersonal relationship between participants.
- *Eliciting and focusing* is not only about getting the work into the room but about identifying the energy or impulse that will make reflection worthwhile (i.e. What is it in particular about this particular issue that makes it worth looking at here today?).
- *Exploring and imagining.* Once a focus has been established, *exploring and imagining* becomes a playful and creatively fertile place in which to try out ideas and ways of working. It is also the place in which stray thoughts, fantasies, images and metaphors can be aired.

- *Tracking and monitoring.* Tracking is both a discreet moment in the reflective cycle and something that runs through the whole session. It is a way of monitoring that what is happening is matching what it is needed within the allotted time.

- *Bridging and enacting* are reminders that we reflect on work from the *past* in the *present* in order to change and enhance work in the *future*. Towards the end of the supervision session, a bridge is built back into the world of everyday practice; enacting names the first steps to be taken. In group contexts there needs to be room for everyone to name what they are taking away.

- *Reviewing and closing* is the process of drawing a line under the particular issues explored today. In supervision, closing well is just as important as beginning well.[1] It is important to ensure there is space for reviewing how the supervision relationship or group is going and making sure future arrangements are in place.

Having a clear structure for each supervision session enables both parties to know what is expected of them and offers a guide for the time together. It operates in much the same way as any broad liturgical structure, which begins with gathering, moves through listening to God's word, invites response and concludes with God's people being sent out in mission. Although different Christian traditions have developed different liturgical structures, each of them guides worshippers through worship and tells them what is expected of them. A clear sense of beginning, middle and end helps the work of the liturgy – the glorification of God and the transformation of humanity – to be accomplished. In similar fashion, a broad structure helps to shape a supervision session so that it can achieve its purpose of reviewing past practice in the present in order to shape practice for the future.

A broadly helpful structure is evident in the conversation between Jesus and the two disciples on the road to Emmaus, in which Jesus comes alongside the disciples on their journey; elicits their story; widens the focus of their understanding; allows opportunity for them to see with their own eyes, with the result that, finally, they return to the mission field with renewed energy and insight. The six processes offered here, tailored to the practice of pastoral supervision, follow a similar trajectory to that of the Emmaus story.

### Figure 2.2  Structuring a supervision session

| | | | |
|---|---|---|---|
| Before the session | **Hosting and containing**<br>(getting room and self ready)<br>*Tracking and monitoring*<br>(reading notes; thinking about shape of the session; identifying any deadlines, e.g. reports to be written) | | |
| First 5–10 minutes | *Hosting and containing*<br>(welcome; check-in; prayer) | | |
| 5–10 minutes | *Focusing and eliciting*<br>(identifying the focus for the session) | | |
| Bulk of the session | *Exploring and imagining*<br>(tell me; show me; using words, images, stories, communication by impact; objects; body work to shed light on the work) | | |
| | *Bridging and enacting*<br>(identifying possible ways forward) | | |
| Last 5–10 minutes | *Reviewing and closing*<br>(summarizing of key 'take home' points)<br>(checking arrangements for next session and any other administration) | | |
| After the session | *Tracking and monitoring*<br>(making notes; identifying any issues that might need addressing or taking to own supervision) | | |

Spanning the full height of the table (rotated columns):

*Tracking and monitoring* (being alert to what the context, the supervisee and the focus of the session require; making interventions to facilitate the best use of the time; keeping an overview of the usefulness of the supervision relationship; taking notes)

*Hosting and containing* (being alert to the relational dimensions of the supervision; being alert to one's own ability to be present; being alert to the hosting and containing that God is doing)

## Process One: Hosting and Containing – Supervision as Hospitality

To enable supervision to be transformative requires it to be conducted in an air of hospitality in which 'every stranger and every strange utterance is met with welcome'.[2]

At the start of a supervision relationship a robust and mutually hospitable container needs to be co-constructed by the supervisor and the supervisee – or the supervision group – that will enable the work to be held so that it can be explored. As in the process of weaving a basket, a strong container will consist of key radials that give it structure and around which a relationship can be woven. In the case of pastoral supervision those key radials include:

- *Clarity about the purpose of the time together.* This is often lacking in pastoral supervision. Since the territory and contours of supervision are still largely unknown in the pastoral sphere, the first task of supervision is to teach people what the space is for. In Chapter 1 we offered some definitions of pastoral supervision and some core functions (normative, formative, restorative). Clarity of purpose frees supervisees to know what to bring to sessions and what to reflect on with others elsewhere. It also frees supervisors to note issues that are overtaking the work space and really need to be taken elsewhere.

  Such clarity of purpose is also important when the supervisor and the supervisee share a work context, as in the case of a student placement or a curacy. In such a context, although there will be other times of meeting (to pray together; plan shared work; share in the leading of worship; engage in mission activities together; meet in a wider staff team; socialize), in the time set aside for supervision, the supervisor needs to concentrate on being available for and to the supervisee in order to focus on their practice for the sake of their future development. In this way supervision is an exercise of **eccentric** ministry: the supervisor creates a space within which the supervisee's practice is allowed to be central.

- *A mutually agreed covenant for the work.* The covenant or contract *for working* needs to be co-constructed. What is the supervisor responsible for? What is the supervisee responsible for? How often are they to meet? How long will meetings last? Are expectations clear about payment and how it is to be made? Is there a cancellation policy? Is there a contract for dealing with issues of fitness to practise and breaks in practice? Is the work ongoing or finite? Is review built in? (For further information about how to do this, see Appendix 2.)

- *A framework of ethical practice underpinning everything.* The entire relationship and all the processes that serve it need to be held within an explicit ethical framework rather than a vague desire to do good and cause no harm. By what code of practice does the supervisor operate? To whom could a supervisee raise issues of concern about the supervisor? Conversely, is the supervisory contract a hermetically sealed private affair between the two parties or are there contractual or organizational factors to consider? Are reports to be written? Are there any legal implications for the work? Is the supervisor covered by professional indemnity insurance and so on?

  Considering together all the relevant dimensions of the context in which the supervision is taking place helps to create a robust set of radials that stands the best chance of holding the supervision relationship in the right place for the work of supervision to proceed.

- *Being emotionally and spiritually available.* A relationship will only develop, though, when both parties are willing to be present. Although the supervisor cannot determine how present the supervisee will be, the supervisor is responsible for their own ability to give their full attention. Being a reliable presence is not about omnipresence, however; it is about being physically, cognitively, emotionally and spiritually available at particular times and in particular spaces, and in this way, being able to point to the God who *hosts and contains* all time and space.

  Supervisors are truly present when they have cleared a space within their own busy heads and hearts to 'lend' themselves mentally, affectively and spiritually to the other. Without this inner spaciousness, supervisors will be unable to make intentional use of themselves and will leave their supervisees cheated.

Part of the way to safeguard this availability is to ensure that you – as supervisor – have had the opportunity to be listened to recently so that you are not tempted to fill the supervision session with your own need to be heard. Further, just as, in pastoral work, when we are overwhelmed by the needs we face, it is easy to rush into trying to make a difference, the same is true in supervision. Burdened by the need to solve the problem presented to us, we can forget that supervision is primarily about accompanying the person we are with, and listening deeply to them and with them to what God is saying, remembering that even if we struggle to contain some of the distressing and anxiety-provoking things we hear in supervision, God is able to hold them.

- *Physical environment.* The physical environment is often neglected in the literature of supervision, but the kind of welcome being offered in pastoral supervision affects the kind of work that can unfold, and this is partly communicated by the physical environment. Before inviting someone into a supervision space, it is important to consider questions such as: 'If I were coming to this space with something that really mattered to me, would this room help or hinder my exploring it? Are these the kind of chairs that encourage the exploration of work or a cosy chat? Is the room warm enough for a comfortable hour together? Will we be disturbed? Have intrusions been anticipated (phones switched off, 'room in use' indicated and so on)?

  Furthermore, if we understand the practice of pastoral supervision to be happening in the presence of the God who hosts and contains us, how might that be signalled appropriately within the room so that there is a point of reference when the going gets tough?

- *Appropriate time set aside.* Hospitality also implies the setting aside of appropriate amounts of time at appropriate intervals and at appropriate times of day: being late, needing to cut sessions short, failing to plan ahead with dates in the diary or being unclear about how long the session will last can give the supervisee the message that you are not a reliable presence; that they cannot count on your being truly available even when you are in the room. This will not only raise questions in their mind about how much of themselves it is safe to bring to the supervision session, but may also teach or model the 'acceptability' of poor presence in the life of ministry. As part of this thinking it is important to consider the times you offer for supervision – if you are routinely tired it will be difficult to give your full attention, so try to think ahead about your diary. It also means thinking about what you do immediately before and after a supervision session. Will you be rushing from something else, still processing what's been happening there, or will you have time to sit down and think about the person you are supervising; to read through any notes you have made from the last time and remember what is happening for them; to pray for them and for your time together; to gather as much of yourself as you can to concentrate on the task of listening? Similarly, after the supervision session, will you head off straight away to something else, or will you plan some time to write some notes about what happened; what seemed significant or might need following up; what made an impact on you and might need further work?

• *Attention to this supervisee.* Although the functions and processes are generic, each supervision relationship is unique. What supervision time should be allocated to finding out about *this* supervisee's circumstances, priorities and sense of vocation? Can you use an exercise such as Exercise 1.4 at the end of Chapter 1 before you launch into the detail of particular issues?

Therefore at the start of each supervision relationship, and before each supervision session, there is work for the supervisor to do in becoming fully present and in setting up the space and time in such a way that the supervisee can be welcomed and their work contained so that it can be explored for the sake of their future practice.

This work also extends into the opening of each supervision session as the supervisee arrives and is helped to bring as much of themselves into the room as possible.

- *Arrival time:* How far has your supervisee travelled? Do they need anything before the work can start?
- *Check in:* How long since you last saw each other? What are the headlines of what is happening in your supervisee's life/work that it would be helpful for you to know?
- *Full presence:* How can you help your supervisee/group to be as fully present as possible? It is useful to offer some physical form of exercise like guided breathing or meditation to help them 'arrive'.
- *Allowing God to host and contain you both:* Is this something that can be done ritually by lighting a candle? By reading the Scriptures together? By beginning in prayer? Think about what you feel comfortable with. Establish with your supervisee what they would find helpful.

## Process Two: Eliciting and Focusing

Nothing does more to kill the energy in supervision than an anxious supervisor who alights on the first thing a supervisee says in a session and presumes to make that the focus for the session. Sometimes supervisees come knowing exactly what they want to talk about and what they are looking for in wanting to explore it. Sometimes they come knowing that a particular incident or encounter has 'stayed with them' and tugged at their mind or heart but cannot identify why it matters or what it relates to. And sometimes people come not knowing where to begin. This can be for a variety of reasons: those new to supervision may not have the tools to sift through weeks of practice to know what to bring; those overwhelmed by their work may be aware that a decision to bring one issue to supervision closes the door on a cluster of others, and may find it difficult to know which to choose; others may be so detached from their work that they are not allowing it to impinge upon their mental and spiritual energies.

45

The process of *eliciting and focusing* what the issue is that should take the time today can be accomplished in seconds or may need ten minutes or more. It is worth spending the time on getting this right so that the session has direction and purpose and is directed to the needs of the supervisee rather than to any other agenda. After the initial welcome, the supervisor needs to change gear and ask specifically, 'What are you bringing today?'

- *What are you bringing?* The first duty of the supervisor is to teach the supervisee how to use the space called 'supervision', within which eliciting a supervisory question or issue is paramount. The question 'What are you bringing to supervision?' can be answered in a number of ways. Oftentimes a supervisee will alight on a particular experience: 'being bored listening to someone's story'; 'chairing a meeting and going blank when asked a question'; 'not knowing my way round something'. At other times what supervisees bring is not so much a particular issue as an aspect of themselves in the work: 'I used to love ministry, but right now the pressure is unbearable'; 'I feel at a professional crossroads'; 'I have had a busy month since we last met, but right now I feel blank'.

- *Why are you bringing it here?* Wherever supervision takes place, the word 'work' is written above the door. Personal and spiritual issues do arise in supervision but need to be respectfully and reverently handled in so far as they impinge on the supervisee's ability to work effectively. There is a humility built into supervision, which recognizes that it is only one form of supportive relationship with its own particular focus and set of skills. Pastoral supervisors need to protect the integrity and limitations of their role, no matter how hard supervisees push them to play the therapist or spiritual guide. Nevertheless, establishing the legitimacy of an issue is only the first step in supervision. Further exploration is needed to know why someone chooses to bring an issue to supervision rather than to a line manager, work colleague or personal friend.

- *Why are you bringing it today?* The question may seem pedantic and may not always be asked in such an explicit

46

way, but supervisors will do well to listen between the lines for hints of an answer. Is the issue urgent and requiring immediate solution? ('I am giving a talk next week about X and feel stuck.') Is the issue recurring and therefore presenting itself for exploration now? ('That was the third time that week I had told a parishioner they had no idea what pressure clergy were under.') Is the issue impeding other work from taking place? ('I can't get what has happened to L out of my mind and feel I am neglecting all the other kids in the youth club.') Asking 'Why today?' will help focus the use of time.

- *What do you want in bringing it?* A supervisee who can answer this question is well on their way to insight. 'I am looking for a second opinion that what I did was not off the wall' (supervision as validation). 'I feel ashamed about messing up at work and need to unravel the mess' (supervision as catharsis). 'I feel chuffed that I managed to confront my fears for a change and speak up for myself' (supervision as bearing witness). 'I have been over this again and again in my head and even talked it through with colleagues, but I fear I may be deceiving myself' (supervision as courageous conversation). People have many reasons for bringing their work to supervision, only a fraction of which are voiced explicitly. Practitioners' developmental stages have a part to play in what they might be looking for. For example, a novice practitioner may be seeking direct instruction ('What do I do?' 'What do I say?'), whereas a mature practitioner may simply be looking for someone to afford them the quality of hearing that they themselves offer others (consultative support). (See Chapter 5).

- *Agreeing a focus.* Agreeing a focus is an expression of hospitality. Just as a host would not give a guest who requested a coffee a cup of tea, so too a supervisor who has elicited a focus needs to respond to that focus and not follow their own interests. In practice this means that once the supervisory issue or focus has been established, every subsequent intervention needs to be attuned to that issue. This requires discipline (in keeping to the agreed agenda); repertoire (a range of ways of going deeper into the issue that has already been identified) and monitoring (are we dealing with the real issue here or getting sidetracked?).

## Process Three: Exploring and Imagining

Exploration is the heart of the practice of supervision. In many contexts, faced with a problem, people immediately begin scrambling around for a solution. While this is sometimes exactly what is required, overuse of quick-fix solutions renders exploration redundant. When it comes to pastoral supervision, we are not dealing so much with problems that need to be fixed as people who need to be accompanied. This is based on the wisdom that the first authority on practice is the care-seeker (the client or person on the receiving end of care). The second is the practitioner. The supervisor comes third and last! Admittedly, supervisees do not always present themselves and their dilemmas in that way, but effective supervisors do well to remember that and resist the **projections** to which they – and care-seekers – are sometimes subjected.

Without due attention to exploration, supervision risks becoming an advice shop in which a wise all-knowing person (the supervisor) dispenses wisdom to a less experienced person (the supervisee), who is expected to be grateful. Such outdated models of supervision accentuate the power dynamic between the two parties and invite dependency and obedience rather than professional development and transformative learning. Exploration should normally account for about two-thirds of the time allotted for supervision. Our primary tool for exploration, the three levels of seeing, will be outlined in detail in Chapter 3; here we note a variety of ways work can be brought into the supervision space, as well as some of the key tools for its exploration.

- *Tell me.* The 'telling' approach favours speech and cognition. Thus a supervisor might say: 'Describe the scene for me.' 'Who was there?' 'Where were you in the room?' 'Were you standing or sitting?' 'Tell me how you were feeling before the incident occurred.' 'Talk me through your thought processes, the inner commentary running in your head as the scene unfolded.' 'Tell me your stray thoughts or fantasies about the person you were dealing with.' 'Tell me what you would say if there were no holds barred.' 'Tell me who she reminds you of.' 'Tell me about other times in your life when you have had to face similar things.' Supervisors need to be attentive to the possibility that the 'telling' approach may establish a pattern of question and answer or be experienced as forensic investigation, and use it only in so far as it enables exploration. Further material for working in this way is offered in Chapter 6.

- **Show me.** 'Showing' approaches invite people to get underneath the stories they tell, to the heart of the matter. Asking supervisees to 'show' the situation they are trying to explore using images, objects, art, music or movement can free them from the 'tunnel of words' to find colour, energy, creativity and a sense of mystery so often lacking in the practice of supervision.[3] A supervisor might say: 'Using any of the objects you have in your pocket/handbag, show me the team you are referring to.' 'Show me that knot in your stomach that you are describing.' 'Show me what losing the thread means.' 'Show me where in your body that feeling resides.' 'Close your eyes and make a sound which expresses that moment you are trying to get me to understand.' 'Choose a card to depict what it was like to be in the chair at that meeting and another to indicate where you would rather have been.' When situations are explored like this, new meaning can emerge in quite surprising ways. This is what Tony Williams calls the 'boo' factor of expressive supervision.[4] Supervisors working with 'showing' approaches need to offer gentle but firm containment since the unconscious is often accessed quickly and deeply through this manner of exploration. Remaining true to the role of supervisor may involve some delicate negotiation here. Supervisors will also need to be aware that some of their supervisees will be 'act hungry' and relish the opportunity to show their work in this way, but less keen to draw out the implications for action that result from insights gained. Further material for working in this way is offered in Chapter 6.

- *Exploring the impact.* Every story impacts upon its hearers. Some stories excite us, some bore us. Some intrigue, some capture our imagination, some appal or horrify us. The **impact** of a story told in supervision provides invaluable information. Social convention allows for certain impacts to be voiced. Stories that generate a 'wow' factor are welcomed, while those that leave us feeling 'yuk' are often left hanging in the air. Feeding back to a supervisee the impact the particular fragment from their 'there and then' professional story has had on you 'here and now' can be very illuminating. Further material is offered for working in this way in Chapter 5.

- *Somatic resonance.* Strictly speaking, somatic resonance is a particular form of **communication by impact**, but we have singled it out here in order to accentuate the importance of the supervisor being fully present – including bodily and energetically – to those with whom they work. Thus, for example, a supervisor may suddenly be overwhelmed by tiredness – tiredness with no basis in fact since they have slept well and were feeling rested until the supervisee began to speak about their work with a particular person or situation. This tiredness may in fact be communicating something about the work being presented or its impact on the supervisee. While somatic resonance should not be sought in supervision, it should not be resisted when it emerges unbidden. Not all supervisors are susceptible to this form of communication by impact, but those who are would do well to monitor this in supervision on supervision. We also explore this way of working in Chapter 5.

- *Image and metaphor.* Sometimes the impact of what is presented manifests within those who listen as stray thoughts ('Must check my bank account to see if she's paid'), distractions ('Wonder what's on TV tonight?'), images ('She looks haunted today') or metaphors ('Humpty Dumpty all over again'). A supervisor who failed to clear their head and heart to make room for and become truly present to the supervisee before the session began would be disabled by such occurrences and unable to discern whether they arise out of the supervisee's material or from their own lack of presence. Conversely, a supervisor who is ready to greet their guest will know that this strange and apparently random information belongs not to themselves but to the supervisee, and can therefore tentatively offer it for exploration. Further material for working in this way is offered in Chapter 7.

Deciding how to work will depend on a number of factors:

1. What have you agreed with this supervisee/group depending on their preferences?
2. What is the supervisee's developmental stage as a practitioner and what is their experience as a supervisee? (See Chapter 5.)
3. What is the best method to facilitate the exploration of the material being brought? This will depend on your assessment of the kind of issue being presented. See Chapters 4, 5 and 8; and for a summary of the issues, Figure 5.3.

## Process Four: Tracking and Monitoring

Tracking is both a discrete moment in the reflective cycle of pastoral supervision and a way of monitoring and paying attention to what is happening in the supervisory space as a whole. Tracking has two components: charting the progress of the supervisory issue, and monitoring that what happens within the allotted time by way of *exploring and imagining* meets the needs of the presenter and does not dissolve into a general discussion of a topic more appropriate to a seminar than to supervision. The five aspects of *tracking and monitoring* are:

- *Interest.* Something caused the presenter to choose this rather than some other issue to bring to supervision. If the *eliciting and focusing* stage has been well handled then it will have become clear why this particular issue is of interest to the supervisee. Monitoring what happens to that interest as the session progresses will help maintain momentum. Similarly, supervisors should track their own interest level, noting when they become more interested and when less. If supervision is conducted in a group, it is sometimes worth explicitly asking what interests the group in what they are hearing.

- **Energy.** Tracking energy is closely related to monitoring interest. A loss of energy in supervision may indicate a number of things: that the issue lacked sufficient 'charge' to merit sustained reflection (in which case the option of revising the supervisory question always exists); that loss of energy is a factor in the issue currently being presented (a form of **parallel process**); that the situation carries within it an investment in remaining stuck (for example, a patient in a hospital context who does not want to get better). As with all interventions, *tracking and monitoring* energy is best used as a form of noticing or wondering that gives the presenter room to manoeuvre.

- **(Re)Focusing.** A focusing intervention could be along the lines of: 'You said you wanted to explore why you find it so hard to visit the care home. With the group's help you clarified that it was not the care home itself that you found difficult but having to deal with Molly the manager. For the last five minutes you have been talking about the youth club you visit, and I am wondering if there is some connection for you between your work in the care home and in the youth club, or if we have gone off track.'

- **Engagement.** Pastoral supervision is an affair for consenting adults in private. As such it requires engagement. One of the paradoxes of the drive to encourage more widespread take-up of the practice is that some people now come without really being either invested in building the relationship that is required or committed to the search for insight aimed at improving their practice. As a consequence, supervisors can find themselves overcompensating and tiring themselves out by doing too much of the work in the session. Ambivalent engagement can also arise when the supervisor or group inadvertently press a button within the psyche or soul of the supervisee, causing them to retreat in self-defence. When it becomes clear that this has happened and that the supervisee is not willing to explore that defence within the supervision session, the supervisor has little hope of going any further. In a group setting the supervisor might choose to close the presenter's work at this point and take the remaining time to work with the resonances group members have found in the story originally presented. This will take the spotlight off the presenter, allowing them time to regroup and (possibly) re-engage. There is further material on working with resistance in Chapter 9.

• *Timing.* Tracking time relates to safe containment. Simple interventions are helpful here: 'We have an hour together today. I wonder what the best use of that time is for you?'; 'We are half way through our time together, so I just want to check that we are doing what you need us to do with you today'; 'We have ten minutes left, so I want to ask if you are any closer to finding a way forward.'; 'I am afraid we are now out of time and there are still unanswered questions. But we do have to stop there. Thank you.' Another aspect of tracking time is to monitor who is taking the air space and who might not have been able to speak: 'We are half way through our time and I notice that we have only heard from three people in the group. Would anyone else like to come in at this point?' Or in individual supervision: 'I notice you have spoken continuously for the last 30 minutes and just wonder if you want anything from me before we finish, besides a listening ear.'

## Process Five: Bridging and Enacting

*Bridging and enacting* are reminders that supervision is fundamentally future facing. At this stage in the session we seek to build a bridge from reflection on action to the world of everyday practice to which the supervisee will return when they leave the supervisory session. Enacting is about supervisees articulating first steps expressive of the insight they have found in the session. The literature of coaching offers a great deal of practical insight and wisdom in this area. The five stages of *bridging and enacting* are:

• *Building a bridge.* Bridges span space. Supervisory bridges span the space of exploration and discovery (the supervision session) and the space of enactment (work). Bridges can be permanent or temporary, made of stone, steel, wood or rope. So too supervisory bridges may be emergency solutions or elaborate constructions that will take many years to complete. However constructed, bridges build professional confidence in helping supervisees recover a sense of empowerment in returning to the workplace.

- *Building what is needed.* Some bridges are built within supervisees themselves: 'I know I can't do anything to change the situation, but knowing that you will be standing there cheering me on from the sidelines already makes a big difference. That is the bridge I'm going to hold on to.' Other bridges are conceptual: 'I am going from here today, laying down the stones I chose to express the weight of responsibility I have been carrying, with the image of a windmill in my mind to represent the kind of free flow of energy I want to recover in my work.'

- *Support for building.* Coming as it does at the end of a session, the question of support is deliberately framed positively ('What will support you?'), without the expected rejoinder ('What will impede you?'). This is partly to do with the supervisory process (the time of exploration has come to an end and we are now in a time of decisive action) and the economy of time (to look at the question from both sides would take longer and impact on the earlier stages in the session.) Much more importantly, however, the positive tone of the question is expressive of a philosophical stance that focuses on assets rather than deficits and sees supervisees as highly resourced people capable of making informed choices for themselves. Using the tools of appreciative enquiry, asking what makes for well-being enables the session to end on an empowering note.

- *First steps.* This is often self-evident, in which case it does not have to be asked. However, if the bridge that has been articulated is overly ambitious, asking about first steps may induce a sense of reality into the equation and therefore save the supervisee from a sense of failure or inadequacy. 'In a few minutes this session will end and you will leave here to go back to work.

What baby step could you take to enact that much bigger desire you have?'

- **Next steps.** Again this is often self-evident. Simple interventions may help: 'You have realized today that you feel inadequate as a preacher, because you haven't kept up with theological and spiritual reading. So what would you like your next step to be – and by when will you have done that?'

## Process Six: Reviewing and Closing

Reviewing is the process of naming what has been learnt through reflection. Closing is the drawing of a line on the exploration. In supervision, closing well is just as important as beginning well. Reviewing works at different levels. In the here and now of the session that is coming to an end, it traces the journey in which both parties have shared from the supervisee's arrival through to their imminent departure. It notes cairns and signposts along the way: that moment of stuckness; the belly laugh that took us both by surprise; the stray thought that moved things on; the silence shared for a few minutes; the moment of connection and so on. Reviewing also works at another level in fostering the supervisee's internal supervisor and reflexivity, and in implicitly offering them another potential tool to use in their own practice.

- **Insight gained by the supervisee.** Being able to name the learning that has taken place is a key moment in supervision understood as transformational learning. Sometimes insight is crystal clear: 'I am no longer a four-year-old in the play-ground. Bullies should be resisted.' At other times insight may be embryonic and inarticulate: 'I can't quite put my finger on it, but I know it's something to do with recognizing the difference between caring for my colleagues and being a complete sponge that soaks everything up.' Leaving supervision able to name insight gained provides a reparative experience for people whose professional lives are often entangled with stories of diminishment or loss of one kind or another.

- *Insight gained by the supervisor/group.* There is an alchemy in pastoral supervision that often results in mutual reciprocity: when one person takes the risk of bringing their work to the loving and critically supportive eye of another, both parties benefit from the encounter. In group supervision this is sometimes articulated as follows: 'When one person is supervised, every member of the group receives supervision.' Underlying this is the truth that when supervision is conducted within an 'air of hospitality', the truth-telling risk of the presenter evokes (albeit at times unconscious) reflection within their hearers. In group supervision it is good to leave time at the end of the session to invite those present to name any insights gained for their own practice as a result of accompanying the presenter in an exploration of his or her issue. Supervisors need to contain this well, lest it turn into grandstanding or competing stories. Insight is what is invited, not further storytelling. (Further help with groups is offered in Chapter 9.) Even when a group is not present, as in individual supervision, it can sometimes be very valuable for supervisees to hear what the supervisor has learnt or been reminded of through today's work. Even when it is not appropriate to voice this with supervisees, a hospitable supervisor can note to themselves what gift their guest brought home to them today.

- *Practicalities.* Being clear about the date of the next meeting and any expectations involved helps supervisees know that their work lies within an ongoing intentional rather than opportunistic relationship. Dealing with practicalities within the time together always protects against leakage into phone calls and emails between sessions and models the kind of containment that pastoral practitioners need to practise in order to leave one situation in a good enough place to be able to concentrate properly on the next.

- *Saying goodbye.* Unnegotiated endings play havoc in people's lives. Many people end up in pastoral need due to unsatisfactory endings: a sudden death; unexpected loss of a job; relationship breakdown; the hanging up of a phone; the slamming of a door. People who have known care as a result of such events often go on to become carers themselves. Supervision offers a chance to model endings that can be healthy, anticipated and negotiated. (There is more material about this in Chapter 10.) Managing the micro-endings of each session well will incrementally strengthen the quality of the relationship – for as long as it continues – and play a part in enabling the final supervisory goodbye when it comes to an end. As with all aspects of supervision, knowing who you are working with will determine when those goodbyes come. Some supervisees will continue the session right to the front door, no matter how many goodbyes you voice. Others will be alert to the time themselves and make the first move.

# Exercises

The exercises offered in later chapters will focus on various aspects of exploration, the main task of supervision. Those offered here relate to the first two phases: *hosting and containing* and *eliciting and focusing*. The last exercise gives an example of a structure that reinforces the six processes of supervision outlined above.

## Exercise 2.1 The Physical Environment

*For reflection*

Think of the physical space in which you either offer or receive supervision – or might. Is there anything about the room that speaks to you of God's *hosting and containing* presence? In what ways does it foster vocational and missional reflection? What could be done to make it more conducive to its transformative purpose? Even in ugly functional settings, an object of beauty carefully placed can help focus attention on a person's aspirations.

## Exercise 2.2 Becoming Present

*For reflection*

How do you prepare to be 'present' in supervision? How do you clear a space from your own busyness to make room to welcome the other? Do you take time to mark the transition from what you were doing prior to this or does one activity leak into the next? Try standing on the threshold of the door of the room you use and asking yourself what you are carrying into the supervisory space that does not belong there. Mentally leave outside the door anything that belongs elsewhere, and only then cross the threshold.

## Exercise 2.3 Identifying the Supervisory Question

*To try*

Allow ten minutes for this exercise.

• Gather some objects together (from a drawer or your desk).
• Without pausing to think, choose one object to represent each of the situations you are currently involved with that might possibly form the subject of a supervision session.
• Looking at the objects you have chosen, which holds the most *interest* for you?
• See if you can answer the following questions:
  • What is the question/issue I am identifying?
  • Why is that a *supervision* issue (rather than a spiritual direction or counselling issue)?
  • Why is that an issue for me particularly at the moment?
  • What might I hope to gain from exploring this issue?

If you are supervising someone else, you might try using this exercise with them at the start of your next supervision session.

## Exercise 2.4  The Six-Shape Supervision Structure[5]

Figure 2.3 Six-shape supervision structure

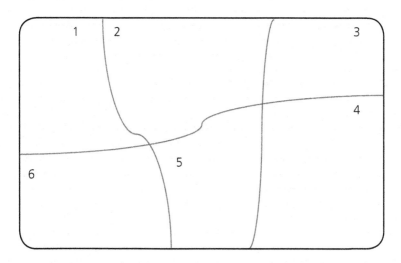

*To try*

### Hosting and containing

- Welcome the supervisee/group and ensure they have time to check in and arrive.
- Provide some A3 pieces of paper and some coloured crayons.

### Eliciting and focusing

- Invite your supervisee(s) to take a piece of paper and divide it into six irregular segments with a crayon or pen. Ask them to choose a number of coloured crayons or pens with which to work. Guide them through the following exercises at a focused but generous pace, so that your supervisees have time to think.
- In the first box, tell your supervisees to write a number '1' and to draw something that represents the situation, person or group of people they want think about. Don't let them worry about

artistic competence. Stick people are fine. Just invite them to make some marks on the page that will act as a reference for them. Encourage the use of colours and shapes to give a sense of mood.

- In the second box, ask people to write a '2' and find a way to draw the question or issue that is their real focus of concern.

## Exploring and imagining

- In the third box, ask them to write a '3' and draw something that gets in the way of solving the problem or addressing the situation.
- In the fourth box, ask them to write a '4' and to focus on their feelings about this situation, using colours and shapes to express this.
- In the fifth box, ask them to write a '5'. The invitation is for your supervisees to take a step back and think about the factors in the situation they have overlooked. Having expressed their feelings, what thoughts do they have about the situation or the wider context that haven't yet been brought into play?

## Bridging and enacting

- Finally, in the last box, your supervisees have the chance to think about a next step. Ask them to review the journey from 1 to 5 and then make some marks that represent something concrete they can do next.
- Invite your supervisees to share any insights they have gained.

## Tracking and monitoring

- Depending on the time you have available you might move straight to *reviewing and closing* or give time for further exploration. It can be useful to give the supervisee(s) a chance to embody one or more of the images they have created, as a way of presenting what has most struck them to their supervisor or to the group (see Chapter 6 for more discussion of techniques of embodiment).

- Alternatively, the journey expressed on the page can become a document supervisor and supervisee can look at together, noticing and wondering and identifying any areas that merit further exploration by another means.

## Reviewing and closing

- Make sure people are clear about the arrangements for next time and that there is time to review the group covenant if necessary.

## Notes

1 This process model of supervision is inspired in part by the work of Steve Page and Val Wosket outlined in *Supervising the Counsellor and Psychotherapist: A Cyclical Model*, 3rd edn, Hove and New York: Routledge, 2015. Our process model adds attention to hospitality, presence and wisdom, all of which are essential if supervision is to be soulful.

2 Parker J. Palmer, 1993, *To Know as We are Known: Education as a Spiritual Journey*, San Francisco: HarperSanFrancisco, pp. 71–5.

3 Antony Williams, 1995, *Visual and Active Supervision: Roles, Focus, Technique*, New York and London: W. W. Norton, p. 210.

4 Williams, *Visual and Active Supervision*, p. 209.

5 This supervisory tool was devised by Anna Chesner and is described in more detail by her in 'The six-shape supervision structure', 2014, in Anna Chesner and Lia Zografou (eds), *Creative Supervision across Modalities: Theory and Applications for Therapists, Counsellors and Other Helping Professionals*, London and Philadelphia: Jessica Kingsley, pp. 71–87.

# 3

# Attending in the Present

## Summary

In the first chapter we highlighted the importance of attending to the horizon of God's purposes and to each supervisee's sense of vision. In the second chapter we paid attention to the process and structure of a typical supervision session, concentrating on the *hosting and containing* and *eliciting and focusing* phases. In this chapter we look more closely at the *exploring and imagining* phases of supervision. Two tools are offered for helping supervisees explore their work – these are faithful to the vision of pastoral supervision set out in the first chapter and invite reflection on the past for the sake of future learning.

Early on the first day of the week, while it was still dark, Mary Magdalene came to the tomb and saw that the stone had been removed from the tomb. So she ran and went to Simon Peter and the other disciple, the one whom Jesus loved, and said to them, 'They have taken the Lord out of the tomb, and we do not know where they have laid him.' Then Peter and the other disciple set out and went towards the tomb. The two were running together, but the other disciple outran Peter and reached the tomb first. He bent down to look in and saw the linen wrappings lying there, but he did not go in. Then Simon Peter came, following him, and went into the tomb. He saw the linen wrappings lying there, and the cloth that had been on Jesus' head, not lying with the linen wrappings but rolled up in a place by itself. Then the other disciple, who reached the tomb first, also went in, and he saw and believed.

John 20.1–9a

This passage is about the first witnesses to the resurrection. That there is a story to be told at all arises because Mary and Peter were willing to be present at the tomb of Jesus. The importance of being physically, cognitively, emotionally and spiritually present to a supervisee has been emphasized in the last chapter, as we looked at the processes of *hosting and containing* and *eliciting and focusing*. Mary and Peter are willing, however, not just to be present at the tomb, but to explore it. They are willing to confront their own fears and bewilderment, to go into the darkest and most mystifying place and face even death. It is through doing this that they become witnesses not only to death, but to the reality of new life.

As we have already suggested, supervision may be about helping people to face whatever is difficult in their work, but it always requires the supervisor to maintain faith in the possibility of new life; to keep their eyes on the horizon of resurrection, even when the route is unclear.

There is more to be gained from this passage though, because the means by which Mary and Peter and John come to be good witnesses to resurrection is through the deployment of three kinds of seeing, all of which are important in the process of coming to understand the way God is working. In the English version we have here, all three kinds of seeing are translated the same, 'she/ he saw', but in the Greek – the original language of John's Gospel – the three words used connote different levels of seeing.

## The Three Levels of Seeing

### Noticing

First, when Mary (v. 1) and John (v. 5) go to the tomb they *take note of* the literal, physical things going on. Mary notices that the stone has been rolled away and that the body of Jesus has gone; John notices the linen wrappings lying in the tomb. The

Greek verb used in both instances is *blepō* – observing in detail the situation as it appears. Observation without interpretation is the first level of seeing.

The relevance of this level of seeing to supervision is that supervisors and supervisees are first of all witnesses in the literal sense that they need to listen to what they hear and notice what they see – the kind of listening and noticing that requires real concentration. When this happens, attention can be drawn to things that are currently eclipsed from the supervisee's sight.

An example is provided by a supervision session with Donna. Jane was responsible for Donna's training, and observed that when Donna had been assisting at communion she had issued the invitation to share the peace without making eye contact with the congregation, and also that in sharing the peace with Jane – and, Jane thought, others – Donna had looked past her. Jane thought it important to help Donna reflect on the possible impact of this for ministry – the mismatch between pronouncing peace or blessing or forgiveness and not being able to embody it to the extent of meeting people in the eye.

When they met for supervision, Jane simply observed what she had seen. 'Donna, I noticed that when we shared the peace in chapel on Thursday you didn't meet my eye. Can you explore with me what that is about?' At first Donna didn't really believe this had happened. The strength of bearing witness in supervision to what Jane had seen with her own eyes, rather than dealing with the reports of others, was that Jane was sure of what she had seen – even if not its significance. But before long Donna was offering her own interpretation: that she didn't really think she was worthy of offering Christ's peace; and then, on further reflection, that she wasn't sure she was really receiving Christ's peace when it was offered to her. Jane and Donna were then able to talk about how this might become more possible and the impact it might have on her ability to embody peace and forgiveness and blessing for others – not just in leading worship but in other aspects of her ministry.

When a ministry context is shared with a supervisee it is possible for the supervisor to bring their own observations about the supervisee's work directly into the supervision session. However, often supervision takes place remotely from the working environment, and when supervision is not part of training or line management, the supervisor and supervisee may only see each other in the context of the session. In this case the supervisor still needs to bear witness to what they see and hear – although this will be restricted to what happens in the supervision session. An example is provided by a supervision session with Malcolm. When Malcolm was telling his supervision group about his boss in the hospice where he worked he became distracted, picking at his trousers and swinging on his chair. His sentences became fragmented and his tone flat, and he lost eye contact with the group. When the group pointed this out, Malcolm was at first surprised but immediately said that his boss was really poor at communication, and that it meant he never felt listened to or secure in his presence. This deepened the conversation about Malcolm's relationship with his boss, which moved into his strategies for maintaining his own identity and sense of safety when meeting with him. More will be said in Chapter 6 about how we can communicate by impact as well as in words, but at the moment it is important simply to note the importance of bearing witness as supervisors to what we see, in order to help our supervisees be aware of more of what is going on for them.

## Wondering

In both instances cited here the importance of the first level of seeing, plain noticing, is borne out. Beyond this, however, there is another level of seeing that is important and to which the story of the empty tomb points. Returning to the text, in John 20.6, when Simon Peter comes to the tomb, he sees a whole series of things: the linen wrappings lying there; the cloth from Jesus' head – not with the other wrappings but lying separately by itself, rolled up. In English this is unremarkable, and yet the Greek verb used is not *blepō* (I notice) but *theōreō*, from which we get the English word 'theory'. Simon Peter is not just noticing these things, but wondering about them; constructing theories about how things came to be like this; looking from different perspectives and asking questions.

This is the second level of seeing that is important in supervision – looking from different perspectives to make sense of what we observe and wondering about the meaning of what is happening. Sometimes – perhaps often – our theories can be wrong, and yet offering them as simple wonderings or theories rather than as definitive interpretations can help supervisees stay responsible for their own pastoral work and its interpretation. In the end it is they and not us who will need to go back into the original situation. Nevertheless, our wonderings can help supervisees think about things differently from how they might have thought about them alone and try out a range of perspectives.

In Donna's case, had Jane started by saying, 'I'm worried that you don't believe you're good enough to be a minister and embody God's grace for others', it would have allowed little room for exploration and would have imposed Jane's interpretation on what she had noticed. Donna's options would have been either to agree with Jane, and doubtless feel shamed (potentially reinforcing what may have been behind the lack of eye contact in the first place), or she could have defended herself or demanded to know how on earth Jane could know that. By choosing to present Donna first with what she had noticed – that Donna couldn't meet her eyes – and then inviting Donna to explore with her what that might be about, Donna was able to deepen awareness of her own pattern and find her own interpretations. Jane's private theory had been that Donna didn't feel worthy of offering others peace. By presenting it to Donna as a possibility and not the 'truth', Donna was able herself to take the interpretation a step further and realize she needed to work on receiving Christ's peace herself.

## Realizing

The use of the word 'realize' brings us to the third level of seeing. In John 20.9 the beloved disciple goes into the tomb. The verb used this time is *horaō*. Sometimes in John's Gospel this verb is interchangeable with *blepō* and means literal seeing, but often –

as in the case of blind Bartimaeus – it refers to a deeper level of insight. In John 20 the spiritual meaning is emphasized by its coupling with the word 'believed': 'Then the other disciple, who reached the tomb first, also went in, and he saw and believed.' For John, the third level of seeing involves seeing in kingdom perspective – perceiving things as they really are; realizing the truth; seeing in action the broader motifs of the gospel. In one sense this level of seeing is a reminder to pastoral supervisors that our work is not simply about helping supervisees with the practicalities of ministry or to come to psychological insight, but to understand their work in kingdom perspective. It is important sometimes to be explicitly theological, to ask the theological questions (and more will be said about this in Chapter 7), but the third level of seeing is also a reminder that we cannot realize things for other people. What matters generally in supervision is that a supervisee comes to their own realizations about their work.[1] This may come about through weighing up the witness and the wonderings of others, but in the end insight needs to belong to the supervisee if it is to be effective in their ministry.

The three verbs of seeing used in John 20 provide a helpful and memorable way of establishing the ethos of pastoral supervision, and they recall the supervisor – or members of a supervision group – to the importance of being a witness. Being a witness requires both our reliable presence and our willingness to make interventions: saying what we see and what we wonder, and keeping our eyes on the spacious horizon of God's grace.

## The Supervisor as Witness

Supervision happens as the supervisee tells the story or shows the supervisor what is happening in their ministry. This 'getting the work into the room' may be by means of a simple verbal account or it may be done through a variety of media, as described in outline in Chapter 2. Whatever the medium, the role of a supervisor is first to help supervisees see what is happening in their work as succinctly as possible and then to bear witness to what they see and hear and experience. This sounds simple, but what we see depends in large part on what 'lenses' we as supervisors are wearing. If we look with *restorative* lenses at what someone is saying, we will see where they are depleted or fragmented; if we look with *formative* lenses, we will notice what we think they need to learn; if we look with *normative* lenses, we will pay attention to issues of boundaries and codes of ethics. For the pastoral supervisor, however, the role of witness has a particular dimension, highlighted in the literature of spiritual direction:

A witness is one who is, above all, present. A witness looks as well as listens, sees as well as hears. A witness to the marginalized is present to see and hear those who are often invisible and inaudible.[2]

In the supervision context, the 'marginalized' may be factors in the situation the supervisee is describing that the supervisee has overlooked. For example, in reflecting with Michael on a sermon she had preached, Julie, a Reader, was focusing on the one piece of critical feedback she had received and becoming depressed about her ability as a preacher. By asking about other responses and comments Julie had received, Michael was able to draw Julie's attention to the more positive feedback she had pushed to the edge and then help her think about the sermon in a more balanced way.

Being a 'witness to the marginalized' may also be about helping the supervisee attend to the small voices within them that need to be brought into focus in order to be heard. Simply observing how your supervisee seems physically may help them 'hear' what their bodies are saying. 'You seem tired today.' 'Is your back hurting you?' 'Your voice seems strained.' Often our bodies carry information of which we are only peripherally aware. A witness who says what they see can help us focus our attention where perhaps it needs to be. Careful listening to the language that supervisees use can also be helpful. 'You have used the word "careful" three times. Is that important? Is it a positive thing here or are you fearful of something?' It is often the case that as supervisees we are unaware of the significance of the words we are choosing until someone draws our attention to them and we can hear the truth they contain.

It may also be the case that the voice that has become marginalized for the supervisee is the still, small voice of God's Holy Spirit, assuring them of their identity in Christ. James Neafsey writes of supervising spiritual directors:

> If the capacity to 'see beyond' is central to supervision, then the primary focus of supervision will be the deep spiritual identity of the [spiritual] director, who he or she is in God rather than correct or incorrect performance at the behavioural level. The supervisor's role is not so much to measure the [spiritual] director's behaviour against extrinsic standards of right and wrong but to behold the unique image of God at the core of the director. Within this open, spacious spiritual horizon, attention can be given to whatever level of the director's experience needs attention at the moment, including issues of performance or skill.[3]

Part of the responsibility of the supervisor, no less in pastoral supervision than in spiritual direction, is to bear witness to the supervisee's identity before God and indeed to the nature and character of God: not to allow the shame and guilt and regret and anger and resentments supervision can help unearth to have the final word or become the defining reality, but to help the supervisee to experience these feelings within the spacious horizon of God's healing and transforming power and reliable presence. This is not to dismiss the importance of allowing negative feelings and difficult issues to come to light, but it is important that the supervisor – at least in their own mind, and when appropriate in speech – remains aware of the identity of their supervisee as a child of God, a disciple of Christ and a person with a vocation within the body of the baptized.

When establishing the ethos of a supervision group it is also important to find a way of inviting the group into an atmosphere of exploration rather than of problem-solving or advice-giving.

Using the three levels of seeing encapsulated in discovery of the empty tomb in John 20 can help supervisees map the journey from seeing and noticing, through wondering and exploring, to realizing and perceiving what is going on in the supervisory issue.

## Noticing and Naming

Figure 3.1 First level: noticing and naming

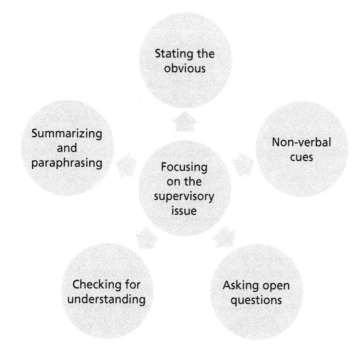

The first level of seeing works with the incontrovertible, the facts of the matter, the kind of thing CCTV would pick up if a supervision session were recorded and played back:

- I notice that today you're clutching on to that cushion.
- I notice that we're only four minutes into our time together and you've already named many issues, any one of which could fill the hour.

- I notice that I can't get a word in edgeways today.
- I notice that you told that story without pausing for breath.
- I notice that you haven't made eye contact with me since you started talking about J.
- I notice that I'm fidgeting more than normal.
- I can normally follow what you're saying but today I notice that I'm losing the plot.
- I notice a flatness in your voice today that isn't normally there.

Sometimes it is easy to neglect this level of seeing since it appears to be too simple and offends our need to appear sophisticated. In reality, being able to state the obvious can result in a breakthrough of insight for the supervisee. For example, in group supervision someone noticed that Mary, a hospice chaplain, ended all her conversations with 'See you later' rather than 'Goodbye'. That insight became transformative in helping Mary to realize that her concerns about her partner's health were preventing her from hearing issues of loss and death in her work with dying patients and had led her to become emotionally unavailable to those in her care.

## Wondering and Musing

The second level of seeing focuses on whatever arouses curiosity. Stories provoke our imagination and cause us to wonder and to turn things over in our minds.

- I wonder how you got through that awful situation you've just told me about.
- I wonder what supports you from the inside when you work with distress like that.
- I'm really curious about your throwaway remark, 'That's men for you'.
- I find myself wondering what 'good enough' work is for you.
- I wonder who taught you to be hard on yourself.
- If you had a magic wand, I wonder what you'd wish for.

Figure 3.2 Second level: wondering and musing

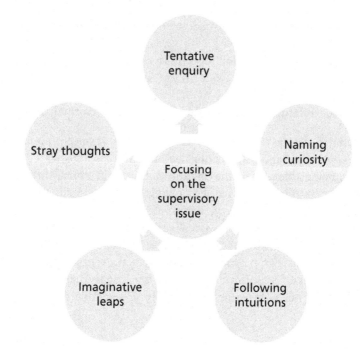

- I wonder what your dream job would be, since you find this one so difficult.
- If ethics didn't prohibit it, what would you really like to do or say to X?
- I wonder what a professionally permitted response to X could be.

Wondering is not the same as analysing or interpreting. Within the overarching context of hospitality, wonderings need to be treated as offerings that supervisees are entirely free to pick up and run with or discard. Supervisors and group members need to pitch their wonderings and musings in ways that open and enlarge space for exploration rather than close and shut it down. The more clever an interpretation in a supervisor's head, the less likely it is to be of use to a supervisee. Wondering allows spaciousness to grow within the supervisee's frames of reference. Interpretation tells them what they should have been thinking about. The subtle difference is important if supervision is to be about transformative learning and not about coming to an expert for a diagnosis and prescription.

## Connecting and Realizing

Figure 3.3 Third level: connecting and realizing

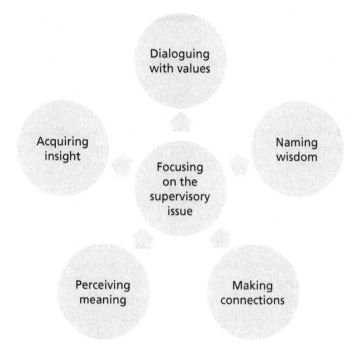

The third level of seeing focuses on making connections between self and work, values and wisdom. It looks for insight, for the penny to drop, for things to fall into place, the fog to lift and clarity to dawn. Realizing the significance of the part within the whole is the whole *raison d'être* of supervision. While exploring things for their own sake may be intellectually stimulating, unless it results in insightful ways to improve future practice it will be of limited value. What Parker Palmer says of education can also be said of supervision: 'space needs to be charged'.[4] The 'charge' running through supervision is the commitment to ensure that those on the receiving end of the supervisee's care receive the best care possible.

- How does what you're describing connect with your value system?
- What do you realize about the values of the organization you're working within?
- What are the internal stories that give you meaning and purpose?
- How does this piece of work connect to your own sources of wisdom?
- What throws you off balance in your work?
- Where do you find your equilibrium?
- What's the worst that could happen; the best that could happen?
- What do you realize by engaging this little story with the macro stories of your practice, life, spiritual tradition?

## Framing Questions

Naming what we see and what we wonder, and inviting supervisees to make connections, are the first steps in pastoral supervision towards making interventions that invite exploration. Many of these interventions are framed as questions.

The following five questions are a suggested framework for exploring prayerfully with a supervisee any situation they bring to pastoral supervision. They are derived from a model of theological reflection known as Pastoral Theology as Attention.[5]

1. Whose voices can you hear, and whose are silent or silenced?
2. What are the wider issues here?
3. What is the situation doing to you?
4. What does the Christian tradition have to say?

74

5. What, in the light of all this, is the mission of the Church, and within that, what is your role, here and now?

## Attending to the Voices

The first question draws the supervisee's attention to other voices than their own in the situation they are describing. It may be helpful to ask them to clarify what people have actually said and what the supervisee imagines others think or feel. It may be important to ask whether there are other voices that are not being heard, that are being silenced or are being heard only through the mediation of others. The supervisor may have direct knowledge of the situation and use this to ask about characters who seem absent from or misrepresented in the supervisee's account. The purpose of these kinds of questions is to help the supervisee achieve some distance and see the situation from various perspectives.

## Attending to Wider Factors

The second question broadens the focus. If pastoral supervision is about helping people see in broader perspective, at this point the supervisor would help the supervisee think about features of the situation that are common features of human behaviour in general, the culture in question or the organization for which they work. Some supervisees may personally have a lot of expertise to draw on and with which to interpret a given situation – perhaps from psychology, group theory or cultural studies – and once the questions have been asked they may realize connections for themselves. Other supervisees may need some formative supervision arising from these questions in order to help them interpret more accurately how people are behaving or how the culture they are ministering in operates.

## Attending to the Supervisee's Own Feelings

The third question concentrates on the feelings and instincts of the supervisee. This may well mean returning to what the supervisee began with: their anger or frustration or sense of humiliation may be what prompted them to bring the situation to supervision in the first place. Having broadened the focus, however, feelings and instinctive responses may have shifted or clarified; it is a good idea not to lose sight of these and to bring the supervisee's attention to them – especially if being in touch with their feelings is not something that comes naturally. Unexpressed feelings are likely to be highly influential in ministry situations. Supervision is a good place to explore them so that the supervisee can be responsive rather than reactive. This is a restorative aspect of pastoral supervision but one that helps to clear the supervisee's field of vision. It is also worth noting that the supervisor may have experienced a strong reaction to the material being presented in supervision because of the resonances it has with their own situation. Supervision is not the place to explore these feelings, but it is important that their influence be noted and checked. More will be said about this dimension of supervision in Chapter 5.

## Attending to the Theological Tradition

The fourth question looks explicitly at what the theological tradition has to offer. This may be the Bible, church teaching or a spiritual resource of some kind. The initial stages of exploring the situation may have already been couched in theological language, but this is an opportunity to think more broadly and more deeply. Is there any wisdom from the tradition that might shed new light? This might come from the supervisee, prompted to think about relevant biblical passages, what they are reading or their prayer life in relation to the situation; or it might be that the supervisor can offer something for the supervisee to explore. There may well be formative work to do here as the supervisee moves from an embedded (previously unconsidered) theology to a more deliberative[6] (considered and owned) theological position that makes sense to them in the context.

## Attending to the Supervisee's Role and Influence

The final question invites the supervisee to narrow their focus as they think about returning to the situation or how they will handle similar issues in future. This requires a clarity about what the Church is for in general and the boundaries and responsibilities of their own role in particular. These are normative issues. It is always important in supervision to end with an opportunity to think about the next steps the supervisee will take, to help them make a bridge from the expressive and sometimes playful treatment of a situation in supervision to a realistic and manageable action or strategy they can try.

Structured reflection using all five steps of the method in a supervision session may be useful to supervisees who are training or who have a particularly complex situation to respond to. More generally, these questions offer areas for exploration that can be used in a tailored way, depending on what the supervisee most needs on a particular day. More guidance is provided in Exercise 3.3 at the end of this chapter.

## Conclusions

In this chapter we have been focusing on the importance of supervisors being a reliable presence, fully available to listen to their supervisees in order to help them interpret their context and role and discern the way forward in their practice. We have looked at the supervisor as witness – both to the supervisee's identity in Christ and also to what they see and what they notice – and we have begun to look at the interventions supervisors might make: sharing what they notice and wonder with supervisees and asking questions that broaden the supervisee's focus and help them reflect on their own feelings and role in theological perspective.

The exercises that follow ask you to think about the quality of your presence in supervision and invite you to practise paying attention to the five steps by reflecting on a piece of your own ministry. Exercise 3.3 then suggests how this tool might be used in supervising others. Finally, for those whose who work well in other modes than talking, Exercise 3.4 outlines a creative method for getting the supervisee's work into the room.

# Exercises

## Exercise 3.1 Seeing in Three Dimensions

*To try*

Sit comfortably in a room and let your eye fall upon any object. Allow yourself to attend explicitly to:

- What you see or notice about it (its colour, shape, size, scale, design etc.).
  *This is the first level of seeing, which is about observation without interpretation.*

- What it makes you wonder about (its history, who made it, where it came from, how it came to be sitting where it is, what difference it would make if it were turned upside down etc.).
  *This is the second level of seeing, which attends to what makes us wonder or arouses curiosity or questions.*

- What you realize about it (whether it fits in or clashes with the other objects in the room; whether its setting does it justice or whether it would be better against a different background or in a different position; what the object is for; what meaning it has etc.).
  *This is the third level of seeing, which looks for the meaning in things.*

## Exercise 3.2 Being a Witness

*For reflection*

Think about yourself as supervisor.

### Noticing and naming

1 What kinds of thing do you notice and what might you miss?

> Physical things – how a room is set up; body language; the way someone dresses.
> Emotional states – how someone is feeling; how you are feeling.
> Ideas – the content of what someone is talking about.
> Language – the words people use.

Is there anything you want to practise noticing more?

2 Supervision involves noticing and naming things that in social conversation would be considered rude. Are there any things you notice in supervision that you struggle to name?

> I notice you're looking tired.
> I notice you're holding yourself quite stiffly.
> I notice you seem quite buoyant even though this is a difficult subject.
> I notice you keep repeating the word 'typical'.

Can you name any obstacles you experience to naming what seems relevant?

### Wondering and musing

> How do you widen the space for exploration?
> Are you able to allow other interpretations than your own of what you notice, or do you close down the space?
> Are you able to offer your own interpretations of what's happening for the supervisee to weigh up, or are you reluctant to offer an opinion?

➢ If you supervise groups, how do you help group members offer appropriate 'wonderings'?

Is there anything you want to change about the way you introduce your perspectives and theories?

## Connecting and realizing

➢ Can you remember a time when a supervisee has come to a realization in a supervision? What role did you play? What role did they play?
➢ Do you deliberately ask your supervisees to name where they have got to as they leave as part of *bridging and enacting*?
➢ When supervising groups, do you make space for the connections group members are making with their own material, even when it is not they who are presenting?

Is there anything you can do to help your supervisees take more ownership of the supervision process?

## Exercise 3.3 Pastoral Theology as Attention

*To try*

This is a tool best used when a supervisee is trying to work out the way forward in a particular situation or to discern their role. Informally, the framework provides some possible questions and areas of discussion. To use the method formally in supervision you will need about an hour. We encourage you to use it for self-reflection before using it with others.

*For reflection*

➢ Begin in prayer or silence, asking for the guidance of God's Holy Spirit.
➢ Look at Figure 3.4.

## Figure 3.4 Interpreting the situation

<table>
<tr><td rowspan="5" style="writing-mode: vertical">Exploring and imagining: Prayerful attention to who God is and what God is saying</td><td>Step 1:<br>Attending<br>to the<br>'voices'</td><td>• Whose voices are part of the conversation?<br>• What are they saying?<br>• What feelings are being expressed?<br>• Whose voices are absent or being silenced?<br>• Whose voices are being mediated by someone else – how does that nuance them?</td></tr>
<tr><td>Step 2:<br>Attending<br>to wider<br>factors</td><td>• What trends in culture are exemplified here?<br>• What kinds of human behaviour are exhibited here?<br>• How has the past shaped the present?<br>• What academic disciplines (sociology, psychology, history) or witnesses from the context (doctors, local politicians, children) might help us understand the dynamics and issues better?</td></tr>
<tr><td>Step 3:<br>Attending<br>to my own<br>'voice'</td><td>• What is your role?<br>• How do you feel?<br>• Where do you locate yourself in relation to the issues emerging?<br>• What are your instincts about the 'real' issues here – where do these instincts come from (personal experience; Scripture; what you've been taught … or read)?</td></tr>
<tr><td>Step 4:<br>Attending<br>to the<br>theological<br>tradition</td><td>• What ethic(s) are being practised in this situation – what is their implicit theology/ideology?<br>• What biblical texts resonate or set up a challenge in this encounter/situation?<br>• Why these texts and not others?<br>• What has your church tradition said about the issues identified?<br>• How helpful/realistic is the stance taken for dealing with this situation?<br>• What other theological resources can you bring to bear (theologians; liturgies; hymns; practices of the church)?</td></tr>
<tr><td>Step 5:<br>Attending<br>to role</td><td>• What is the calling of the church in (every) and this situation?<br>• What is/was your role in this situation?<br>• What do you want to govern your response in the future?<br>• What that is within your power do you want to do next?</td></tr>
</table>

Work through each step in sequence, noting what seems important. You do not have to answer all the sub-questions. They are intended as prompts to help you reflect, not as a comprehensive list. You may find that, as you move on, other issues surface that belong in an earlier section, so leave room to make additions.

> Do not leave out step 3. Sometimes feelings are well buried, but they are always significant.
> At step 4 you might want to do some intentional reading to help you reflect.
> At step 5, review the other steps you have taken. Considering the nature of your role, what – that is within your power – do you need to do next as a result of this reflection? Try to be really concrete, even if it is only a small step.

*For use in supervising others*

> First, frame the supervision as an act of discernment. This might be done through the lighting of a candle; listening to God in silence; the reading of Scripture together; prayer for attentiveness to God's Holy Spirit.
> Next, invite your supervisee to describe the situation they are bringing to supervision (often this will be a situation that has arisen in an earlier supervision (*eliciting and focusing*) but that you have agreed together to give extended treatment).
> Using Figure 3.4 as a framework, work through steps 1 to 4 as ways of *exploring and imagining*. Do not try to use all the prompts. Ask only those questions that seem particularly pertinent to the situation described. In some contexts it may be helpful to share the framework with your supervisee, or to ask them to have worked through the five steps in advance.
> When you reach step 5, this step focuses on the identity and role of the supervisee and reminds the supervisor that, whatever the situation is, it is not a problem to solve, rather you are working with a person who needs to discern what God is asking of them in this particular situation.
> Finish by asking your supervisee what they will take away from today's session. This might be issues for further thought,

conversations they need to initiate or other actions they need to take. Help them work out their next step (**bridging and enacting**).

## Exercise 3.4 Picturing Exercise

*To try*

Some people work well with words, but for others images will speak louder. Try this exercise yourself before inviting those you supervise to try it.

You will need A3 paper and felt-tipped pens in a range of colours.

- Invite people to spread out, with plenty of personal space.
- Give each of them an A3 sheet of paper and a range of coloured pens.
- Ask for a minute's silence.
- Then say:
  - Think of someone you work with with whom you would like a better relationship.
  - What is it like to be in their presence? What is it about that person or that relationship that bothers or concerns you?
  - Now take an imaginative leap and imagine that person as a building; briefly sketch that out on paper using the coloured pens. To indicate you have finished, please put down your pens.
  - Now on that sheet of paper, place yourself in relation to that building. A stick person will do – but think about your size and colour and position in relation to the building you have drawn. And again, to indicate you have finished, put down your pens.

Invite people to come and sit together. Explain that each person is invited in turn to present their work to the group without any words, so that those who receive the presentation can simply say what they see and what it makes them wonder about, but will not get any answers from the person presenting.

The presenter needs to listen to what is said and weigh it in their mind. Some feedback will be off the mark and can just be discarded. Some will resonate and help the presenter realize something. Some will disturb – this may be because it is spot on and has hit a blind spot. Try not to dismiss in your mind feedback that is difficult to hear.

After everyone has presented and received feedback:

> Ask people to go back to their private space and, in the light of the feedback they received, make one adjustment to their drawing that represents a way of improving the relationship between them and the person depicted. It is important that the change they make is within their power and not just a wish that the other person would change.
> Once again, ask people to put their pens down when finished, and then regroup.

Finally, each presenter – in the briefest of terms – says what they brought and what they learnt. Encourage people to avoid telling the story of this relationship or explaining their drawing – especially the parts people didn't interpret well. What matters is the insight received by the presenter – not that the group find out the background.

## Notes

1 Although there may be occasions when the supervisor will need to give clear direction, particularly if the safety of the supervisee or of others is at stake, this is not the preferred way of working under normal circumstances. It is particularly important in group supervision for the group to be prevented from giving advice or trying to impose their meanings or ways of working on a peer.

2 Norvene Vest, 2003, *Still Listening*, New York: CPI Morehouse, p. 93.

3 J. Neafsey, 2005, 'Seeing beyond: a contemplative approach to supervision', in Mary Rose Bumpus and Rebecca Bradburn Langer (eds), *Supervision of Spiritual Directors: Engaging in Holy Mystery*, New York: CPI Morehouse, p. 21.

4 Parker J. Palmer, 1998 *The Courage to Teach: Exploring the Inner Landscape of a Teacher's Life*, San Francisco: Jossey-Bass, pp. 73–7.

5 An expanded version of this framework is provided in Exercise 3.3. This model of theological reflection was first published in 2007 – see J. Leach, 2007, 'Pastoral theology as attention', *Contact: Practical Theology and Pastoral Care* 153, pp. 19–32.

6 Drawing on the work of Howard W. Stone and James Duke in their 1996 book *How to Think Theologically* (Minneapolis, MN: Fortress Press), Carrie Doehring expands on the relationship between embedded and deliberative theologies and the role of the pastoral care giver in helping people to deepen their faith in this way – Carrie Doehring, 2006, *The Practice of Pastoral Care: A Postmodern Approach*, Louisville, KY: Westminster John Knox Press.

# 4

# Attending to the There and Then

## Summary

In order to work effectively, and to focus on the *work* of the supervisee, pastoral supervision needs to find ways of getting the supervisee's work into the room. The most obvious way for the supervisee to do this is to talk about it and for the supervisor to ask questions that *elicit* the story, *focus* its relevance and help them together to *explore* its significance. Starting from the way Jesus draws the story from the woman at the well, this chapter outlines three ways of attending to what is happening in the supervisee's work. Tools are offered for helping the supervisee to distil and bring significant work to supervision and for helping the supervisor to execute the *eliciting and focusing* processes necessary to effective supervision.

So he came to a Samaritan city called Sychar, near the plot of ground that Jacob had given to his son Joseph. Jacob's well was there, and Jesus, tired out by his journey, was sitting by the well. It was about noon.

A Samaritan woman came to draw water, and Jesus said to her, 'Give me a drink'. (His disciples had gone to the city to buy food.) The Samaritan woman said to him, 'How is it that you, a Jew, ask a drink of me, a woman of Samaria?' (Jews do not share things in common with Samaritans.) Jesus answered her, 'If you knew the gift of God, and who it is that is saying to you, "Give me a drink", you would have asked him, and he would have given you living water.' The woman said to him, 'Sir, you have no bucket, and the well is deep. Where do you get that living water?' Jesus said to her, 'Everyone who drinks of this water will be thirsty again, but those who drink of the water that I will give them will never be thirsty. The water that I will give will become in them a spring of water gushing up to eternal life.' The woman said to him, 'Sir, give me this water, so that I may never be thirsty or have to keep coming here to draw water.' Then the woman left her water-jar and went back to the city. She said to the people, 'Come and see a man who told me everything I have ever done! He cannot be the Messiah, can he?'

Many Samaritans from that city believed in him because of the woman's testimony, 'He told me everything I have ever done.'

John 4.5–11, 13–15, 28–29a, 39

In this Gospel story, human, physical need brings two people together. Tired from the journey, Jesus needs a rest. To provide for herself and her household, the woman needs water. And yet the very ordinary experiences of everyday life provide an opportunity for dialogue, exploration and insight as two people whose paths should not cross renegotiate a boundary and encounter each other with humour and respect. Naming her need for a drink, the woman opens the conversation. Restating the norms that prohibit him from meeting such a request, Jesus widens the conversation from the 'here and now' of this present moment and sets it in the wider context and dynamics that have been forged in the 'there and then' of history. Jesus elicits from the woman the deepest and darkest truths of her life and offers her a space for 'truthful non-shaming speech'.[1] He helps her to explore the deeper meaning of her request and to see things differently (v. 19, *theōreō*). He enables her to explore layers of meaning to such an extent that the encounter becomes transformative not only for her but also for the others whom she bids come and see with their own eyes (v. 29, *horaō*).[2]

Some of the hallmarks of what we have already identified as good pastoral supervision practice are clearly detectable here. *Hosting and containing* are expressed in the meeting of fellow travellers, the negotiating of boundaries and in bringing 'fresh air to the most vulnerable and hidden aspects of ourselves'[3] through a commitment to truth telling and hearing from both parties. The naming of ordinary everyday experiences more puzzling than they would first appear constitutes the *eliciting and focusing* stage of the supervisory process. Broadening the focus of enquiry to allow people to wonder and be curious about alternative ways of understanding what is happening characterizes the *exploring and imagining* process, which is continuously *tracked and monitored* until the supervisee has found the kind of transformative insight that offers them a *bridge* from the place of exploration (supervision) to the place of enactment (work setting) with renewed energy, motivation and focus (*reviewing and closing*).

Often, when thinking about what to bring to supervision, supervisees can be at a loss to know where to begin. The experience of our practice may seem 'ordinary'. We may regard ourselves as dealing in nothing more exciting than patterns of tiredness and thirst. When this happens we can struggle to know what would count as significant enough to bring to supervision. At other times we struggle to know how best to use the time because we are too busy and there is simply too much unprocessed material in our heads. Perhaps due to the emotional ups and downs of our work we have lost our own sense of self among the stories and emotions of those we have listened to. Alternatively, we may not know where to begin because we are uncertain of the reception we will receive if we present a particular issue or reveal some level of unknowing in our practice. At times we may experience a sense of paralysis arising from the awareness that in choosing to present one thing we will not have time to explore so many others and lack clear criteria by which to choose – all the more need, then, for supervisors to help those who come to them to elicit a focus that has sufficient cognitive, spiritual or affective charge to make best use of the time available.

Jane remembers a session at the end of a very stressful period of ministry when, as a supervisee sitting with a new supervisor, she simply sat for almost the whole hour trying to focus what she needed to say. Telling all that had happened in the preceding nine months would have been impossible, but how could she convey the impact of it all in a few words? The process of trying to distil what she needed to say was what was important. The wisdom of her supervisor was in not interrupting the silence, until Jane raised her head and said: 'I thought I had a lot to say.' Drawing attention to the fact that she had folded herself into the chair, covered her head and wept silent tears, her supervisor simply and gently acknowledged: 'You have said it.'

This example points out the importance of allowing time in pastoral supervision to get to what really matters, although it would not be usual to take the whole session doing this. Sensitivity is needed to know when to interrupt a silence or a torrent of words with questions or activities that might help the supervisee start sifting and focusing their material using other **tools for distillation.**

In Chapter 2 we outlined this kind of *eliciting and focusing* as the second process in the supervision session and offered a series of prompts to enable this to be established as early in the session as possible. To help the supervisee condense and find the important threads in what they are bringing, further questions can also be used as the supervision progresses:

- Tell me in no more than ten words what it is about this person that has got under your skin.
- Present the various people you are talking about without words, using whatever you have in your pockets or handbag or objects in this room.
- If you were to write on a postcard the bare bones of this story, what would it say?
- Thinking back over that situation, where would you say was the eye of the storm?
- Can you give this encounter/situation a title?

In her book *Reflective Practice*, Gillie Bolton recommends the practice of writing for six minutes.[4] The aim is to produce a stream of consciousness in writing and, if you can't think what to write, to write about that. After six minutes you are invited to read back to yourself what you have written and highlight what seems significant. Useful as a tool for self-supervision, the technique can also provide a way to help focus a supervisee at the beginning of a session, beginning with what emerges from the exercise. You might ask a supervisee to journal for six minutes under the heading: 'The thing that has replayed in my mind or heart from my practice in the last few weeks is ...' Detailed instructions for this and other such tools are offered in the exercises at the end of this chapter.

Such tools and questions teach the supervisee to focus on the purpose of the supervision session and help the supervisor steer a steady course between being drowned in a torrent of detail and kept floating on the surface with generalizations that reveal nothing.

## Interpreting the There and Then

Having succeeded in getting important material into the room, the supervisor needs to know how to handle it in ways that are not judgemental or threatening, but challenging and formative. To facilitate this process, Peter Hawkins and Robin Shohet, in their seminal book *Supervision in the Helping Professions*, outline a seven-mode approach to supervision. This approach offers seven possible foci within the supervisory material. Each mode produces a different range of questions and suggests different ways of working. The choice of mode should be appropriate to the supervisory question identified. Six of the seven modes fall into two spheres.[5]

Figure 4.1 sets out the two spheres with which this model of supervision is concerned. The bottom circle represents the there and then of the supervisee's relationship with their ministry context. The upper circle represents what happens between the

Figure 4.1  The spheres of supervision

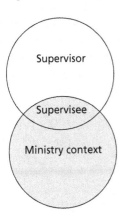

supervisor and the supervisee during supervision sessions. The lower circle is in shadow because to a large degree this is only available to the supervision session by report. Mostly it is the supervisee who will report on what is happening in the ministry context, although where supervisors and supervisees share a ministry context the supervisor will have their own access to information. The question of how to handle such complex dynamics is treated in Chapter 8, but for the moment we are focusing on how the supervisor can help the supervisee bring the there and then of their work into the supervision session and broaden the supervisee's interpretation of what is happening there. For this reason, in this chapter we will focus only on the first three modes in Hawkins and Shohet's **process model**, in which the spotlight falls on what is happening in the supervisee's ministry context. The next three modes, which shine a light on what is happening between the supervisor and the supervisee, will be discussed in Chapter 5. Mode 7, which considers the contextual dynamics underpinning the work (and therefore stands outside the two spheres), will be discussed in Chapter 8.

## Mode 1: Focus on Diagnosis

Working in this mode, the spotlight in supervision shines on the lower circle of Figure 4.1. The focus of attention is not on the supervisee but on the people with whom they work. The task of the supervisee is to represent as accurately as possible the situation or relationship for which they seek insight, so that the supervisor can help them interpret what the issues are and suggest ways forward. The supervisor will ask questions like:

- Can you tell me what happened?
- How do you interpret what is going on?
- Are there other ways to look at this situation?
- Are there other factors to consider?

In summary, what the supervisor is asking the supervisee to do in this mode is 'Paint me a picture' so that interpretations can be examined and broadened.

When working with inexperienced practitioners, some of the motive of the supervisor in choosing to operate in this mode may be quality assurance – to check there is nothing dangerous happening that needs to be stopped; to check out how a supervisee is interpreting the ministry situation they are encountering, in order to help them work out how to act. In this case a danger of the diagnostic mode is that the supervisor will be tempted simply to tell the supervisee what the situation is and how to respond to it. Although this may short-circuit potential problems, it also short-circuits the learning process and prevents a supervisee developing their own sense of pastoral identity and skills. Even when novice supervisees are seeking reassurance ('Tell me I'm doing this right' or 'Tell me what to do'), it is important for the supervisor to help the supervisee broaden their own interpretation of their own context. Ways to achieve this are to ask questions rather than make statements; to give multiple options for possible interpretations and invite the supervisee to weigh them up; and to use tools that explicitly ask the supervisee to work through a range of lenses (such as the pastoral theology as attention model introduced in Chapter 3).

In lots of ways those new to ministry who seek reassurance are easier to supervise than those who are afraid to let their supervisor see what is really going on for fear of being told they are 'doing it wrong'. Such supervisees may benefit from group supervision in which the support of peers makes the risk of exposure more bearable. If gentle persuasion and the use of structured tools do not begin to convince the reluctant supervisee of the value of transparency, the issue may need addressing explicitly (for some discussion of how to interpret and handle resistance, see Chapter 9). The diagnostic mode may be particularly prominent when working with those new to ministry, but in fact it has a place in most supervision sessions. Often even experienced supervisees will be asking, 'Help me interpret what is going on', although increasingly it will be the unusual situations they confront that they need help with, or those in which their own involvement prevents them seeing clearly. In almost all supervision sessions, whatever the subject matter, the supervisor will need to ask the supervisee some questions that arise from looking through Mode 1.

An example is provided by Rachel's presentation of her work to a group of fellow ordinands. Rachel told the story of meeting a couple at a funeral. The minister she was shadowing was busy talking with the funeral party, and so she moved away to allow them some privacy. This left her vulnerable to conversation with a couple who had arrived quite late, but she ended up feeling 'stuck' in the conversation with them and torn, as she was now separated from the minister by the hearse. The conversation fizzled out, leaving Rachel feeling guilty and a failure. Having told the story of the encounter, Rachel was asked to give the 'situation' a title. 'My failure to evangelize', was her answer. Asked why she wanted to bring this to supervision today, she replied that she wanted to learn how to speak of God naturally in ways that make sense to people.

The diagnostic mode of supervision is a reminder that asking questions about 'what happened' is an important aspect of all supervision work. In Rachel's case, before proceeding with any formative work about how to speak of God, the supervisor invited clarifying questions. The group asked, 'What was your role at this funeral?' 'Where did this conversation take place?' 'Had you been to a funeral before?' 'Did you feel trapped?' 'Do you think this couple felt trapped?'

The group learnt that Rachel's understanding of her role was to watch and learn from the minister, and that they hadn't talked much about the dynamics of funerals in advance. When Rachel got separated from the minister (which she hadn't anticipated happening), she felt vulnerable and unsure of what to do as she had never been to a funeral before and hadn't thought much about who would be there and what funerals bring up for people. The group also learnt that the whole encounter took place outside the church as the hearse was approaching and the coffin was being removed. Rachel said she felt trapped on the 'wrong side' of the hearse, but also that this couple who were late were probably very uncomfortable about not being able to slip into the church, and possibly upset by the sight of the coffin. She thought, on reflection, that they had probably felt trapped too.

Having established much more about 'what happened' than she had initially offered, Rachel was asked if she wanted to stick with her title or whether she felt there was a more appropriate one. 'Getting stuck' was the answer. Asked if she wanted to refine what she wanted to learn, Rachel said she realized her time at Bible college had taught her that every encounter should be a mission encounter. Although she still felt she needed to learn about how to speak of God in natural ways, she questioned whether this was ever going to be a fruitful conversation if everyone was feeling stuck and distracted. What she now wanted to learn was, 'How to disengage from a conversation that needs to end.'

In this example, simply by asking attentive questions about what happened and using the distilling technique of giving an encounter a title, the group were able to help Rachel reframe her encounter. The more realistic description of the situation allowed Rachel to reinterpret her learning needs and broaden her sense of the various kinds of encounters she would need to be skilled in as an ordinand. The group were then able to help her think about ways of ending conversations, as well as about discerning when it is right to seek to deepen a conversation and when to bring it to a close.

## Mode 2: Focus on Interventions

In this mode the supervisor's attention is still on the lower circle of Figure 4.1. It is an extension of Mode 1. The focus is still upon 'what happened' but the field of view narrows to look at the interventions made by the supervisee with the aim of increasing the range of pastoral skills employed. Questions are used such as:

- What did you say?
- How did they respond to your saying that?
- What happened next?
- What do you think might happen if ...?
- How about trying ...?

In this second mode the focus is on evaluating what did or did not work and offering creative suggestions. The supervisor asks the supervisee: 'Show me your strategies'.

In order to do this effectively some access is required to the interventions supervisees have actually made. Short of video/ audio recordings, the most helpful tool for this purpose is the **verbatim** method first devised in the 1920s in the context of training for ministry in the USA. Through his own experience of mental illness, Anton Boisen came to believe that ministry students have most to learn from encountering themselves as they make relationships with those who are ill. He began training ordinands in 'clinics'; that is, places where a concentration of people with particular needs could be found (at first psychiatric hospitals, then acute hospitals, hospices and prisons). By the 1960s, under the influence of figures like Seward Hiltner, the model developed into what has become known as **Clinical Pastoral Education (CPE)**. Students spend time on the wards, time in **clinical supervision** looking at their own reactions and development, time learning theory and time in groups looking at verbatim accounts of their own encounters.

Although it was developed as a training tool, verbatim is a good way of reflecting on any encounter in which we want to improve our practice or understand better what was going on. Good situations to include are those which have left a deep impression on us for reasons we can't quite grasp; which seem dense and which we can't quite recall; or from which we feel we have something to learn.

The method requires the writing down of a key passage of conversation for further reflection. The supervisee is invited to recall their feelings as they approached the encounter – which could be a one-to-one encounter, a meeting or even a phone call. The conversation is recorded like a drama, the practitioner recalling as nearly as possible the actual words used. Body language, interruptions and the practitioner's own internal dialogue should be recorded in brackets or italics. Then the practitioner is invited to reflect on the encounter in retrospect and consider what they want to learn from bringing it to supervision. A template for preparing a verbatim for supervision is provided at the end of the chapter.

The value of the verbatim method is that it gets the detail of supervisees' conversations into the room and offers some access to the actual interventions they have made in encounters. It is still, of course, mediated by the supervisee, and yet in our experience the method reliably brings to light important formative work. Michael found it telling, for example, to supervise a hospice chaplain whose verbatim reports of visits to patients' bedsides invariably ended 'See you later' and never with, 'Goodbye'. Given that all her visits were to people whose deaths were imminent, focusing on her interventions – in this case the avoidance of 'Goodbye' – revealed a whole area of which she had no conscious awareness.

Attention to the actual words used, and the examination of different possibilities for future reference, can also happen informally without a verbatim having been prepared in advance. In Rachel's case above, through the supervisor's use of Mode 1 she identified a new focus for learning that was about strategies and interventions: 'How to disengage from a conversation that needs to end'; using Mode 2 the supervisor might then have developed the supervision by asking Rachel to recall the actual conversation she had had with the couple at the funeral. This would have enabled an examination of the points at which she might have been able, appropriately, to end the exchange and facilitated a rehearsal of a variety of ways of doing that, drawing suggestions from the group for Rachel to try out for size.

## Mode 3: Focus on the Relationship between the Supervisee and their Context

In this mode the spotlight is still on what is happening in the lower circle but now focuses in a broader sense on the relationship between the supervisee and the person with whom they are working in their ministry:

• Tell me about your relationship with this person (or group).
• How did you meet?
• How has the relationship developed since then?
• What did you first notice about this person (or group)?
• Can you give me an image or metaphor for this relationship?
• If you were cast away on a desert island together, what kind of relationship could you imagine ensuing?
• What would a fly on the wall have noticed about your last meeting together?

In summary, in this mode the supervisor asks the supervisee, 'Tell me about your relationship'.

Asking a supervisee to view the particular encounter or situation they are describing in the light of their ongoing relationship with the person or context enables patterns and dynamics that might otherwise escape notice to be seen. Telling the story of how a relationship began and developed can shed new light on particular incidents and the behaviour of one or more parties. An exercise to draw out the historical dimension of relationships is outlined at the end of the chapter. Mode 3 also offers an opportunity to focus on unconscious dynamics that may be at work and may be unearthed by looking at repeating patterns in a relationship or at what seems peculiar in the light of the history of a relationship:

• Is this how you and this person normally relate?

- Do you feel there is anything going on in the relationship that cannot be talked about?
- How do you think this person responds to your authority as pastoral counsellor/minister?
- Do you think you might remind them of someone else?
- What do your relative sizes feel like?
- Do you have a sense that you are being demonized or canonized in this relationship?

Such questions reveal the dynamics of what psychologists call **projection** and **transference**, whereby the feelings and behaviours attached to one relationship or situation can be felt and enacted in another.

In Rachel's case, she had no ongoing relationship with the mourners at the funeral. However, some attention to her 'relationship' with funerals had been revealing. If Rachel had identified a different objective, such as 'understanding why I felt vulnerable', it might have been appropriate to conduct the supervision through Mode 3, looking at her associations with funerals, with death or perhaps with new situations. There might also have been room to explore the way her ongoing relationship with her supervisor was affecting her ability to function at the funeral.

The importance of addressing unconscious dynamics is illustrated by this example of Michael's supervision session on his work with Jack. Michael explained to his supervisor that Jack was an ordinand in residential training who would come to tutorials and be very polite and co-operative, yet Michael never felt he was getting to know what was really going on in his work and development. Whenever a tiny amount of progress was made, at the next supervision Jack would withdraw and seem angry but be unable to voice it. He would then visit other staff members to question the nature or the form of supervision offered, while avoiding eye contact and conversation with Michael.

Michael's supervisor asked him, 'What is your sense of your relative sizes when you interact with Jack?' Michael answered that Jack often seemed very small, making him feel too powerful. Michael's supervisor asked him whether he thought it possible that

98

Jack was transferring his feelings about authority figures in general onto the supervision relationship. He suggested that Michael ask Jack how big or small he felt when coming to tutorials. At the next tutorial Michael asked Jack whether he was aware of his size in any sense during tutorials. He said that being asked questions made him feel as if he was pinned against the wall. Michael asked whether this had ever actually happened to him and Jack agreed that it had. Michael asked whether there was any way that the supervisions could be structured to avoid making Jack feel like this. They agreed to try walking instead of sitting together. The release of the pressure Jack was feeling allowed him to approach the tutorials in his adult self and made it more possible to open up areas of work.

In this way, because Michael's supervisor approached Michael's work with Jack through Mode 3, the focus was on the relationship between Jack and Michael and the way Jack may have been prevented from making good use of the tutorial space by a negative transference. This approach was initiated by the 'size' question.

The issue of 'size' is a useful tool in gaining access to unconscious dynamics that make an impact not only on supervision sessions but also on the work supervisees are engaged in and bring to supervision. Another helpful tool for attending to unconscious processes in the relationships supervisees have with those they work with is the drama triangle devised by Stephen Karpman in 1968.[6] He described the way, in stressful situations, complex feelings that belong together can become split off from one another. For example, unable to bear our own anger in a stressful situation we may project that anger onto a colleague, parishioner or supervisor; while the other person is then experienced as a persecutor, we are left as a powerless victim, believing there is nothing we can do for ourselves. Unable to bear our own vulnerability in the face of the persecution we are experiencing, we may then look for a rescuer to come to our aid. The dynamics of splitting off anger and vulnerability are presented in Figure 4.2.

The invitation to a pastoral worker faced with someone who is feeling like a victim is to get hooked into playing either the persecutor or the rescuer. When working in teams, the dynamics of this

Figure 4.2 The drama triangle: splitting off anger and
vulnerability and becoming the victim

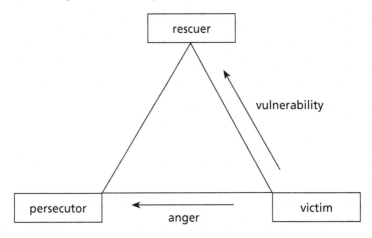

process can be easy to enact. In a hospital situation, for example,
if a patient is complaining about their treatment by nursing staff it
can be easier to play the rescuer and join in with condemning other
staff than to help the patient face up to their own vulnerability
and anger caused by being ill and feeling impotent. Supervision
can help by being alert to such dynamics and asking the chaplain
whether they feel they are being canonized or asked to demonize
colleagues in such a situation. This does not preclude the possibility that there might be situations of maltreatment or injustice
in which a chaplain might act as an advocate for a patient, but
alerts the chaplain to the possibility of **countertransference**; that
is, the awareness of acting out of what is triggered by the patient
in oneself.

Pastoral workers can also be asked to play the role of persecutor. In Jack's case, his sense of smallness when coming to
tutorials was an indicator that he was feeling like a victim. His
superficial co-operation with Michael was likely to be an attempt
to keep the potential persecutor at bay, as he transferred his
feelings from other situations into the supervision relationship.
Unable to experience his own anger (which might provoke the

potential persecutor), he projected it on to Michael. As soon as Michael presented a challenge, therefore, Jack was likely to interpret this as persecution. He demonstrated this by the withdrawal of his co-operation – avoiding eye contact, becoming monosyllabic, courting other members of staff in the hope they would rescue him. What he was not able to do was own his anger at being put on the spot and communicate this directly to Michael.

The challenge for a pastoral worker when on the receiving end of such a strong transference is to avoid playing out the role that they are being offered. In this situation Jack was unconsciously inviting Michael to play the persecutor. Consequently Michael was constantly worried that he was indeed persecuting him. Michael's own supervision was important in providing a context in which he could describe his interventions and check out with his supervisor whether the report he was writing on Jack seemed persecutory. The supervisor was able to confirm that Michael was not persecuting Jack and to point out that there was a strong invitation to countertransference happening. In paying attention to the unconscious dynamic being played out in the tutorial relationship, Michael's supervisor was able to help him resist the countertransference and stick to the learning covenant.

Another possibility offered by the drama triangle is that the pastoral worker may be turned into a victim by the person they are working with. Jane remembers visiting Albert, an elderly church member, in hospital when he had been run over. Instead of being welcomed as someone willing to listen and offer prayers, she felt verbally attacked by the old man. She came away hurt and mystified and reluctant to go back.

Looking at the incident now in the light of the unconscious dynamics represented in Figure 4.3, it becomes possible to see that, unable to bear his own feelings of vulnerability, Albert projected that vulnerability onto a victim (Jane) in whom it could be attacked and kept at bay. Spotting the countertransference at the time would have helped Jane locate her feelings of hurt and fear where they belonged – that is, in situations where she *personally* had been vulnerable – and then concentrate on what was happening for Albert and how she might respond pastorally to him.

## Figure 4.3 Splitting off vulnerability and becoming the persecutor

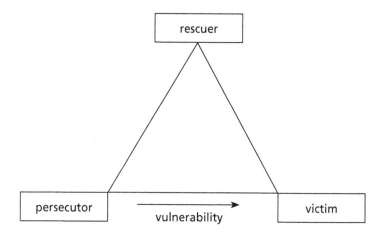

Figure 4.4 outlines the third role in the triangle. 'Rescuers' find it difficult to bear both their vulnerability and their anger and therefore seek both someone to rescue and someone else to identify as the persecutor. This leaves them with the role of rescuing the victim from the clutches of the persecutor. Rescuers are quite common in Christian communities. They can often appear in situations brought to pastoral supervision, as a result of the frustration of those who are 'looked after' and prevented from finding their own power, or of the conflict they have caused by painting others as persecutors. Supervisors will need to help their supervisees to spot when 'rescuing' is happening within their congregations and teams, and to face their own feelings of vulnerability and hostility.

Helping supervisees recognize and understand the dynamics at work in any given situation can go a long way to discovering a way through presenting difficulties and a way of 'interrupting stuck narratives'.[7]

The drama triangle operates as one such stuck narrative, in which the conversation is controlled in a rigid way by the only three options available: to act as persecutor, victim or rescuer. That rigidity arises from the refusal of each of the protagonists to

Figure 4.4 Splitting off anger and vulnerability and becoming the rescuer

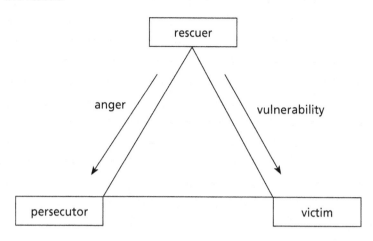

take responsibility for their own actions and feelings, as a result of which the toxicity is passed from one person to another. A redemptive alternative to the drama triangle is offered by Allyson Davys and Liz Beddoe in what they term the 'empowerment triangle'.[8] In contrast to the drama triangle, the empowerment triangle breaks the destructive pattern by offering constructive alternatives to each of the roles. Thus the persecutor ceases to undermine others by becoming appropriately assertive. The rescuer stops soaking up all the debris and psychic fallout and acts from an appropriate level of care, which includes care for self. And the victim puts an end to self-absorption by embracing a sense of vulnerability appropriate to the issue and context. The turning point from stuckness to fluidity, from drama to empowerment, is appropriate ownership and a sense of proportion commensurate with the situation.

Michael remembers working with Sharon, who had been asked by her bishop to give a keynote address at a diocesan conference with less than 24 hours' notice, after the original speaker fell ill. In supervision Sharon reported the fateful phone call from the diocesan office, in which she said 'yes' with her lips and 'no' with her heart. After a sleepless night she delivered the best she could

Figure 4.5 Empowerment triangle: unlocking stuck narratives

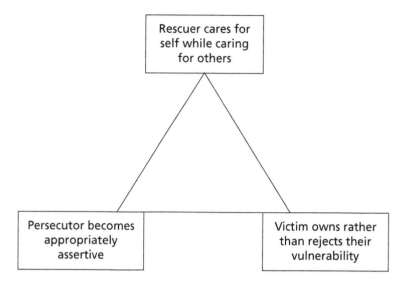

do in the allotted time and asked for questions or comments from the audience. The first contribution from the floor sounded a note of dissatisfaction that there was no 'handout' to accompany her talk, at which point Sharon became enraged and publicly rebuked her hearers for their failure to recognize the pressure she had been under to deliver anything at such short notice. In exploring this in supervision, Sharon recognized that while she was happy to rescue the bishop (after all, it gave her a sense of being noticed and validated), she had switched from rescuer to persecutor in an attempt to ward off feeling victimized by the comment from the floor. Using the empowerment triangle as an alternative way of framing what had happened, Michael was able to help Sharon see other ways she could have handled the request. Her desire to help (albeit with mixed motivations) came from a good place but her rescuing was based on the promise (in this case not delivered) of gratitude. Flipping the drama triangle on its head, rather than rescuing the situation, she could have expressed care (caring role) by doing something manageable (assertive) that honoured her own vulnerability. By looking at the situation this way, Sharon realized she could have responded to the invitation by offering to use her considerable skills as a group facilitator to do some live work with the group rather than accept the invitation to do the impossible – give a keynote address at such short notice – and not only allow herself to get caught in other people's dynamics but try to rescue them.

So far we have looked at the drama and empowerment triangles as tools for helping supervisors identify and help their supervisees work with the unconscious dynamics operating in the pastoral situations they are bringing to supervision. The focus in Mode 3 is upon helping supervisees spot projections onto them and disentangle their responses from the invited countertransferences. It is also possible, however, for the transferences in pastoral relationships to originate with the pastoral worker. More will be said about this in Chapter 5.

Unconscious dynamics are always at play in human relationships and it is therefore important that these can be explored in pastoral supervision. Those seeking supervision for their ministry often have to choose to work either within an ecclesial context, where theological and spiritual issues will be taken seriously but unconscious dynamics ignored, or with a secular supervisor, who will help them recognize unconscious dynamics but be ill equipped to help them think theologically. Good pastoral supervision pays attention to both.

That Jesus was able to work with hidden motivations and unconscious dynamics is illustrated time and again in the Gospels. An example of the dynamics of projection operating within Scripture is provided by the story of the woman caught in adultery (John 8). In this incident Jesus was invited to take sides: to side with the scribes and Pharisees in stoning the woman; or to defend her and prove himself unfaithful to the law of Moses. Instead Jesus invited the Pharisees to face their own feelings of hostility towards the woman and become present to their own fallibility: 'Let anyone among you who is without sin be the first to throw a stone at her' (John 8.7b). Once in touch with their own vulnerability, the scribes and Pharisees melted away and stopped pressuring Jesus to take the role of persecutor. Having resisted the persecutor role both in relation to the scribes and Pharisees and in relation to the woman they wanted to stone, Jesus was then free to respond to the woman with integrity as one who embodied good news: '"Woman, where are they? Has no one condemned you?" She said, "No one, sir." And Jesus said, "Neither do I condemn you. Go your way, and from now on do not sin again"' (John 8.10–11).

## Conclusions

The point Peter Hawkins and Robin Shohet make in outlining the different supervisory modes is not that supervisors should choose one and refine it according to temperament or inclination, nor that they should employ all the modes in a linear progression, but that the skilled supervisor should move freely between them, doing whatever it takes to get the work into the room, offering bespoke supervision, according not to personal preference but to the needs of the supervisee and their context.

If you are already engaged in pastoral supervision you will probably already be operating within all three modes. Separating them out is in some senses artificial, but becoming aware of the modes as distinct approaches offers more possibilities for choosing appropriate strategies in supervision: 'Is the supervisee present to enough of what happened to interpret it effectively, or do I need to get more into the room?' (Mode 1); 'Is the supervisory question about strategies and interventions?' (Mode 2); 'Do I need to help the supervisee focus on their relationship with a person or other aspect of the situation?' (Mode 3). In each case the mode chosen will suggest different ways of *exploring* the material. Mode 2 lends itself to verbatim and to **symbolization** for rehearsing future strategies. Mode 3 might lead a supervisor to choose to work with the picturing methods outlined at Exercise 3.4 or below at Exercise 4.4.

In the encounter between Jesus and the Samaritan woman at the well Jesus offers the woman a way out of the cyclical narrative in which her life is stuck and empowers her for a new role as a witness and evangelist. Supervision that effectively enables supervisees to examine what has happened in particular situations in the there and then of their practice, and that is alert to the ways in which they can get stuck playing roles that are unhealthy for them and for those they seek to serve, can be an agent of transformative learning. The first three modes of Hawkins and Shohet's seven-mode model have been explored here in order to help pastoral supervisors focus on the there and then of supervision. The exercises presented at the end of this chapter invite you to concentrate your attention on each of the three modes in the lower circle in order to embed these before we move on to Modes 4, 5 and 6 in the next chapter. (Mode 7 will be covered in Chapter 8.)

# Exercises

## Exercise 4.1 Six-Minute Journaling (Getting Work into the Room)

*For reflection*

> The moment one gives close attention to anything, even a blade of grass, it becomes a mysterious, awesome, indescribably magnificent world in itself.
>
> Henry Miller

Time-limited journaling provides a medium for self-supervision. The act of 'turning life into text' can be revealing as we see things on the page that we cannot hear ourselves say so easily. A short piece of focused writing provides material you can take to supervision as a starting point for reflection with someone else. You can write on any subject that impinges on your work or ministerial life. If you cannot think of anything, try one or more of the following topics:

- A working relationship I find difficult.
- An aspect of my work that makes me feel really alive.

- A moment of truth.
- Conflict.
- A piece of work I would love to initiate/complete.
- The last straw.

Whichever topic you choose, try to write continuously for six minutes. This will help concentration. Treat it as an act of discernment, expecting that God will reveal something to you as you write or reflect afterwards.

When the six minutes are up (set a timer), read through what you have written.

- Which words or phrases seem significant?
- Does anything surprise you?
- How do you feel now?
- Is there anything you want to spend some time thinking about in more detail?
- Is there anything you might approach differently in the light of this reflection?

## Exercise 4.2 What Happened? (Mode 1)

Figure 4.6 Timeline of ups and downs

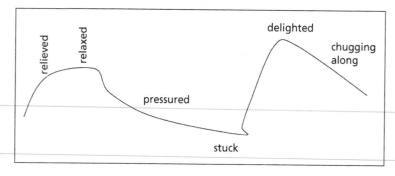

*To try*

- Invite your supervisee to spend six minutes drawing a labelled timeline of their ups and downs in their pastoral practice since you last met for supervision, using no more than ten words. (See Figure 4.6.)
- Invite your supervisee to share the timeline with you and anything they noticed or wondered.
- Share with them what you notice or wonder – for example: 'I notice at your lowest point you seem to be going backwards'; 'I wonder what changed "stuck" into "delighted"'; 'I notice the line has turned downwards again and I wonder if "chugging along" tends to turn into "pressured".'
- Last, invite your supervisee to choose the focus for the supervision session today.

The distillation of the timeline allows the supervisor to interact immediately with the significance the story has for the supervisee and not merely its superficial details. The supervisor may well need to ask the supervisee to say what happened at particular points, but the thread of significance will already have been established in the supervisee's mind, helping them to choose what, among all that might be said, it is important to tell.

## Exercise 4.3 Facilitating Supervision Using the Verbatim Method (Mode 2)

*For reflection*

As ever, it is good practice to have tried writing a verbatim account yourself and taking it to supervision before asking others to bring a verbatim account to you. Try doing this using Figure 4.7.

## Figure 4.7 Verbatim Template

| Your name | |
| --- | --- |
| Date of encounter/meeting/ visit | |
| Setting | |

1  **About yourself** (How were you feeling before this encounter/meeting/visit? What had happened immediately beforehand? What was your aim for this encounter? What did you anticipate your role would be?)

2  **Your knowledge of the situation** (What do you know about the situation before you enter it? This may vary from nothing at all to a great deal. Write what will be helpful to your supervisor when reading this.)

3  **Your initial impressions** (What do you notice, e.g. body language; tone of voice; set-up of the room; atmosphere already established? Does anything surprise you or make an impact on you?)

| 4  **The conversation** (Write here a key extract from the conversation as you recall it. Set it out like a play. Number the contributions people make for ease of reference. Include pauses, tone of voice, interruptions and your own internal dialogue at the time in italics or brackets.) Use separate sheets if necessary but do not exceed three sides of A4. | 5  **Review** (As you write down the conversation, record your current observations, feelings and questions here. How do you interpret what was happening? How do you evaluate your interventions?) |
| --- | --- |
| Example Layout: | |
| Me 1:  Hello, good to see you again.<br>SP 1:  Oh hello.<br>Me 2:  How are you feeling today? | *I think my manner was probably quite 'breezy' and perhaps not appropriate.* |
| *(SP looks down and tears fall into his lap. I feel a bit shocked as last time he was quite upbeat.)* | |

## Figure 4.7 cont.

| Conversation | Review |
|---|---|
| | |

### 6 Evaluation

| a) What do you think are the key issues here? | b) What do you think were the strengths and weaknesses of your interventions? |
|---|---|
| • Theological<br>• Ethical<br>• Psychological<br>• Structural/systemic<br>• Cultural<br>• Other | |

c) What do you hope to learn from bringing this encounter/meeting/visit to supervision?

We are grateful to Derek Fraser and the UK Board of Healthcare Chaplains for the basic outline of this form.

*To try in a group*

- The practitioner should have prepared the verbatim account in advance, with clear guidance about how to do this – for example, according to the template attached in Figure 4.7.
- The facilitator should open with prayer/Scripture, and locate the session as an act of discernment in which we allow ourselves and our practice to be seen by others, trusting that as we discuss together, God's voice will be heard (***hosting and containing***).

1. Invite the first presenter to give a copy of their verbatim out to the group. Ask the group to read through questions 1–3. Are there any questions of fact to the presenter?
2. Invite the presenter to read the verbatim encounter out loud, giving a sense of their own feelings/internal commentary where appropriate; alternatively, the presenter may choose to hear the encounter read by others.
3. Invite the presenter to share anything that struck them through reading/hearing the conversation again. Is there anything that others noticed?
4. Invite the group to read the rest of the comments and evaluation.
5. Invite the presenter to share *why* they have brought this encounter and to say what they hope to learn from the discussion. This is very important in order to give shape and focus to the reflection (***eliciting and focusing***).
6. Invite the group to interact with the verbatim material. Ask them to frame their comments in close connection with the text (for example, 'I notice ...') and to ask non-threatening questions (for example, 'I wonder ...'). Remind the group that although they may have opinions and ideas about the 'meaning' of the encounter, only the presenter was actually there and can *realize* things about their own work. Noticing and wondering can include the feelings and reactions the verbatim evokes in the supervision space (***exploring and imagining***).
7. Invite the presenter to say whether the exploration is yielding

any insight (***tracking and monitoring***). If so, continue; if not, revisit the stated focus.

8. At a natural end, or when the time is coming to a close, ask the presenter what they will take away from the process – *realized* either during preparation of the verbatim or during discussion (***bridging and enacting*** for the presenter).

9. Invite members of the group in turn to note anything they have realized about themselves and their own practice (***bridging and enacting*** for the group).

10. Recall the group's attention to the biblical passage and invite the group to name any resonances for them with the material presented or the issues raised.

11. Thank the presenters and the group and close in prayer if desired (***reviewing and closing***).

## Exercise 4.4 Story Board (Mode 3)

*To try*

Having established that proceeding with the supervision through Mode 3 might be fruitful, invite your supervisee to tell the story of their relationship with this person or context in story-board form (see Figure 4.8).

This might involve inviting them to draw the story in comic strip form by dividing a page into four and using stick figures to depict four stages of the relationship:

- The beginning
- The norm
- An incident
- The latest

Alternatively, a series of drama cards might be used, inviting the supervisee to choose four cards – or more if necessary – to help them tell the story of the relationship.

Figure 4.8 The relationship story

| Meeting: | Early: | Mid: | Now: |
|---|---|---|---|

Ask questions such as:

- What do you notice about your telling of the story of your relationship?
- Are there any scenes missing?
- How would the other party tell the story?

What do you notice:

- about you?
- about the other person?

Do you feel there is anything going on in the relationship that cannot be talked about?

- How do you think this person responds to your authority?
- Do you think you remind them of someone else?
- What do your relative sizes feel like?
- Do you have a sense that you are being demonized or canonized in this relationship?

Invite the supervisee to think about the next scene in the story. How would they like it to be? What could you they do differently? Invite them to add a final box, or to choose a final card (see Figure 4.9).

Figure 4.9 Next step

Next:

# Notes

1 Margaret Bazely and Ruth Layzell, 2014, 'Pithead time for pastors: training in pastoral supervision', in Michael Paterson and Jessica Rose (eds), *Enriching Ministry: Pastoral Supervision in Practice*, London: SCM Press, p. 122.

2 The authors acknowledge their gratitude to Anne Tomlinson, the Principal of the Scottish Episcopal Theological Institute in Edinburgh, for her highly creative reflections, in an unpublished paper, on the dialogue between supervision and John 4.

3 Nicola Coombe, 2011, 'Fear and stepping forward anyway', in Robin Shohet (ed.), *Supervision as Transformation: A Passion for Learning*, London: Jessica Kingsley, p. 181.

4 Gillie Bolton, 2005, *Reflective Practice: Writing and Professional Development*, 2nd edn, London: Sage, p. 145.

5 Peter Hawkins and Robin Shohet, 2012, *Supervision in the Helping Professions*, 4th edn, Buckingham: Open University Press. Subsequent to their original 1989 edition, Hawkins and Shohet added a seventh mode – or what they now term 'eye' – that pays attention to context. They acknowledge themselves, however, that this is a different kind of mode from the other six. We have found it more helpful to deal with the contextual issues in supervision separately, in Chapter 8.

6 Stephen Karpman, 1968, 'Fairy tales and script drama analysis', *Transactional Analysis Bulletin* 7.26, pp. 39–43. For an extended discussion of the drama triangle, see Lynette Hughes and Paul Pengelly, 1997, *Staff Supervision in a Turbulent Environment: Managing Process and Task in Front-Line Services*, London and Philadelphia: Jessica Kingsley, chapter 6. The theory on which the triangle is based originates in the work of Eric Berne, 1964, *Games People Play: The Psychology of Human Relationships*, New York: Grove Press.

7 Sheila Ryan, 2004, *Vital Practice: Stories from the Healing Arts – the Homeopathic and Supervisory Way*, Portland, OR: Sea Change, p. 47.

8 Allyson Davys and Liz Beddoe, 2010, *Best Practice in Professional Supervision: A Guide for the Helping Professions*, London: Jessica Kingsley.

# 5

# Attending to the Here and Now

## Summary

In the last chapter we introduced the use of Hawkins and Shohet's Modes 1, 2, and 3 as tools to help the supervisor *elicit and focus* material and begin to *explore* it. However, there are further tools the supervisor can use to assist with the *exploration* of the supervisee's material. Hawkins and Shohet's Modes 4, 5 and 6 focus not on the 'there and then' situations supervisees report, but on the 'here and now' dynamics of the supervision relationship itself. This chapter, therefore, pays attention to unconscious dynamics and offers tools for paying attention, as the supervisor, to the impact of the supervision on oneself and using this information appropriately in supervision sessions. The last section introduces a way of thinking about the developmental stages of your supervisee(s) and of helping you evaluate what kinds of interventions are likely to be most helpful to them.

When Jesus had crossed again in the boat to the other side, a great crowd gathered round him; and he was by the lake. Then one of the leaders of the synagogue named Jairus came and, when he saw him, fell at his feet and begged him repeatedly, 'My little daughter is at the point of death. Come and lay your hands on her, so that she may be made well, and live.' So he went with him.

And a large crowd followed him and pressed in on him. Now there was a woman who had been suffering from haemorrhages for twelve years. She had endured much under many physicians, and had spent all that she had; and she was no better, but rather grew worse. She had heard about Jesus, and came up behind him in the crowd and touched his cloak, for she said, 'If I but touch his clothes, I will be made well.' Immediately her haemorrhage stopped; and she felt in her body that she was healed of her disease. Immediately aware that power had gone forth from him, Jesus turned about in the crowd and said, 'Who touched my clothes?' And his disciples said to him, 'You see the crowd pressing in on you; how can you say, "Who touched me?"' He looked all round to see who had done it. But the woman, knowing what had happened to her, came in fear and trembling, fell down before him, and told him the whole truth. He said to her, 'Daughter, your faith has made you well; go in peace, and be healed of your disease.'

Mark 5.21–34

One of the striking things about this story is the ability of Jesus to respond in the present moment even when he has a busy – indeed life-and-death – schedule. As the narrative makes clear, Jesus has been asked by a man of importance to do something really urgent and yet, in the busyness of the task, he is touched by someone and is immediately aware that power has gone out of him. Something unconscious, pre-verbal and beneath the surface has taken place. How easy it would have been to let it pass and continue with the important and urgent task of healing. But Jesus has felt something that needs to be brought to consciousness. He knows it is important even though at first he does not know its significance. Stopping in his tracks amid the business of the day and the busyness of the crowd, he makes this slight, fleeting impression central.

One of the things that makes this narrative uncomfortable to contemporary hearers is that Jesus places the woman right there in the middle for all to see. Although it may seem potentially humiliating, somehow, the fullness of her healing will not be effected until what has happened surreptitiously between them can be named. What she has taken from him, she needs to receive as gift. Though physically healed, she is still frightened and trembling, unsure of her place in the community. But as now she has the courage to name what a few minutes ago she could not ask for, so Jesus is able to declare not only to her, but also to the community from which she has been excluded, that her faith has restored her, and allow her to go in peace.

This chapter is about getting beneath the story, the task, the programme of supervision, to become more attentive as supervisors to the things that touch us: those fleeting mental, emotional or bodily impressions that something is going on we cannot necessarily name and yet is important; that sense or intuition that something unarticulated is being asked of us, perhaps even draining us of power, that must be named if fullness of life is to be received by those with whom our supervisees work.

## The Presence of the Supervisor

There is a common illusion that supervisors, like other pastoral workers, should leave themselves outside the supervision room as if they were a blank canvas, neither expecting nor allowing what is brought to supervision to impact upon them. This illusion rests on a mistaken belief that being fit to practise means that nothing they see, hear or sense in the supervision space should affect, interest, attract or repel them. But if relationship lies at the heart of ministry, then the most important factor that will determine the usefulness of supervision is the quality of the relationship between the parties involved. Part of that requires that supervisors work in an ongoing way to integrate the various parts of themselves so as to be present in the supervisory space, not as neutral automatons, but as whole people rooted and at home in their own histories, personal, spiritual and ministerial stories and experiences of life. Supervisors need to be people who have known – as supervisees – the vulnerability of trusting themselves into the loving hands of another as well as the power of being met with redemption rather than condemnation in admitting their weaknesses and mistakes.

If supervisors are to be *usefully* objective in supervision, though, it is imperative they resist having their own needs met through the encounter, since nothing detracts more from the spaciousness of supervision than a needy supervisor who fills the sessions with their own issues or uses them to impart their own pent-up wisdom. For this reason, as we outlined in Chapter 2, it is important that supervisors have been and continue to be supervised themselves.

## The Intentional Use of the Self

While not denying that supervisors need to develop a certain degree of objectivity, an understanding of the supervisor as reliable presence strongly advocates that supervisors need to develop their capacity to use their *subjectivity* for the good of those they accompany. As Harold Searles notes, 'One does not become free from feelings in the course [of supervision]; one becomes, instead, increasingly free to feel feelings of all sorts.'[1] So it is not so much that supervision makes us more objective (though a degree of that is necessary), rather it makes our own subjectivity more useful and trains us to use ourselves as tools that might be of use to others. When all of the supervisor turns up to supervise and the supervisor does their best to practise real presence in the here and now of the supervision space, then all sorts of surprising things can and will be happening.

A supervisor who is fully present, therefore, can become aware of a whole range of feelings and sensations. While none of these can be manufactured or conjured up, common phenomena include:

1. feeling responses (anger, envy, boredom);
2. bodily and behavioural responses (physical sensations, loss of energy, pain);
3. fantasy responses (strange mental images, stray thoughts).[2]

The role of the supervisor as reliable presence and as witness is simply to name what they see, hear, sense or intuit and to offer it to the supervisee to mull over rather than to presume to interpret the meaning. Thus pastoral supervision involves the intentional use of the self of the supervisor for the deep well-being of the supervisee and those among whom the supervisee works. Naming stray thoughts or bodily sensations is but one intentional use of the self.

As Jesus names a bodily sensation in his encounter with the crowd and seeks to discover its meaning for the sake of the healing of the other, so supervisors can use their feelings and bodily responses as information to feed into supervision sessions. Michael remembers working with a supervisee for several years who struggled with anorexia. After each session Michael would eat three biscuits until he realized that the hunger he was feeling was not his own but his supervisee's. The hunger then became something Michael was able to disentangle himself from and use as information to bring into supervision sessions.

Likewise Jane remembers a supervisee whose presence would make her head feel too heavy to hold up. When she realized that this sensation only happened with this particular supervisee, she named what was happening: 'As you're talking, I'm finding it difficult to hold my head up – it feels too heavy. I'm wondering if that sensation has any resonance for you?' As soon as she mentioned it, the supervisee started holding up her own head, and the sensation in Jane's body disappeared. After a few minutes of thought the supervisee said: 'I think I feel like this, when I'm at the hospital. It's like the whole hospital is a baby that can't hold its head up. Somehow it can't take responsibility for itself and I feel like I have to carry it.' Once the supervisee had articulated the feeling and identified that it didn't belong to her either, the weight shifted, and they were both able to start thinking about what it might mean for 'a whole hospital not to be able to support its own head'.

In using feelings and bodily sensations (**somatizations**) as information in pastoral supervision, it is important for the supervisor to be constantly alert to the question of whose feelings these are. It may well be that the feelings triggered in the supervisor belong to them and need processing elsewhere. In this case, the supervisor needs to note the feelings, check they do not belong to the supervisee and put them on one side for attention later. Those feelings, thoughts or sensations that seem unrelated to the supervisor's inner life, however, can be offered tentatively to a supervisee to see whether they hold any resonance.

So far we have discussed the importance of the full presence of the supervisor in the here and now of the supervision session in order to be a witness to what is going on. Like all relationships, supervision is an art that demands supervisors pay careful attention to what supervisees' need, what they can cope with and what will overwhelm them. A good supervisor is one who is flexible enough to coach when needed, counsel as required and be a consultant, evaluator, monitor or model as and when the learning needs of their supervisees require it.[3] Towards the end of this chapter a map of the stages of development of supervisees is set out to help you think about appropriate strategies in supervision for people at different stages in the development of their ministry.

## Working with the Here and Now in Supervision

Figure 5.1 Hawkins and Shohet's Supervision Modes

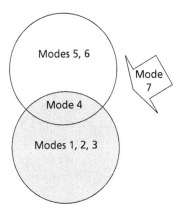

In the previous chapter we outlined three modes of supervision that focus on the there and then of a supervisee's pastoral practice, represented by the lower circle in Figure 5.1: diagnosis (Mode 1), interventions (Mode 2) and the story of the supervisee's relationship with their context (Mode 3).

Modes 4, 5 and 6 of Hawkins and Shohet's process model pick up the theme of attending to the here and now of what lies beneath the surface or between the lines in supervision (represented by the upper circle in Figure 5.1): those fleeting mental, emotional or bodily impressions that something is going on, such that it can be named, brought out into the light and incorporated rather than suppressed.

## Mode 4: Focus on the Supervisee

Towards the end of the last chapter we began to explore the kinds of unconscious processes that might be operating in the ministry context as we looked at Mode 3 of Hawkins and Shohet's model. Our focus then was on the projections that individuals and groups might make onto those in ministry. There we were asking questions about the attitudes towards authority of members of congregations, or the sense of reduced or increased size a student might experience when coming for a personal tutorial. We were focusing on how it is important in supervision to help your supervisee be alert to the ways the people they work with might be transferring feelings and attitudes from one context into their relationship with their chaplain, minister or pastoral counsellor. Being alert to this helps to avoid countertransference.

In Mode 4 the focus remains on unconscious processes, but now the spotlight falls not only on what supervisees or those they seek to help might be carrying into encounters but *what might be triggered in them* by the projections onto them. In other words, what is the impact on the supervisee of the work they are doing?

To access these dynamics a supervisor might ask questions such as:

- Does this person remind you of anyone?
- How do you feel waking up on the day you see that person?
- How do you feel when you hear them ring your doorbell?

- What thoughts or fantasies go through your head about him or her?

Behind these questions is the realization that most of us, by our very calling as Christians, filter out our more primitive responses to people only to be surprised when they jump up and bite us. Of course, such responses might, on the face of it, be positive. In response to being asked, 'Does the old lady you are visiting remind you of anyone?' a supervisee might answer: 'Yes, she reminds me of my late grandmother whom I miss dearly.' Bringing that transference or human echo into awareness allows the supervisee to disentangle and separate out the person they encounter in pastoral visiting – the parishioner – from their *real* grandmother, permitting both people valuable yet distinct existences in the life of the supervisee.

Naturally, positive transferences or human echoes are usually easier to manage appropriately but, if we are honest, some of what goes on in our hearts and minds about people in our pastoral care can be much harder to deal with. Admitting to ourselves that we find a certain person repugnant or someone else sexually desirable can test the limits of our own self-awareness long before we get to the stage of trusting that information to our supervisors.

Michael will never forget a supervisor, sensing that he could not allow himself to name his true feelings about someone, asking him the question: 'What would you like to say to this person if there were no holds barred, and you were not her pastor?' The momentary silence that followed was broken by a torrent of venom from his lips that shocked both of them. Once they had both recovered, Michael's wise supervisor asked if there was anything within what he had said that it would be ethically and pastorally responsible to say to the woman concerned. They then spent the rest of the supervision session role-playing and refining what Michael might say next time they met.

Bringing what lay hidden and buried out into the open was not only cathartic for Michael personally, but led to a much more creative and pastorally healthy relationship with the person concerned. As Sheila Ryan writes, 'Supervision can re-connect us with our experience, to what we knew before we censored, interpreted and changed it to fit this way and that.'[4] That is not to say, however, that I have the right to offload my uncensored raw experience onto those with whom I minister. Supervision, as a place of truth-telling, catharsis and confession, is a good place to deal with that and to examine the effects unprocessed material can have on pastoral relationships.

An example is provided by Gail, a curate who was part of a verbatim group Jane was running. An analysis of her interventions when visiting a woman called Janice, whose husband was in the last stages of Parkinson's disease and living in a nursing home, revealed that Gail was not really listening to Janice.

Although Janice and Gail took it in turns to speak, there was no real connection between the two speakers. When asked whether Janice reminded her of anyone, Gail said no, but what she did talk about was the fact that her own mother had died of Parkinson's disease. When asked what she would really like to say to Janice, Gail said she should stop being so selfish. In answering these questions Gail realized that she was so consumed with her own feelings about how important it had been to care for her own mother at home rather than in a nursing home when she was dying, that she was unable to hear what Janice was saying.

Such questions reveal the dynamics of projection and transference, whereby the feelings and behaviours attached to one relationship or situation can be felt and enacted in another. Being asked questions like those listed above enables a supervisee to focus on their relationship with the person they are visiting or dealing with by disentangling them from those they remind them of. As a result of this supervision session, for example, Gail was able to disentangle her feelings about her mother and appreciate that Janice's feelings, constraints and options might be quite different from her own. Gail was then able to visit Janice again with quite a different approach.

Although this is an example from a training context, focusing on what a supervisee carries into and away from their work is an important dimension of all supervision. The drama triangle was presented in the last chapter as a tool for helping supervisees explore the dynamics of their pastoral relationships. It is also useful in helping supervisees think about their own tendencies under pressure. Helping them to identify whether they are most likely to become rescuers, persecutors or victims can help them resist countertransferences and be effective in their roles.

In an ongoing supervision relationship, the possibilities for spotting patterns of relating that crop up again and again is much higher. In order to do this, supervisors need to be attentive not just in each supervision session, but from one session to the next. Keeping notes of themes and key phrases used and ongoing questions is an important way of being able to bear witness to what you notice across sessions.

## Mode 5: Focus on the Relationship between the Supervisor and the Supervisee

Mode 5 draws attention to unconscious dynamics happening in the supervision relationship itself. **Projections, transferences** and **countertransferences**, as outlined in Mode 3, are as likely to be happening here as in the situations supervisees are bringing to supervision. Being in supervision yourself can help you spot and work with these dynamics, but there is one unconscious dynamic – **parallel process** – that is worthy of exploration.

Parallel process is worthy of a whole book in itself. Originally identified within the literature of psychoanalysis, the term has had a chequered history, with as many advocates as enemies. At its most basic it describes the process in which the here and now of the supervision session mirrors the there and then process of the pastoral encounter being presented.[5]

Spotting such a parallel process at work involves identifying unusual patterns of relating or behaviour in a supervisee. So, for example, if a usually chatty supervisee starts clamming up when describing a particular colleague, it may be that the 'clamming up' is one way the colleague's behaviour is manifested – and becomes present and visible right here and now – in the supervisory room, and has nothing to do with the relationship between the supervisor and the supervisee, or with the supervisee's own emotional state.

What happens in parallel process is that some piece of information is presented in supervision in disguised form. The supervisee, at some level, has the information, but it is out of their line of vision. As James Neafsey suggests,[6] the attentive supervisor can bear witness to that which is marginalized and help make it central so that its insight can be heard.

An example from Michael's practice arises from his work with Tom. As Tom was talking about his parishioner, Trish, he was upbeat and positive, but the more he talked the harder Michael found it to believe him. Suspecting there might be a parallel process at work, he said to Tom: 'Everything you are telling me about Trish is upbeat and positive, but the more you go on about how well she is doing, the more heavy I feel and the harder I find it to believe. I wonder if that is significant?'

Although Tom was quite shocked by the question, after some conversation he volunteered that Trish herself was very upbeat about the children's work in the church, for which she was responsible. Tom acknowledged that he wanted to believe that it was all going well but, if he was honest, he had some real questions about it that he had been afraid to ask.

What Tom had done was **communicate by impact** what he couldn't quite bring to consciousness on his own. By unconsciously paralleling what was happening in his pastoral relationship with Trish, Tom allowed Michael to pick up an unspoken anxiety about the children's work in his church. By naming what he suspected was a parallel process, Michael gave Tom the chance to explore his fears about raising his anxieties with Trish.

As Tom's shock indicates, naming a possible parallel process involves some trust and maturity on the part of the supervisee. Supervisors need to consider how to use the information a potential parallel process offers in relation to the developmental stage of their supervisee (see later in the chapter).

Counsellors and psychologists differ over their interpretation of what accounts for the phenomenon they term parallel process. Theologically speaking, parallel process might be seen as 'an attempt to penetrate and open up matters which are present but hidden'.[7] Michael Carroll cautions against the overuse of parallel process, which 'can too easily become a magical formula for clever interpretation and woolly connections'.[8] Yet as one aspect of the ministry of supervision, and in common with all forms of theological reflection, it is a useful tool if applied appropriately. It is also worth bearing in mind that a supervisor can introduce material unconsciously into a supervision session and enact a parallel process that has nothing to do with the supervisee's work, or that reflects something of the dynamic of the context in which the supervision is happening. (To explore the impact of context on supervision further, see Chapter 8.)

## Mode 6: Focus on the Supervisor

In Mode 6, the supervisor becomes aware of the ways what is being presented in supervision – the relationship the supervisee has with someone in their pastoral care – enters into their own internal world. Often this process is akin to Jesus' realization that, amid all the pushing and shoving, one person in particular – the woman with the issue of blood – has touched him. Similarly, an experienced supervisor might sense a sudden change of mood or have a surprising image or picture flash through their mind while supervising. Nowhere is self-knowledge more important than at this moment when trying to discern whether what is in your head is unusual, spontaneous and out of character – and therefore potentially a response to the supervisee's story – or simply personal material begging to be addressed in your own supervision and not that of the supervisee.

Michael had been supervising Karen for some years. He looked forward to her appointments and found energy in working with her. However, in a recent session she was talking about a new piece of work she was doing, supervising a spiritual director named Paul. Unusually, he found himself struggling to pay attention and drifting off to sleep. Knowing he was not in fact tired and certainly not uninterested in what she had to say, he interrupted her by saying: 'You are talking about being with Paul (there and then) but, here and now, I am feeling really drained and heavy. I don't normally feel that way working with you, and so am left wondering whether Paul leaves you feeling heavy or drained?' A brief pause ensued while Karen thought about what he had said. She then broke into a big smile and said: 'I have just realized that, because he won't pick himself up, I have been trying to carry him myself. I need to put him down and simply walk beside him, or at least just sit with him if he doesn't want to move. I haven't got the strength to carry both of us.' What happened next was that they both felt palpably lighter and relaxed their tensed body postures. It was as if a gust of fresh air had just entered the room and driven out the staleness.

Often such experiences are characterized by a real risk on the part of the supervisor which, as in the example above, once named and brought out into the light results in physical and psychological relief. Sometimes that risk is heightened by the power of the imagery or fantasy in the supervisor's head.

For example, a narrative brought to supervision may, on the face of it, be about a supervisee's sense of helplessness at having nothing to say that could comfort a distressed family. Meanwhile, in contrast to the supervisee's calm and moderate language and tone, the supervisor's mind may be filling with extreme images of violence and trauma. If the supervisor simply pushes away such images as if they were irrelevant, an opportunity can be missed. If the supervisor can find the mental space to identify whether the images belong to them or not, they can be offered as information that might assist the *exploration* of the supervisee's narrative and its meaning.

In an example of precisely this type, when Michael told a supervisee who was a chaplain about the images of guns that were in his mind as he listened to him, the supervisee proffered the suggestion that he had been in the direct line of fire of a bereaved family. Sensing there was more going on, Michael asked him to stay with the image a little longer. What finally emerged through tears and anger was that he was fed up with having to make excuses for God, and wasn't it about time God stood in the firing line for himself?

Offering the extreme images that were in Michael's mind for *exploration* allowed the chaplain to get in touch with feelings that were difficult to express, but the exploration of those images allowed him to realize his need for a break from the hospital, and to develop a more realistic sense of what he was and was not responsible for.

## Using the Seven Modes

The various modes of working outlined here – and Mode 7, outlined in Chapter 8 – offer different focuses for the supervisor's attention, but all with the aim of bringing into consciousness that which is out of focus or into light that which needs to be revealed, so that the supervisee can see more clearly and make responsible choices about how to proceed.

Which mode to use will depend partly on the preferences and skills of the supervisor and partly on the developmental stage of the supervisee. Someone new to ministry and to supervision might be very surprised if at a first supervision session the supervisor began talking about the stray images in their own head, for example.

What is needed, as in all relationships, is a sensitivity to the needs of the people with whom one is working, and to the material being presented. This will help to determine which mode to select and the method of working that is most appropriate, whether it is with words, images, narratives, objects or role.

So in Gail's case, as the prescribed method was verbatim, a way to help her separate out her transference from her grandmother (Mode 4) would be to help her focus on her visitee Janice's experience – rather than on her own experience of her grandmother – by pointing to Janice's responses in the verbatim text. An alternative way to work would be using the technique of **role-reversal**, asking Gail to inhabit Janice's shoes by setting up a chair for Janice and a chair for herself (see Chapter 6 for information about this way of working).

## Figure 5.2 Choosing the appropriate method for working

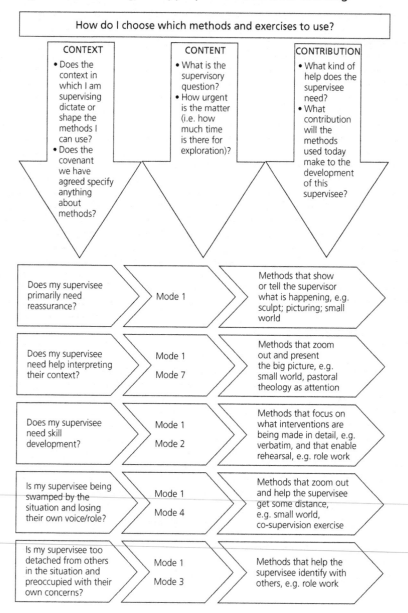

How do I choose which methods and exercises to use?

**CONTEXT**
- Does the context in which I am supervising dictate or shape the methods I can use?
- Does the covenant we have agreed specify anything about methods?

**CONTENT**
- What is the supervisory question?
- How urgent is the matter (i.e. how much time is there for exploration)?

**CONTRIBUTION**
- What kind of help does the supervisee need?
- What contribution will the methods used today make to the development of this supervisee?

| | | |
|---|---|---|
| Does my supervisee primarily need reassurance? | Mode 1 | Methods that show or tell the supervisor what is happening, e.g. sculpt; picturing; small world |
| Does my supervisee need help interpreting their context? | Mode 1 / Mode 7 | Methods that zoom out and present the big picture, e.g. small world, pastoral theology as attention |
| Does my supervisee need skill development? | Mode 1 / Mode 2 | Methods that focus on what interventions are being made in detail, e.g. verbatim, and that enable rehearsal, e.g. role work |
| Is my supervisee being swamped by the situation and losing their own voice/role? | Mode 1 / Mode 4 | Methods that zoom out and help the supervisee get some distance, e.g. small world, co-supervision exercise |
| Is my supervisee too detached from others in the situation and preoccupied with their own concerns? | Mode 1 / Mode 3 | Methods that help the supervisee identify with others, e.g. role work |

In the case of parallel process (Mode 5) and impact on the supervisor (Mode 6), these do not so much dictate the appropriate medium through which the supervision might work as become part of the *tracking and monitoring* the supervisor is doing throughout the session. Whether or not the supervisor chooses to name what they notice will depend on the agreed supervisory question and the developmental needs of the supervisee. Having such a map in mind when first meeting a supervisee helps a supervisor assess (a) what the needs of the supervisee are likely to be and (b) how best to respond so that there is a fit between those needs and their manner of working.

## Stages of Development of a Supervisee

### Stage 1

Supervisees at this level are often novices in pastoral ministry who come to supervision anxious, fearful and needing considerable reassurance about their performance as pastoral workers. Ultimately, their plea to the supervisor amounts to: 'Help *me* survive rather than drown in the work *I* do.' Implicitly they ask the supervisor to help them diagnose what is going on and to prescribe interventions that will remedy the situation. Often such supervisees hang on every word that falls from the supervisor's mouth and take copious (mental) notes as to what to do next. Alternatively, such anxiety may be covered by bravado and an unwillingness to let the supervisor tell the supervisee that 'they are doing it wrong'. In both cases the assumption is that the supervisor is in charge.

Such supervisees need a supervisor who:

➤ knows the context in which the supervisee is working;
➤ welcomes the expression of anxieties;
➤ focuses upon skills development;
➤ builds up the supervisee's confidence and self-belief;
➤ helps the supervisee to trust the supervision space;

> can work in the diagnostic mode of Hawkins and Shohet's Mode 1 and help the supervisee interpret the contexts in which they are working and being supervised (Mode 7).

## Stage 2

Having gained some confidence, supervisees at this stage are less anxious and fearful and are more able to tolerate open explorations of what might have been going on with specific people in pastoral encounters. At this stage, the supervisee is beginning to ask: 'How can *I* – as opposed to you, my supervisor – help this particular person *I* am working with?' They are also beginning tentatively to speak with their own voice, stand in their own shoes and express *themselves* as opposed to mimicking the supervisor in their pastoral work. While such supervisees find their own balance, supervisors become like stabilizers on a child's bike that can be attached and detached as needed. Not surprisingly, with confidence ebbing and flowing and not yet firmly established, personal and spiritual issues are often triggered in this phase. Since these issues have arisen out of the work context and perhaps also impact on that work, it would normally be advantageous if they can be sensitively handled within the supervisory relationship itself rather than through referral to another external party.

Such supervisees need a supervisor who:

> can help them get detailed work into the room;
> can tolerate difference and allow them to find their own voice;
> can work with personal and spiritual issues arising from the work;
> can, additionally, help a supervisee work with Modes 2, 3 and 4.

## Stage 3

Having acquired significant pastoral experience, the supervisee is *beginning* to see their individual work in its wider context, to understand the various dynamics at work in a given situation and to deal with the relationship processes in their ministry. It is no longer a case of simply *surviving* pastoral ministry but of coming to feel at home in it. Unconsciously competent, what becomes evident in supervision is the personal skill and flair of someone able to bring their own personal signature to the work they do. Stage 3 supervisees, while grateful for the support of their supervisors, are generally able to trust themselves and their own decisions. As a result, what is brought to supervision is more likely to be more complex or multifaceted pastoral situations rather than the detail of ordinary aspects of ministry.

Supervisees need a supervisor who:

➢ can rejoice in the independence and expertise of the supervisee;
➢ can attend to unconscious processes;
➢ can attend to wider contextual and organization issues (see Chapter 8);
➢ can, additionally help a supervisee to work through Modes 4, 5 and 6.

## Stage 4

Such a supervisee is not only a well-seasoned pastoral practitioner but someone with a highly developed capacity for critical self-evaluation of their ministry. Such a person will by now have developed an internal supervisor that holds them in check, encourages them and acts as a guide and inner mentor. Supervision is still sought regularly but is valued primarily as a place of collegiality with a peer in which subtleties are explored, blind spots revealed, practice tweaked, identity strengthened and integration sought. This stage is often characterized by contemplation in action as supervisees sense the action of God in their work, see gospel stories unfold before them and make connections between theology and life.

Such supervisees need a supervisor who:

➢ is not threatened by an equal;
➢ can tolerate the complexity of situations to which there are no easy answers;

➤ can work with all seven modes from Hawkins and Shohet's model.

## Conclusions

Just as the story of Jesus' healing the woman with the issue of blood demonstrates but one among many of his responses to human need, so too working to bring what is seen 'in the dark' (Matthew 10.27) into the light of day needs be embedded within a wider repertoire of care and attention, according to what is needed at any given time. But what is equally true is that a failure to incorporate things marginal, inaudible and invisible will short-change supervisees and consequently the people with whom they minister, and deny them the chance to get beneath the surface and heal those many factors that hold us captive in our patterns of relating.

The first exercise at the end of this chapter invites you to think about the developmental stages of your supervisees – and your own – and the modes for supervision that might be appropriate in each case. The further exercises suggest ways of embedding the three modes on which we have focused in this chapter.

# Exercises

## Exercise 5.1 Mapping Developmental Stages

*For reflection*

Look at Figure 5.3 and think about your own needs in supervision.

Figure 5.3 Developmental stages of supervisees

| Developmental stage of supervisee | | Needs a supervisor who: |
|---|---|---|
| **Stage 1:**<br>**The novice practitioner** | Experiences the supervisor as an expert who will tell them what to do (this may be experienced positively or resisted).<br><br>Seeks someone who can help them survive rather than drown in the work they do.<br><br>May blame the supervisor if the advice given doesn't work. | ➤ Knows the context in which the supervisee is working.<br>➤ Welcomes the expression of anxieties.<br>➤ Focuses upon skills development.<br>➤ Builds up the supervisee's confidence and self-belief.<br>➤ Helps the supervisee to trust the supervision space.<br>➤ Teaches the supervisee how to use the supervision space to *explore* their work for the sake of future practice.<br>➤ Can work in Mode 1 of Hawkins and Shohet's model and in Mode 7 (context). |
| Developmental stage of supervisee | | Needs a supervisor who: |
| **Stage 2:**<br>**The apprentice practitioner** | Oscillates between wanting:<br><br>An experienced practitioner who can help them develop their own skills, interpretations and strategies, and<br><br>Someone who can reassure them and direct them. | ➤ Can help them get detailed work into the room.<br>➤ Can tolerate difference and allow them to find their own voice.<br>➤ Can work with personal and spiritual issues arising from the work.<br>➤ Can work in Modes 2, 3 and 4 of Hawkins and Shohet's model.<br>➤ Can work with personal and spiritual issues arising from the work. |

Figure 5.3 cont.

| Stage 3: The independent practitioner | Seeks an experienced supervisor whom they can consult about difficult cases and dynamics. The supervisor need not necessarily be acquainted intimately with the work context of the supervisee. | ➤ Can celebrate their supervisee's independence and expertise. ➤ Can attend to unconscious processes. ➤ Can attend to wider contextual and organization issues (Modes 6 and 7). |
|---|---|---|
| Stage 4: The senior practitioner | Seeks supervision as a place of collegiality with a peer in which subtleties are explored, blind spots revealed, practice tweaked, identity strengthened and integration sought. | ➤ Is not threatened by an equal. ➤ Can tolerate the complexity of situations to which there are no easy answers. ➤ Can work in all modes. |

- Where do you see yourself?
- What kind of supervision do you need?
- Is there anything you need to review with your supervisor or supervision group?

Having considered the various stages,

➤ What kind of supervision do those you are supervising need?
➤ What skills development might you need to concentrate on in order to meet their needs?
➤ Is there anything you need to review with your supervisees?

## Exercise 5.2 **Making a Process Report**

*To try*

Bearing in mind Hawkins and Shohet's process model of supervision and Figure 5.3, write a process report on a supervisee you are working with. This involves identifying the modes with which you are working and the processes in play in the supervision you are offering. Think back to the beginning of the supervision relationship and review the development of the work using the form in Figure 5.4.

Figure 5.4 Process report form

| Name of supervisee | |
|---|---|
| Period and frequency of meeting (e.g. monthly since May 2015) | |
| Covenant | ➤ What have you covenanted to work on?<br>➤ What structure of session/methods of working have you agreed?<br>➤ At what developmental stage was your supervisee? |
| Early sessions | ➤ What did you establish about your supervisee's vision motivation for working?<br>➤ What did these sessions focus on?<br>➤ What tools did you use for getting the work into the room?<br>➤ Which modes did you use?<br>➤ How effective were these? |

## Figure 5.4 cont.

| Now | <ul><li>What is the work focusing on?</li><li>What tools are you using for getting work into the room?</li><li>At what developmental stage is your supervisee now?</li><li>Comment on a recent session in terms of Hawkins & Shohet's six modes:</li></ul> | |
|---|---|---|
| | Mode 1: Diagnosis<br><br>'Tell me what happened . . .' | |
| | Mode 2: Interventions<br><br>'Show me your strategies . . .' | |
| | Mode 3: Relationship<br><br>'Tell me about your relationship with this person/group/context . . .' | |
| | Mode 4: Supervisee<br><br>'What are carrying into/away from your work?' | |
| | Mode 5: Parallel Process<br><br>'Is the way you are with me here and now mirroring what was happening there and then?' | |
| | Mode 6: Supervisor<br><br>'Is what I'm feeling anything to do with the way you're feeling or what was happening there and then?' | |
| Review | <ul><li>What have you noticed or realized?</li><li>Is there anything you want to discuss with your own supervisor?</li><li>How will you approach your next supervision session with this supervisee?</li></ul> | |

## Exercise 5.3 Working in the Here and Now (Mode 4)

*To try*

This exercise is designed to help a supervisee reflect on their experience of their role at the moment in general terms, and to consider how their mood about their work might impact on their practice. It focuses on what the practitioner might be bringing into the room when they engage in pastoral or other ministry work.

### Eliciting and focusing

1. Spread some picture postcards (or other images of art, people and scenes) around the room and invite your supervisee(s) to choose one that speaks to them about how they are experiencing their work as a minister/chaplain/pastoral worker at the moment (perhaps a merry-go-round or a tussle or plain sailing might emerge).

2. Invite each person in turn to present their postcard as a **sculpt**. This involves asking other members of the group to take up positions to represent the significant elements of what is happening in the postcard – or to use cloths or objects to represent the scene if there is no group (a merry-go-round might be reproduced by four people revolving in a circle joined by their right hands; a tussle might be expressed in a tug-o-war; plain sailing may need to involve cloths for the sea and people forming a ship – or perhaps several ships). What matters is not a carbon copy of the postcard, but the presenter deciding what matters in the scene and finding a way to present that.

### Exploring and imagining

3. The role of the supervisor is to help the supervisee create the most resonant tableau they can and to ask clarifying questions: Are the characters the right distance apart? Where is the energy in the scene? What is the mood between these two characters? Is this aspect of the original postcard important?

4. When the presenter is satisfied that they have evoked what

they mean, invite them to step back and observe what they notice, wonder or realize. Invite any of the group who are observing to share their observations or to wonder aloud.

5. Ask the presenter whether there is anything, within their power, they would like to alter about the scene that would represent a more satisfying way of relating to their work (there may not be)?

## Bridging and enacting

6. Ask the participants to return to their seats and the presenter to de-role any objects used. Give opportunity for those who have taken roles to reflect on anything they experienced in role that might be information for the presenter.

7. Finally, ask the presenter to review the exercise and see what they have realized about how they are experiencing their role at the moment, how that might affect their work, and any next steps they want to take towards any changes they want to make.

8. Give opportunity for all members of the group to note aloud any resonances for them in their work.

## Reviewing and closing

This involves picking up any administrative issues such as arrangements for future sessions or reviewing the group covenant.

## Exercise 5.4 Working in the Here and Now (Mode 6)

*To try*

1. With a peer, take it in turns to read out a six-minute journaling exercise you have prepared. (See Exercise 4.1.)

2. As the other person reads their reflection, concentrate on noticing your own feelings, bodily sensations and thoughts.

3. Allow some silence when they have finished reading.

4. Offer any feelings, sensations or thoughts triggered by their

presentation and ask whether they resonate – for example: 'As you were reading about your relationship with your colleague I started to feel immensely sad. Does that resonate with how you are feeling, or how your colleague seems?'

5. Allow time for the presenter to see whether what you have offered resonates. If not, it is likely that this feeling, thought or sensation belongs to you. Don't worry – the exercise is about being fully present and learning to distinguish what belongs to you and what might be information relevant to what is being presented.

6. Allow time for either of you to name anything you feel the need to explore further that has arisen from each other's work.

This exercise may bring up feelings that belong to you personally rather than to the supervisee. Such feelings need exploration in an appropriate context. In supervision, when we have lent ourselves to others we can be left with resonances that need some time to be explored in a safe place. Peer supervision may be an appropriate place to do that, but if you are facilitating a group or supervising an individual it is not appropriate for you to name those resonances; rather, you need to get in the habit of noting them for yourself and returning to them outside the session.

The exercise outlined above for peer supervision could also be adapted for working with a group. Try, for example, writing a short story about an encounter or situation and reading that out to a group. You will have to be disciplined to prevent the group becoming simply a space to share stories. Even if you find yourself in sympathy with the presenter, the purpose of the exercise is not your own catharsis, but the presenting of your feelings as potential information for them.

## Notes

1 Harold F. Searles, 1966, 'Feelings of Guilt in the Psychoanalyst', reprinted in H. F. Searles 1979, *Countertransference and Related Subjects: Selected Papers*, New York: International Universities Press, quoted in D. Sedgewick, 1997, 'Some images of the analyst's participation in the analytic process', *Journal of Analytic Psychology* 42.1, pp. 41–6.

2 For a fuller discussion, see Andrew Samuels, 1989, *The Plural Psyche: Personality, Morality and the Father*, London: Routledge.

3 Michael Carroll, 1996, outlines the seven tasks of supervision – to set up a learning relationship; teach; evaluate; monitor professional ethical issues; counsel; consult; monitor administrative aspects – in *Counselling Supervision: Theory, Skills and Practice*, London: Cassell, pp. 53–87.

4 Sheila Ryan, 2008, 'Mindful supervision', in Robin Shohet (ed.), *Passionate Supervision*, London and Philadelphia: Jessica Kingsley, p. 71.

5 Michael Carroll offers a very accessible summary of parallel process within the literature of psychological counselling in *Counselling Supervision*, pp. 103–8.

6 James Neafsey, 2005, 'Seeing beyond: a contemplative approach to supervision', in Mary Rose Bumpus and Rebecca Bradburn Langer (eds), *Supervision of Spiritual Directors: Engaging in Holy Mystery*, New York: CPI Morehouse, pp. 17–31.

7 Edward Farley, 1979, *Ecclesial Man: A Social Phenomenology of Faith and Reality*, Philadelphia, PA: Fortress Press, p. 70.

8 Carroll, *Counselling Supervision*, p. 103.

# 6

# Attending to the Body

**Summary**

In the last chapter we noted the way that bodily sensations both of the supervisee and of the supervisor might provide clues for interpreting the dynamics of ministry. In this chapter we show how, during the *exploring and imagining* phase of supervision, the deliberate use of the body can help tell the story of the ministry situation being explored in supervision, and provide clues to its interpretation. In particular, the chapter draws on the concepts of *embodiment, projection* and *role* employed in the creative arts.

We declare to you what was from the beginning, what we have heard, what we have seen with our eyes, what we have looked at and touched with our hands, concerning the word of life – this life was revealed, and we have seen it and testify to it, and declare to you the eternal life that was with the Father and was revealed to us – we declare to you what we have seen and heard so that you also may have fellowship with us; and truly our fellowship is with the Father and with his Son Jesus Christ. We are writing these things so that our joy may be complete.

1 John 1.1–4

In this first letter of John the writer speaks about the way the life of God has been revealed through the human senses: 'we have seen with our eyes ... and touched with our hands'. The way this life was revealed was in the bodily presence of Jesus of Nazareth during his earthly ministry. It was his physical presence among human beings as the Word made flesh that enabled his disciples to come to know God in a tangible way, and to be able to testify to what they had seen, touched and heard. In this way the voice, the tears, the hunger, the shared meals, the touch and all the other aspects of the physicality of Christ's bodily presence enabled the word of life to be revealed as the sick were healed; the outcasts were touched; the shunned were welcomed; the guilty were addressed by name.

Even at the end of his life, the physical body of Jesus was the arena in which salvation was worked and revealed, and so when the Gospels came to be written, the writers directed their readers' attention to physical things: it was by attending to the stripping, the lashes, the nails, the thirst and the spear that new disciples might come to know Christ's humanity; and by noticing the marks of his wounds in his hands that they might know his resurrected body, pronouncing the triumph of peace over violence and of life over death.

The importance of the bodily life of Jesus of Nazareth to Christian faith was established in the creeds and councils of the early centuries of the Church and has remained central to Christian theology and Christian devotion since.

Christians through the centuries have been more ambivalent, however, about their attitudes to their own bodies. It has not always been the case that Christians have thought about their own bodies as being the arenas for God's salvation, despite testimonies of sickness healed, addiction overcome and debilitating anxieties quelled. Although we are not perhaps used to thinking of our bodies as the site of salvation in this way, it is perhaps most apparent to us that God is revealed to us profoundly in our physical life when we are ill or injured. At such times, and at other times of stress, we are aware of the relationship between body and spirit, not least through the bodily rites of the Church, which can speak deeply to us of the life of God as we receive the sign of the cross on our foreheads or eat bread and drink wine.

One of the most fundamental facts about human existence is that it is embodied. Although often the Western philosophical tradition has paid more attention to the development of what Janet Henderson calls the 'critical self' (a way of escaping the body through abstract thought) than the 'aware self' (a way of being present in the 'here and now'), Eastern thought has a more embodied sense of wholeness (holiness), which Rowan Williams echoes when he asks:

> How do you tell the story of your own life? Not simply as a record of what happened to this particular lump of fat and bone. You can tell your story as a story of how you learned to speak and to relate, to respond and to interact. In other words, you tell your story as the story of how your life, how your flesh, became inhabited.[1]

Put another way: bodies matter. Being human is not a question of being a mind in a machine, but of becoming some*body* who is in concrete relation to other bodies. The doctrines of creation and of **incarnation** are doctrines of **embodiment**. Matter is created good and yet suffers; bodies are redeemed through the suffering body of Christ; the bodily resurrection we proclaim in the creed is a matter not only of symbol but of substance.

As we begin to consider pastoral supervision in the light of this thinking it becomes apparent that if being human is about becoming some*body* who relates to other bodies, then this is also true of ministry or chaplaincy. However self-aware pastoral workers need to be about the impact of their physical presence on others – whether through touch, the use of their voice or their physical proximity to someone vulnerable – we cannot exercise ministry as if our bodies were not carriers of messages to others. One of Jane's most profound memories of being ministered to, for example, was of watching the tears roll down the face of the minister who was listening to her tell her story. One of the most powerful statements that can be made at times of crisis is for a pastoral carer physically to go and be present with a person whose world has ended.

## Embodiment

The experience of being ministered to by a chaplain who was moved to tears points to the way ministry happens, not just in the bodies of those to whom we minister – as we lay on hands in prayer or share the peace – but in our own bodies as we sit with those in pain, hold a child we are baptizing or long to comfort someone who is beyond our reach.

In her book *Gilead*, Marilynne Robinson tells the story of an elderly preacher trying to express what happens when a person touches another in blessing:

> There is a reality in blessing, which I take baptism to be, primarily. It doesn't enhance sacredness, but it acknowledges it, and there is a power in that. I have felt it pass through me, so to speak. The sensation is of really knowing a creature, I mean really feeling its mysterious life and your own at the same time.[2]

We have already explored in Chapter 5 the ways supervisees who have been ministering in such situations may bring their work into the supervision space in their body rather than in words. Pressured by time and the sheer volume of human contact, it is not uncommon for those in ministry to carry these experiences in their bodies – an alert supervisor can help the supervisee notice the way they are holding their body and perhaps carrying a burden they need to put down before they can see what it is and examine it, and decide how to respond to it.

If knowledge can be held in the body like this, then something the therapeutic arts have discovered is that the body can be encouraged to help the conscious mind find out what it knows. A simple example of an exercise that can be used in supervision to help a supervisee or group of supervisees is to ask them to think about what they have brought with them to the session from their day or their week; to walk in the space, imagining they are physically carrying those things. How easy are they to carry? Is it a whole range of things? Is it one large thing? How are the things being carried or dragged or juggled? Where is the weight? Is anything in danger of being dropped or of breaking?

In this way a supervisee can be helped through a bodily exercise to locate what unconsciously they might be carrying – and then to put it down in front of them so that they can name what it is and invite others to explore it with them.

This simple exercise is an example of what, in the creative supervision literature, is called embodiment. Such exercises are about getting in touch with what the body is holding, such as tension, pain, anger, others' stories. Such work 'can include sensory work, movement, warm-ups, sounds, dance and all bodily means of expression'.[3]

Creative methods in supervision are largely taken from **dramatherapy** practice. They cluster around the three central tools of **embodiment, projection** and **role**.[4] Both Michael and Jane have found these to be appropriate for *pastoral* supervision because they allow a holistic approach to the person that does not rely so heavily on the spoken word and cognitive processing, but allows what we know in our bodies to become explicit and useful in our work. In broad terms it fits with an incarnational theology that insists that 'we only learn to live in heaven in the presence of our maker, saviour and lover when we learn to live on earth in the here and now, inhabiting the space in which God has placed us.'[5]

Of course, it can be challenging to introduce such techniques into the supervision of those who are used much more to living in their heads and who find that movement makes them self-conscious and inhibited. Yet from a whole range of settings those of us in ministry know that the engagement of the body is important to wholeness – from helping someone relax by offering them a cup of something at the start of a difficult meeting, inviting people to attend to their breathing as part of prayer, to the ways people react when they feel inhibited from engaging their bodies in worship in the ways to which they are accustomed (whether by raising their hands while singing or kneeling to receive holy communion). As in the leading of worship, it is important to judge what is appropriate for each person and context, but often in supervision it can be fun and help people relax and become more 'present' if movement is introduced in the right way. Some examples you might try are given in the exercises at the end of the chapter.

## Projection

After embodiment, the second tenet of creative action-based supervision is 'projection'. Projection has been discussed already in Chapter 5 in the context of the feelings and memories one person can project onto another, transferring reactions and responses from another context into the current one. Human beings can also happily project their feelings onto objects, however, and this can be a safe way to explore the feelings and dynamics that arise in pastoral ministry. According to Sue Jennings, 'projection can include sand play, painting, drawing, clay work, writing, object sculpts and body sculpts.'[6]

An example of the use of projective methods in one-to-one supervision comes from Jane's practice. Vernon brought to supervision a difficult relationship with his curate in which he felt there was a lot of miscommunication. He wanted to think about some different strategies for relating better. From a collection of small figures, animals and other objects, Jane suggested he choose three things to represent himself and three to represent his curate, so that together they could explore the nature of the attributes represented.

For himself, Vernon chose a ruler, a holding cross and a juggling ball. For his curate he chose a jagged piece of pottery, a furry cat and a jigsaw piece. Commenting on what he had chosen, he said the ruler was about knowing he was responsible for writing reports on his curate and being worried that his curate was not making good progress; the holding cross was about his need to hold on to the centrality of faith in God in the midst of a busy ministry; the juggling ball was about the many things he needed to get done.

Commenting on the objects chosen to represent his curate, he said the pottery shard represented the curate's 'prickliness'; the furry cat represented the way others had reported the curate relating well to them in pastoral situations; the jigsaw piece was about him finding the curate to be a puzzle.

Jane asked Vernon to choose the aspect of himself he thought had the best chance of making a connection with his curate, and physically to pick up that object and move it around the objects representing the curate, to see what occurred to him. Having chosen the juggling ball, Vernon noted that there seemed to be a resonance between it and the puzzle piece that he had not originally thought about. 'I chose this because I'm always aware of how many balls I have in the air', he said. 'I wonder how much time I've spent actually present to this person and trying to see things from his perspective. Also, I know he loves games and leads these really well in the youth group, but there never seems to be any element of fun in the way we relate ... and actually juggling might be about fun. I wonder what's happened to the fun in my ministry.'

The use of objects allows for two things to happen. First, the objects become a physical representation of the situation being described in such a way that both supervisor and supervisee are able to look at the situation together. This act of **concretization** allows the supervisor to notice and wonder things as they are literally placed on the table: 'I see the ruler is the largest thing you've chosen, and you've placed it almost like a barrier between you.' 'If the cross represents what's central in your ministry, I wonder what is central to your curate's sense of vocation.' 'I notice that the jagged edges are also broken edges.' The supervisee, however, is also able to 'see' things because the feelings, dynamics and memories that have been circulating in the mind are now projected onto the objects. These feelings and dynamics are now outside of the supervisee, represented such that they are small enough to see and handle. As the supervisee 'plays' with the objects, this gives them the opportunity to assume some agency in the situation. The technique of **symbolization** also means that the objects chosen can reveal aspects of the situation the supervisee has not consciously already noticed: an object may be chosen because it is a particular shape or has a particular conscious association but, further, the colour of the object or the way it is placed may reveal an important unconscious resonance.

Having projected feelings, relationships and dynamics onto an object, however, it is important that the supervisee has the opportunity to reappropriate from these symbols what seems useful as they prepare to go back into the real situation; that is, to name what they realize or perceive – the third level of seeing. As the objects have been given a role, now they need 'de-roling'. One way to do this is to invite the supervisee to put the objects back into the box or onto the shelf from which they came, and ask them to say anything to that object they wish. It is then important to give the supervisee a chance to reflect on where they have got to once the objects have been put away. This enables the phase of playing with options and alternatives to end and the serious business of thinking about the next steps they are actually going to take to take root in the mind.

It is possible to use objects in this way to map a whole variety of situations and aspects of relationships. Sometimes this is best done on a deliberately small scale – sometimes called 'small world'[7] – to help the supervisee gain some distance or 'helicopter vision',[8] so they can see the whole of something and their own role within it more clearly.

Sometimes it is helpful to map the issue on a larger scale so that the supervisee can physically move around it and combine the benefits of embodiment with those of projection. In seeking to help a supervisee identify how they felt about possible future arenas of ministry, Jane asked Charlotte to set up the options in different parts of the room, choosing a different colour cloth for each alternative. Having chosen a green cloth for theological education, a blue cloth for healthcare chaplaincy and a red cloth for local church ministry, Charlotte then chose objects to place on these cloths. She was then able to sit in each space and handle the symbols she had chosen. In each space Jane asked the same three questions: 'What is the focus of your attention in this area of work?' 'What is giving you energy here?' 'What is draining you of energy here?' Having 'inhabited' all three spaces, Charlotte then stood in the centre and articulated what she had noticed: 'The local church ministry rips me apart and I still don't feel safe in it even though I feel attracted to it.' 'It moved me to tears to hold a book in my hand – I don't think I really believe that my intellect can be part of ministry, but I feel bereft because I seem to have left it behind.' Once she had de-roled the objects and the cloths, she identified the next steps she wanted to take: to re-engage with some academic reading and do some more thinking about why it was that local church ministry felt so painful.

In supervision groups it is also possible not only to sculpt with objects (as above), but with people. An example is provided by Deborah Ford, writing in *Practical Theology*.[9] She describes how in a supervision group led by Michael she was asked to take on the roles of patients in the healthcare setting where she was working, including the role of 'Tracey', a woman awaiting surgery on her thumbs, which had been damaged several years before when she had set fire to herself. Throughout the enactment of what had happened on the ward, Deborah and the person holding the role of Tracey had both felt very detached from their feelings, whereas other members of the group, holding more peripheral roles, had reported strong emotions. To help Deborah reconnect with her own feelings and those of Tracey, Michael asked the whole group to tuck their thumbs into their hands. This proved a difficult position to sustain both physically and emotionally. However, the experience of the whole group doing it with Deborah enabled her to face the unbearable feelings the encounter had brought up for her, and to feel supported in going back onto the ward again.

Asking people to hold roles in such a group sculpt raises the importance of giving anyone who takes part an opportunity to reflect on how that has affected them. However, when skilfully led this can be a very powerful mode of supervision. (Chapter 9 offers further exploration of managing these dynamics.) Those who wish to supervise in this way are advised to receive specialist training.[10]

## Role

The example given above bridges the three categories of creative supervision: embodiment (the use of thumbs); projection (the way members of the group 'held' the unbearable feelings Deborah could not get in touch with); and role (the willingness of the group to enact elements of the original encounter).

In practical terms, according to Sue Jennings, 'Role can include improvisation, script work, role play and enactment.'[11] It can involve **doubling** (speaking the role of someone else as closely as one can in order to empathize); **mirroring** (moving from identification within a scene to seeing the scene from the outside in order to analyse it and think about how it might need to change); and **role-reversal** (stepping in and out of the shoes of another or multiple others, better to hold and tolerate the tension of multiple perspectives).

In the example above the group all doubled the experience of having thumbs that do not work. The purpose of this was to help Deborah connect with Tracey's feelings, from which she had distanced herself, in order to bear the unbearable moment. Mirroring – a way a supervisee is invited to see their situation from the outside – can be very useful in supervision. Similarly, role-reversal – the ability to step into the shoes of another person or embody a dynamic active in a situation, such as fear or anxiety – offers a powerful tool not only for group supervision, but also when working one to one. In such situations the supervisor might role-reverse with the supervisee ('For a moment I am going to speak as that part of yourself that is eager to take on this new area of ministry') or the supervisee might engage in role-reversal quite simply by moving between two chairs or spaces in the room.

For example, Colin brought to supervision the problem of how to raise a difficult issue with Mani, a member of his ministry team. Jane suggested that Colin set up two chairs – one for himself as team leader and one for Mani. She invited him to 'dress' the chairs in cloth. He chose sackcloth for himself and a sparkling black cloth for Mani. She asked him to start by sitting in his 'team leader' chair – as distinct from the chair he was using as supervisee. Having interviewed him about the problem he was trying to raise, she asked him, 'What do you really want to say to Mani?' 'I need to tell him that there really can be no more excuses for his behaviour; that I have discussed the matter with my superior, and that now my superior wants to see us both next week.' Jane invited Colin to say this directly to Mani, as if he were in the chair opposite. Turning towards Mani's chair, Colin became physically smaller. He started to wring his hands and jiggle his leg before saying, 'How are you feeling that things are going, Mani?'

Jane invited Colin to swap places and sit in Mani's chair. She asked him to sit in the way Mani sits and to think about how Mani breathes and holds himself. 'Mani,' she said, 'Colin has just asked you how you feel things are going. Can you answer him?' 'Oh – just fine', he said.

Jane invited Colin to sit back in his own – team leader's – chair. 'It's hopeless,' he said, 'I just keep giving him let-outs.' Jane asked: 'How do you need to sit in order to speak to Mani?' Immediately Colin became aware of his posture and sat more solidly. Jane then asked: 'What is the let-out you need to avoid?' 'I need to stop prioritizing his feelings and draw his attention to the effects of his behaviour on everyone else.'

Jane invited Colin to say this to Mani. 'Mani, I am worried about how your behaviour is affecting the rest of the team.' Jane invited Colin to swap chairs again and immediately, as Mani, to respond. 'You don't need to worry, the team and me are good', was the answer.

Invited to look at the situation from a standing position (the mirror position), Colin reflected that he was still being too indirect because the situation had got beyond him exploring Mani's impressions and the conversation needed to result in Mani understanding that he now needed to discuss the situation with Colin's superior. Jane asked Colin to choose a cloth to add to his chair that would represent what he needed in order to be able to communicate what was necessary. Making a joke about bishops, Colin chose a purple cloth.

This time Colin was able to say: 'Mani, we have had several conversations over the last year about the amount of time you take off and how unavailable you are for ministry. I don't feel that the situation has improved, and so I have now reported this to Garth. He wants to see us both on Tuesday next week.'

Having put away the chairs and the cloths, Colin reflected that in the forthcoming meeting with Garth he would wear his purple socks to remind him who he is speaking for: 'I'm no longer just speaking with my own authority', he said. 'Now I've involved Garth, and Garth wants to see Mani, I'm speaking on his behalf as well.'

During this role work Colin was able to show Jane what happens when he tries to confront Mani. Because Jane could see it she could help Colin not just to think differently about the encounter, but to experience it differently in his body – adjusting his posture, for example. Likewise, Colin's choice of sackcloth revealed that this was not a task he relished and that somehow Mani had all the sparkling power; but putting on a different costume enabled Colin to feel the authority with which he needed to speak. By rehearsing in this way instead of conceptualizing the difficulties and imagining the possibilities, Colin was helped to get in touch with who he needed to be in order to fulfil his role as team leader appropriately. This 'rehearsal' went beyond finding the right words (Colin already actually knew what he needed to say), and helped Colin to be in the right mind and body not only to deliver the lines, but convincingly to act as team leader – believing in himself and thus communicating the appropriate authority to Mani.

It is apparent from this example that a good number of metaphors are being drawn here from the world of drama: role, rehearsal, play, act. This does not, of course, imply that ministry is a performance or that supervision is not a serious business. Anna Chesner defines role as 'a way of being … It is not limited as a concept to the idea of donning a mask or persona … In psychodramatic thinking, by contrast, being appropriate to the moment, embodying spontaneity, is dependent on having a wide and flexible enough role repertoire to "be" authentic.'[12] Part of the role of the supervisor is to help the supervisee extend their role repertoire – not only reversing roles with those they bring to supervision, in order to empathize with them and interpret their needs better, but also to help supervisors themselves develop the capacity to adopt appropriate roles in relation to those with whom they work.

The importance of this kind of serious play has been noted in a number of disciplines. In fact Frances Ward uses the metaphor of supervision as play space in her book *Lifelong Learning*, arguing that we all need places where the pressure is off to try out different approaches in a provisional way.[13] To create these spaces, supervisees also need their supervisors to act as playmates – colleagues who will hold roles for them and encourage them to try out different ways of being and thinking in relation to them – as they work out who they are and need to be in the serious business of ministry.

Sometimes, as above, this can be about helping someone grow into the authority that comes with a role; sometimes it can be about exposing the assumptions a supervisee has about a person they are working with so that these can be brought to consciousness and subjected to critique.

Michael was offering team supervision to a group of theological educators. He invited them to identify the roles that between them they needed to play for their students. In a circle he placed a number of roles written on pieces of paper that had been identified by the group: teacher, evaluator, role model, critical friend, fellow disciple, reference-writer. Team members took it in turns to role-reverse with a student with whom they were struggling to find how to work. The other team members were invited to choose one of the above roles to inhabit by standing behind the relevant piece of paper. The 'student' was then invited to approach each person in turn and initiate an interaction with them in role.

Julie chose to 'present' Jasmine, one of the few independent students at the college and also one of the few Asians. As she took on the role of Jasmine, Julie found herself clasping her hands behind her and becoming very tense. Each encounter with a staff member around the circle proved very unsatisfactory, as the staff were unable or unwilling to offer Jasmine what she was asking for.

Afterwards, among the staff this piece of role work produced the laughter of recognition at the accurate representation of their encounters with Jasmine. Julie, however, felt very upset. 'Although I can see why we respond to her in the ways we do, being Jasmine is a horrible experience. I felt so tense and so confused, and the more I tried to get my questions answered the more lonely and rejected I felt.' The conversation then moved on to a deeper level at which the team were able to think about the encounters from Jasmine's point of view and see whether there were ways their responses could be modified to take cultural factors into account, or whether there were some decisions that needed taking either about the structures of the institution or about Jasmine's place in it.

It is important to note that there is no substitute for actually asking someone else – in this case the real Jasmine – how she is actually experiencing a relationship. Role-reversal is no substitute for this. However, what this kind of role work can facilitate is the coming to light of knowledge the supervisee might have about the person they are presenting that is perhaps suppressed or held unconsciously. Julie's role-reversal with Jasmine was a fiction, but it was based on real encounters with Jasmine in which, by Julie's own admission, she had been consciously aware more of her own frustration than of the signals of distress Jasmine had been displaying. By one of the team embodying that distress, the whole team were able to take the student's signals more seriously as they thought about how to proceed. The whole team's role repertoire was enlarged through the experience.

## The Roles of the Supervisor

We also want to mention in this chapter another way the concept of role plays a part in supervision, and this concerns the roles the supervisor plays. In creative action supervision the supervisor acts as a facilitator – or even as the director of an unfolding drama. In this particular way of working, the supervisor is not chiefly a teacher, an expert or a counsellor, but someone who helps create the space for *exploration* by providing a structure and a way of working.

There are very many ways of characterizing the roles a supervisor might legitimately inhabit at different times during supervisions and with different people. During a course that Jane attended, among other suggestions the group brainstormed the following role descriptors for supervisors:

- Fully present attender
- Open-hearted welcomer
- Collaborative re-framer
- Sensitive boundary holder
- Congruent respecter of limitations
- Playful accompanist
- Appropriate knowledge holder
- Intrepid intervener
- Transparent report writer
- Astute seer beyond the surface.

Of course, each of these roles has its equally demanding counterpart in the supervisee. Suggestions from the same group included:

- Prepared contributor
- Interested explorer
- Engaged reflector
- Courageous questioner
- Receptive welcomer
- Ethical monitor
- Balanced acknowledger of strengths and weaknesses
- Frank mistake-owner
- Occasional challenger
- Discriminating assimilator of advice.

More systematically, Tony Williams identifies the four supervisory roles: facilitator, teacher, consultant and evaluator.[14]

## Facilitator

A facilitator creates a structure in which the *exploration* of the supervisory issue can happen. This is literally true in terms of hosting a physical space and making it as user-friendly as possible, but it is most importantly true in terms of helping the supervisee identify a way to use the time that will enable them to explore fruitfully the issues they are bringing. A facilitator is not an expert on the subject in hand and is not obliged to come up with brilliant insights. A facilitator is someone who understands the dynamics of the supervision space and can guide a supervisee or a group through a satisfactory process, whether that is a creative one, using embodiment, projection and role as described in this chapter, or a verbal one, such as verbatim or a model of theological reflection as outlined in earlier chapters.

## Teacher

A teacher is someone who has knowledge that can be useful to the supervisee. This might be theoretical knowledge or knowledge of a context. In the supervision space this knowledge is not systematically presented, as it might be in a classroom; rather the need to teach arises from the supervision itself, out of the 'need to know' of the student. The teaching might involve explaining some concepts and helping the student think about their relevance to the situation in which they find themselves, as an aid to *exploring and imagining* (as Michael helped Sharon to think through her situation using the drama and empowerment triangles, p. 103), or it might involve offering suggestions for reading as part of the *bridging and enacting* phase of the supervision.[15]

## Consultant

The consultant role offers the chance for the supervisor to speak authoritatively from their own experience. This can be useful if used sparingly, but the role comes with a health warning! It can be very tempting for the unsuspecting supervisor to overuse this role and spend the whole supervision giving advice. Novice super-visees, in particular, are susceptible to leaving the responsibility with their supervisor for deciding what they should do, and a supervisor who prefers the consultant mode can stunt the super-visee's development if they are not careful.[16] Nevertheless, it can occasionally be helpful to speak from experience, as long as the supervisee is given room to consider their own response: 'In my experience this is not something that it pays to tackle head on. What experience might you draw on here?'; 'I have learnt through bitter experience that if I don't take a regular day off, everyone suffers. What would be your wisdom on the subject?'

## Evaluator

The evaluator is most obviously the report-writer who has to assess a student's progress for a third party. Evaluation is a much more generic part of the role of the supervisor, however, as they weigh what is being presented and make judgements about the way to work with the issues and material being presented. This aspect of the supervisor's role is most clearly seen as the super-visor helps the supervisee in *focusing* their work and in *tracking and monitoring* the progress of the session so that the conver-sation, interventions and activities serve the agreed agenda.

To have an awareness of a standard scheme such as that of Tony Williams can help the supervisor focus their attention on the kind of presence they need to be at different phases of a supervision session or different stages of a supervision relationship. Auditing one's own role repertoire as a supervisor using a list such as the one above can also help alert us to our own development needs. A supervisor with a good role repertoire is best able to embody a good level of authenticity and create a space in which their supervisees can open up to themselves and to others in the kinds of authentic and spontaneous ways that allow the Holy Spirit to flow. In this way even the attentive physical presence of a super-visor with a supervisee might become an arena in which God's saving work can be experienced and witnessed.

# Exercises

## Exercise 6.1 Over- and Underdeveloped Supervisory Roles

*For reflection*

In this chapter we outlined the supervisory roles of facilitator, teacher, consultant and evaluator. It is easy for supervisors to default to their familiar developed roles. Thus clergy who supervise may find themselves defaulting to pastoral care in supervision, and counsellors to a therapeutic way of approaching what is presented. Effective supervision requires the supervisor to attend to the neglected and underdeveloped aspects of their role.

List the supervisees you see one to one.

With Tony Williams' four roles in mind (facilitator, teacher, consultant, evaluator):

- Which are your default supervisory roles?
- Which do you neglect?
- Which have you overdeveloped?
- Which have you underdeveloped? (For example, you may have a well-developed facilitator role, honed by years of working in your main area of expertise, but resist embracing the role of consultant or teacher when you supervise.)

## Exercise 6.2 Amplification

*To try in a group*

Invite the group to stand in a circle with some space between each person. Explain that you are about to make a movement the next person will need to copy and then enlarge in some way. Make a small and definite movement that can be copied, allowing for the fact that it will need to be amplified as many times as there are people in the circle. If people get stuck, encourage them to think not only about amplifying the size of the movement but its speed or number of repetitions. When the movement has been around the whole circle, you should complete the largest and final version. If time allows, the person next to you can then initiate a second movement, and so on around the circle. At the end, invite the group to reflect on what they needed to be alert to in order to engage in this exercise. The skills are those needed for doubling (attentive watching and listening) and for mirroring (reflecting on what they have seen).

## Exercise 6.3 Eye Contact

*To try in a group*

1 Invite the group to stand in a circle.
2 Demonstrate making eye contact with another person and changing places with them in the circle without eye contact being broken (this will involve walking backwards once past the crossing point).
3 Invite the group to do this in silence.
4 Variations can be added, such as either high fives or jumping in the air at the crossing point; speeding up. These can be built up a step at a time to increase complexity.

The exercise involves multiple series of movements in the room, which have to be negotiated without words. This focuses attention on the body and on the other bodies in the room. At the end of the exercise, invite the group to reflect on what they needed to be alert to in order to engage. Again, the skills are those needed for doubling (attentive watching and listening) and for mirroring (reflecting on what they have seen).

## Exercise 6.4 Bibliodrama

*To try*

Bibliodrama involves the director reading through a selected text, stopping at points of interest to invite people to step into the role of a character. Bibliodrama honours the written text but invites a deep exploration of its impact and meaning. It becomes an embodied vehicle through which the life of an individual or group might interact with the biblical narrative.[17]

In the supervision context the text to be chosen should arise from the content of the supervision material. Having agreed a text with the supervisee (or group), as part of the process of *eliciting and focusing*, the supervisor should read the text and invite the group to adopt postures or articulate the thoughts or feelings of the characters. One possible technique is to invite the supervisee or group to create a space in the room in which to experience each of the different dimensions of a story, using cloths and objects – for example, in the story of Mary and Martha, spaces might be created for Mary, for Martha and for Jesus. A text like that of Psalm 137 might be divided into a series of episodes, each of which might be given a name by the group: verses 1–4 might be titled 'loss'; verses 5–8 'home'; verses 7–9 'fury'. The group might be invited to explore these spaces in their own time, adding objects or quotes or single words on cards; or the group might 'visit' the spaces together, voicing thoughts, feelings, songs and stories that are evoked by that space. Whereas in a teaching context the teacher might decide the breakdown of the verses and the names of the 'episodes', in the supervision context it would be more appropriate for the supervisor to facilitate the supervisee or group in coming to a view because the text is not being explored only in its original context, but in the life of the supervisee or group.

In all cases, at the end the spaces should be de-roled by the individual or group, allowing time for further reflection and assimilation of any insights or changed perspectives and the articulation of next steps as part of the *bridging and enacting* process. There should be opportunity for the individual or group to reflect on what they have experienced and heard, and to make connections with their work. This might also include reflection on the way the biblical text has been 'used' and possible distortions of its meaning in its original context – not primarily to reinforce an abstract orthodoxy, but because these reflections might flag up dimensions of insight missing from the supervision.

# Notes

1 Rowan Williams, 2007, 'A theology of health for today', in J. Baxter (ed.), *Wounds that Heal: Theology, Imagination and Health*, London: SPCK, p. 7.

2 Marilynne Robinson, 2005, *Gilead*, London: Virago, p. 26.

3 Sue Jennings, 1999, 'Theatre-based supervision', in Elektra Tselikas-Portmann (ed.), *Supervision and Dramatherapy*, London and Philadelphia: Jessica Kingsley, p. 67.

4 For a use of this paradigm in supervision, see Jennings, 'Theatre-based supervision', pp. 62–79.

5 Williams, 2007, 'A theology of health for today', p. 13.

6 Jennings, 'Theatre-based supervision', p. 67.

7 A phrase coined in Mooli Lahad, 2000, *Creative Supervision: The Use of Expressive Arts Methods in Supervision and Self-Supervision*, London and Philadelphia: Jessica Kingsley.

8 Katerina Couroucli-Robertson discusses this 'helicopter ability' in her article 'Supervisory triangles and helicopter ability', 1999, in E. Tselikas-Portmann (ed.), *Supervision and Dramatherapy*, London and Philadelphia: Jessica Kingsley, pp. 95–113.

9 Deborah Ford, 2009, 'Are you able to drink the cup that I drink?', *Practical Theology* 2.3, pp. 343–54.

10 Such training is offered by the London Centre for Psychodrama (www.londoncentreforpsychodrama.org) and by Michael Paterson and Jessica Rose (www.creativesupervisiontraining.org.uk).

11 Jennings, 'Theatre-based supervision', p. 67.

12 Anna Chesner, 2014, 'Role as a concept in creative supervision', in Anna Chesner and Lia Zografou (eds), *Creative Supervision Across Modalities: Theory and Applications for Therapists, Counsellors and other Helping Professionals*, London and Philadelphia: Jessica Kingsley, pp. 43–58.

13 Frances Ward, 2006, *Lifelong Learning: Theological Education and Supervision*, London: SCM Press.

14 Antony Williams, 1995, *Visual and Active Supervision: Roles, Focus, Technique*, New York and London: W. W. Norton.

15 The role of teacher relates closely to the second of Inskipp and Proctor's functions of supervision – the formative leg of their three-legged stool outlined in Chapter 1.

16 The role of consultant must be carefully pitched according to the developmental stages of supervisees, as outlined in Chapter 5.

17 See for example Pieter Pitzele, 1999, 'Psychodrama and the Bible: mirror and window of soul', *The Journal of Religious Education* 86.4.

# 7

# Attending to the Story

**Summary**

In the last chapter we looked at various ways supervision
might attend to the tacit knowledge and assumptions that
the body of the supervisee might be carrying, which might be
brought to the surface and examined through the techniques
of **embodiment**, **projection** and **role**. In this chapter we
explore a narrative approach to supervision in which images
and metaphors are the predominant means by which material
is *explored and imagined*. This approach sees supervision
as a place in which the story God is telling is brought into
dialogue with the stories that situations and individuals are
telling. Towards the end of the chapter, further exercises are
offered that use the Bible imaginatively within the supervision
session as ways of helping supervisees interpret themselves,
their choices and the situations they face within the story of
salvation.

The hand of the LORD came upon me, and he brought me out by
the spirit of the LORD and set me down in the middle of a valley;
it was full of bones. He led me all round them; there were very
many lying in the valley, and they were very dry. He said to me,
'Mortal, can these bones live?' I answered, 'O Lord GOD, you
know.' Then he said to me, 'Prophesy to these bones, and say
to them: O dry bones, hear the word of the LORD. Thus says
the Lord GOD to these bones: I will cause breath to enter you,

and you shall live. I will lay sinews on you, and will cause flesh to come upon you, and cover you with skin, and put breath in you, and you shall live; and you shall know that I am the LORD.'

Ezekiel 37.1–6

Dreams and visions may be dismissed by many today, but they are an important part of the way the Bible presents God communicating with his people. In the Bible the symbolic language of dreams and visions, poetry and story is constantly interwoven with dogmatic and historical passages. All are important in meditating on who God is and what God is saying to God's people. In this passage the prophet Ezekiel describes a dream or vision in which he senses God's hand upon him leading him into a dry valley, there to address what was dead and lifeless so that it might live again. To interpret the dream, we need to know something of the historical, political situation into which Ezekiel was speaking – the exile and despair of the people of Israel. We also need to listen carefully to the language of the vision: it is only *ruach*, the spirit of God, who can breathe life into the dead. Nevertheless, the prophetic ministry of Ezekiel is also needed: to go to the place of dryness and deadness; to listen to the story the dry bones are telling; to listen to the story God is telling; to invoke the wind; to encourage the people to hear the story of salvation, but not only to hear it, to allow what is dead within them to be caught up into the story; to allow the story to become enfleshed within their own experience so that they may be filled with life-giving power.

If pastoral supervision is to be attentive to what God is saying, to the story God is telling, it needs to deal in two kinds of narrative: the explicit stories we tell ourselves and can articulate; and the implicit meanings we carry in symbols and images, which are harder to bring to consciousness. As we explored in the last three chapters, pastoral supervision is concerned both with the 'there and then' of what happened and with the meanings we carry unconsciously and express in body language or by impact in the 'here and now'. In this chapter we use the notion of story to consider how, through listening to the there and then and the here and now, we can find ourselves part of the story God is telling.

## Narrative Forms of Pastoral Supervision

The two people who have done most to think systematically about narrative forms of pastoral supervision are Anton Boisen and Charles Gerkin. In the 1920s, in the USA, Anton Boisen was worried that seminarians were learning the language of the Christian story but without making profound connections with their own experience.[1] To try to help his students make deep connections in their own lives and in the lives of others, he spoke of himself and those he listened to in counselling and supervision as 'living human documents'. He saw the listener's task as being not merely to listen with unconditional positive regard but to help the speaker make deep sense of their experience within the framework of the Christian story – or, to use the language of Ezekiel, let the dry bones of the Christian story become enfleshed with their own experiences.

For Boisen, this involved a profound listening to the meanings being made by the person being listened to, listening carefully, in particular, to the language and images in use without assuming we know what they signify. For although we may often be working in pastoral supervision with people who share our general outlook on life as Christians, the deep associations we have crafted out of the myths, stories and language offered to us in our families, schools and churches, and through films, books and fairy stories, will be particular to each of us. Some of the connections we have made will be profoundly life-giving – they will incarnate for us the gospel that gives life. Yet some of the connections we have made will keep us bound and restrict our lives and our ability to be life-giving for others.

More recently, and drawing on the work of Paul Ricœur, the American pastoral counsellor, supervisor and pastoral theologian Charles Gerkin has taken Boisen's work further. Arguing, with Ricœur, that human beings are primarily interpreters, he suggests that pastoral supervision is a ministry of co-interpretation, as supervisors listen with their supervisees for meaning. He suggests that supervisors, therefore, need to listen in three ways:

- for the story *behind* the stories supervisees bring to supervision;
- for the story God is telling;
- for what God is saying in the supervisor's own experience.

The purpose of this threefold listening is that supervisor and supervisee might hear the story of creation, incarnation and redemption not as a theoretical story, but as it is enfleshed in their lives; that dry bones may live. The three dimensions of the listening Gerkin advocates need to happen simultaneously, but in order to think about them they are treated here in sequence.

## Listening to the Story Behind the Stories

For Charles Gerkin, the first task of pastoral supervision is to listen to the story the supervisee is telling. This is not simply to make the point that we need to be accurate listeners (which is assumed), but that we need to listen carefully to the story *behind* the stories we are being told in order to help our supervisees reflect – not at a superficial level, but at the profound level where transformation is possible.[2]

This involves listening in all the ways that Chapters 3, 4 and 5 have opened up. It involves listening to the there and then the supervisee is reporting (Modes 1 to 3) as well as to the here and now of the dynamics in the room (Modes 4 to 6), and it involves listening to and through the body (Chapter 6). It involves listening to the detail of particular incidents but reflecting on them in the longer perspective of the story of a relationship or the broader perspective of the supervisee's other relationships (Modes 3 and 4), and it involves thinking about the significance of this story told in this supervision context.

A helpful way to approach this kind of listening in supervision is to think about why a particular story is being told. A useful mantra for a pastoral supervisor to bear in mind is:

➢ Why this story?
➢ Why today?
➢ Why here?

Often the stories people want to tell in supervision are those that don't fit their explicit 'script' or self-understanding. It will be important to get to the bottom of what the story being told and the person's self-interpretation have to do with one another. The example of Dave telling the story of his curate in Chapter 1 is a good case in point. There may have been many possible avenues to explore in supervision, but the urgent one for Dave related to the reason he was telling the story – because the way he was being made to feel in this situation contradicted his self-interpretation as a person called to holiness. The story *behind* the story was that of Dave's self-understanding and deep sense of call. Anger didn't fit the script, so the script needed revisiting in the light of the Christian story that shapes Dave's commitments.

The first task of the supervisor, then, is to listen to the story behind the stories the supervisee is telling. This is not a superficial or simple task, not least because living human documents are complex multiple and dynamic texts that need subtle interpretation. Echoing the dynamics of the Ezekiel text, Gerkin suggests that there are two strands of story for a pastoral supervisor to listen to: first, the explicit strand, which is what we tell ourselves our lives and ministry are about, a story that has an articulate force and certain structure about it (the historical, narrative thread); second, the more implicit meanings we carry in images and symbols (dreams and visions). It is bringing these two strands of the supervisee's story into dialogue with each other that can be helpful in promoting integration and freedom of response in their work.[3]

A good example of seeing these two levels in operation is in a piece of work Michael did with Geoff. Geoff had been in ministry for 30 years. When asked to tell the group what his vision of ministry was, he simply said: 'Obedience'. When asked to say a bit more about it, he commented on the discussion that had preceded the exercise, saying: 'It doesn't matter whether ministry is life-giving or not; that is not the point. What matters is that I've been obedient.' This was the story Geoff was telling himself explicitly about ministry and life, yet another story was simultaneously being told by his body: as he spoke, Geoff's arm was pulled across the top of his head at a tortuous angle, pushing him further and further down into his chair. The tension between what his words were saying and what his body was saying prompted the group to help Geoff explore his experience of ministry – in what ways it had brought him life but also what the cost had been. This was the beginning of a long and painful process of getting in touch with feelings Geoff had not allowed himself to experience, and yet as he got in touch with anger, loss and isolation, so also was the possibility of joy opened up for him.

It is important for those in ministry to have access to those formative levels of their own personalities that are often carried implicitly in symbols and images or unconsciously in our bodies – if we are to be people who can minister to others. Elizabeth O'Connor warns of the consequences of the alternative:

When we discourage persons from being on an inward journey of self-discovery, we keep them from coming into possession of their own souls, keep them from finding the eternal city, keep them from being authentic persons who use their gifts and personality to mediate God's peace and God's love. He or she who tries to keep another from the pilgrim path of self-discovery is doing the devil's work, and a lot of frightened people are about that work.[4]

To sit with someone as pastoral supervisor is to help them make the journey inwards, so that they have as much of themselves available for the tasks of ministry as possible. Another way to describe this is the language of flat and round characters. Elizabeth O'Connor again:

To have life as vocation is to be aware that there are two ways to go – the wide road and the narrow road ... The wide road is the road of the crowd. Jesus describes the people on it as not seeing and not hearing ... They have lost awareness that there are two ways. They respond to externals only since their attention is outward. They have many answers. When they do ask questions they ask them of others but never themselves ... By contrast with 'round characters' that develop and change, they are what in fiction writing is known as 'flat characters', which means that they do not change.[5]

Even if we begin ministry as rounded characters, aware of the dynamic of God's grace in our lives, transforming and leading us into new depths and heights, there are many pressures that can flatten us and cut us off from important dimensions of ourselves, making us dry and lifeless. In pastoral supervision we need to be alert to the ways our supervisees may be flattened, listening like Ezekiel to the contexts into which God is wanting to breathe new life.

## Listening to the Story God is Telling

It is already clear from Elizabeth O'Connor's words that listening for the story behind the story is bound up with listening for what God is saying. The story God is telling, Gerkin suggests, is the story of creation, incarnation and redemption. It is worth spending some time thinking about how you would characterize the 'bones' of the Christian story. However, to be able to recognize the gospel as it is enfleshed, we need also to be thoughtful about what this story looks like in day-to-day and not just theoretical terms. To use the language of Ezekiel, we need to know what a people that is dead and lifeless would look like when compared to a people full of God's spirit. This cannot be a simple matter of the language people use ('Not everyone who says to me, "Lord, Lord", will enter the kingdom of heaven'), but needs to be an incarnate sense of what Rowan Williams terms spirit inhabiting flesh:

> God's grace makes flesh to be inhabited by spirit: that is, makes flesh something more than the untenanted material which lies around for other people to fall over ... the whole business of theology is to trace how God transforms flesh, how God makes flesh inhabited, by creating relationship with himself.[6]

Pastoral supervisors, then, as they listen for the story that God is telling in the stories their supervisees bring to supervision, need to be people who are fluent in the language of creation, incarnation and redemption and can recognize God at work not only in explicitly religious language or contexts, but in the detail of daily lives.

In listening for the story of salvation, conceptualizations can help:

- Does this story speak of love or fear?
- Does it speak of bondage or freedom?
- What kind of freedom?
- Is there a sense of truth as well as love?
- What is the hope being expressed – is it just for the self or for others?
- Is there a challenge here to the ways I have conceptualized these things?

But the necessary connections are not only intellectual but emotional ones, and pastoral supervisors need to sound out the connections within themselves:

- Does this story speak of the love of God as I have known it?
- Does the freedom this supervisee speaks of resonate with my experience of freedom in Christ?
- Does the here and now of this supervision speak of Christ's mercy and forgiveness as I have experienced it?
- Is there a challenge here to the ways I have experienced these things?

## Listening for God in Our Own Experience

This brings us to the third dimension of Gerkin's listening, because to be able to hear the story God is telling, pastoral supervisors need, themselves, to be living the gospel not only at the superficial level, but at the deep emotional and symbolic level out of which they live and minister. For if pastoral supervision is an expression of ministry, it needs to be exercised by those who are themselves, like Ezekiel, living dynamically out of God's call; who are alive to God's hand upon them, attentive to God's leading and open to the enlivening power of God's spirit; who can recognize God's spirit at work transforming the daily lives of others because they have sensed this same spirit at work within themselves.

Of course, the task is complicated because the version of the Christian story the pastoral supervisor embodies is particular to them, and as with any other disciple on the road of sanctification, it will be idiosyncratically and imperfectly embodied. The task is not for the supervisor to try to impose their version of the story of salvation on those they listen to; rather, the task is to bear witness to what we know and to trust that as the horizons of our stories and the stories of those we supervise meet, the voice of the Holy Spirit will be heard creating a new understanding of the story God is telling. In the process, the meanings of the supervisor are risked just as much as those of the supervisee.

If the pastoral supervisor is able to be deeply hospitable to the person they are working with, this enrichment of their understanding of the gospel will happen regardless of whether their supervisee is speaking a religious language or not. To what extent the supervisor will introduce religious language to a supervision relationship will depend on the faith commitments of the person they are working with and the agreement they have made.

## An Example of Narrative Supervision in Practice

An example of this process in action is provided by a window into Jane's supervision relationship with Sarah. Sarah is a healthcare chaplain who came to Jane for pastoral supervision for an hour once a month. Part of their covenant was to help Sarah reflect on what priesthood meant in the context of her work. Because her father was a priest, Sarah's images had been fundamentally shaped by his own understanding of priesthood. The conversation often ended up being about him and at the level of explicit meaning – yet this did not seem to be sustaining Sarah in her work, and

Jane felt the need to try to help her reach a deeper level at which formative work might take place.

Asking Sarah to think about women in the Bible she might consider priestly in some way was a deliberate attempt to try to access the other strand of her 'story', held more deeply in images, symbols and emotions. Sarah's immediate thought was of Mary who anointed Jesus with oil before his death, but before she could get any further her explicit 'script' told her that this was not an orthodox image for priesthood. Jane asked Sarah to choose a small figure or other object to represent Mary as priest, and another to represent an orthodox image of priesthood.

Sarah chose two figures – one kneeling female figure and one elderly man – and placed them on the table facing each other. Jane then invited her to adopt the physical position she thought Mary had taken as she anointed Jesus' feet. As Sarah knelt forwards she immediately pressed on her own stomach with her hands and said, 'I can't do this. I'm not supported enough.' These words echoed what she had been saying about her work in the mental health context in recent weeks, but the gesture pointed to a connection with her own vulnerability, which Sarah had previously associated with her near death at birth. This is a feeling Sarah locates in her stomach.

Jane was also struck that the story Sarah had chosen is an anointing for death and that 'deadened' is a word Sarah often uses of the service-users she is describing. Back in her own chair (the mirror position – see p. 263), Sarah discussed what she had felt and Jane voiced what she had noticed. They were able to talk about why Sarah chooses work that is about death and what she finds so deathly in her mental health work in particular.

Returning to the two figures she had chosen, Jane asked Sarah if she wanted to change or add anything to the scene she had created with them. Sarah moved the male figure to a supportive place behind the Mary figure, saying, 'I need my father behind me, supporting me, as part of the apostolic succession – generations of support – for this work in confronting death.'

Sarah then started to wonder about what happened to Mary after Jesus' death. What about resurrection for her? She went home to read the resurrection stories and try to trace Mary of Bethany and to think about the other Marys in those stories and see whether they had anything to offer her.

At the next supervision session, Sarah arrived full of energy and life. 'For the first time I can see that life is not all about death', she said. She spoke about feeling held in herself and having more choices in terms of the kind of work she might do. The joy that Jane, as supervisor, felt as Sarah talked resonated with her own sense of what salvation means.

## Risking New Meanings

As the supervisor, Jane needed to make space for Sarah's meanings in order to understand how Sarah experiences and interprets the world and so get to the bottom of what it is she finds difficult about the mental health work. In the process, Jane needed to allow her own world of associations and meanings to be disturbed and enlarged. For example, Jane had no previous association of Mary with priesthood. Furthermore, she needed to sound out at a deep level within herself whether what Sarah was communicating sounded like life in Christ as Jane had experienced it and understood it, or like the bondage from which Christ longs to set people free. But any associations Jane made needed to be offered tentatively. 'I notice you are holding your stomach.' 'I wonder where your father is in this picture?' 'I wonder whether there's a connection for you between anointing for death and the kind of work you are drawn to do?'

Behind these questions were Jane's understandings and associations: priesthood has more to it than anointing for death (though that is not unimportant); the gospel is about life; ministry cannot be exercised alone. By engaging in this way with the deep meanings that key concepts hold for us, the skeleton of Christian faith is enfleshed in our own experience as we allow our own meanings to come into dialogue with the meanings of others. It is such dialogue that makes the Christian community a living community of faith and not a valley of dry bones.

This is also why, when we listen to someone, study their verbatim, look at a picture they have brought or watch them **sculpt** something with their body, we are not primarily trying to correct behaviours, provide solutions to problems or promote orthodox thought. Rather, as supervisors we are seeking to help supervisees examine the story out of which they live so that they may minister more profoundly the good news of Jesus Christ. Crucial in our ability to do this will be the extent to which we ourselves are open to our own deep realities and experiences being so shaped – the extent to which our faith is dynamic and living.

## Remaining a Rounded Character as Pastoral Supervisor

This openness to the spirit of God needs to operate in real time within the supervision we offer, but our engagement as supervisors with the continual process of becoming more deeply embedded within the life-giving story God is telling in Christ cannot be parasitical on those we supervise; we need to be exploring our own associations and meanings – in worship, in prayer, in Bible study and in supervision ourselves.

So in Jane's supervision on the work she did with Sarah, Jane and her supervisor looked at an eleventh-century image of Joseph dreaming that he needs to take Mary and the baby to Egypt. This was a sculpture Jane had photographed while on pilgrimage in Spain and which had been fascinating her. Jane took it to supervision because she was aware that it held meaning for her that was not entirely explicit and because the image kept coming to mind when she was working with Sarah. The image depicts an angel communicating with Joseph by putting his hand on Joseph's stomach.

Gradually her supervisor helped Jane to name a number of things: that her stomach represents her intuition (it is not, for Jane, associated with death as it is for Sarah); and that Jane needed to trust that God can speak to her in this way – and not just through her head. So Jane concluded that she needed to listen to the language of the body and hear the need for that which is vulnerable, precious and life-giving in her to be protected and nurtured and held so that she can do this for Sarah and for others among whom she ministers.

In this way Jane's own pastoral supervision was helping her connect with what Rowan Williams means, in the quotation earlier in this chapter, by the inhabitation of flesh by spirit in our own experience. It helped to keep her in touch with what the life of the spirit feels like so that she could recognize it becoming embodied in others' lives, but it also helped her allow her meanings and Sarah's to remain distinct and not become elided.

Retaining clarity about the two horizons of meaning is particularly important where there are close resonances. For example, for both Sarah and Jane the stomach had become an important symbol, yet it was important for Jane to be clear about what it symbolized to her and to keep exploring with Sarah what it symbolized for her.

Another sense in which pastoral supervision can help supervisors remain rounded is by helping them access parts of themselves that become split off when dealing with supervisees. One way to do this is to work in our own supervision with the stories and images that fund our imaginations when we think of particular supervision relationships. In the case of Jane's work with Sarah this meant working on the image of Joseph, because this image kept surfacing in her mind during their supervision sessions.

In that case an image was surfacing of its own accord, but sometimes work with a particular supervisee can simply feel stuck. In order to access what we know at the level of embedded stories and images, but have suppressed, Mooli Lahad proposes using characters and scenes from films, books or plays.[7] He suggests that this technique can help identify where we have become flattened characters within the supervision, acting a script rather than being fully present.

Because as pastoral supervisors our meanings are embedded not only within films, books and plays, but in the Christian story told in the Bible and enacted in the liturgical life of the Church, exploring the narrative associations we have with biblical characters and stories or characters within Christian history can also be fruitful.

This is not to fall into the trap Stephen Pattison identifies of dressing up perfectly valid ways of working in religious or biblical language in order to give them a falsely elevated authority.[8] Rather, experience suggests that working imaginatively with characters who are embedded in a narrative of God's loving purposes for humanity helps supervisors to hold open the supervision space as a place where God's Holy Spirit might be active in redemption and transformation.[9] Supervision then actively participates in the imperative to hold before ourselves the Christian narrative that it may have imaginative power over our lives, particularly as it comes into dialogue with actual, concrete practices.[10] This is not to suggest that we only imagine the redemptive power of God, but that God works deeply through imagination, symbol, image and feelings.[11]

## Co-supervision with a Biblical/Historical Character

The method is set out in detail in Exercise 7.3, but it is illustrated here from a peer supervision context. Helena felt that her work with Susan, a student training for lay ministry, was stuck. To try to get beyond the 'stuckness', Jane asked Helena to choose a biblical character she thought might be a good co-supervisor for Susan. Helena chose Mary, the wife of Cleopas, who she introduced as 'one of the women at the foot of the cross' and probably the 'other disciple' who walked away from Jerusalem with Cleopas towards Emmaus; 'someone who knew despair and what it is to be lost'.

Jane asked Helena to introduce herself to Mary. 'Hello, Mary, I am a Director of Pastoral Studies, and I need some help thinking about my supervision of Susan'. As Jane listened, she noted that initially she wondered about the identity of 'Mary, the wife of Cleopas' and then was struck by the anonymity of the companion of Cleopas in the Emmaus story. Jane noted that the word 'lost' came up more than once, and that there was a marked contrast between the formal description Helena gave of herself ('I am a Director of Pastoral Studies') and her much more emotive description of Mary ('someone who knew despair and what it is to be lost').

Jane asked Helena to imagine that she was due to meet Susan but instead would send 'Mary, the wife of Cleopas' to see her. Jane asked her, 'How will Susan respond to the fact that she's meeting someone else instead of you?' Helena said she thought Susan would feel betrayed and confused; that she would appear closed. Jane asked Helena how Mary would respond. Helena replied that she thought Mary would either tell her own story to Susan, give an empathic response or give her a hug. She found it difficult to imagine how Susan would respond to this, feeling that telling one's own story and giving hugs are not appropriate to supervision relationships.

As Jane listened she noted that the method had allowed Helena to access possible responses to Susan that she felt were proscribed by their formal relationship. In fact she later admitted that she modified 'tell her own story' to 'give an empathic response' in order to make it more acceptable. In this way, using 'Mary's voice' allowed feelings and conflicts to surface that otherwise might have remained hidden. Helena's explicit narrative came into dialogue with more implicit knowledge held in her association of Susan with Mary the wife of Cleopas.

In terms of helping Helena to reflect on her work with Susan, this technique helped her to access knowledge she had suppressed in her sessions with Susan because of her views about what is appropriate to supervision. By choosing a character to symbolize these 'unacceptable' instincts, they became accessible. Helena was then able to choose consciously how to work with Susan: she identified the ways she might 'psychologically hug' Susan, but also the need to help Susan find a therapeutic context in which she might explore some of the interpersonal issues Helena intuited needed work. This insight came about in particular from thinking about Mary's identity as a 'wife'. Helena felt that her own knowledge of personal and intimate relationships was telling her there was work for Susan to do here. Although telling Susan her own story in the way 'Mary' had advocated was not appropriate, it was important to help Susan attend to this dimension of herself – even if this needed to be outside the formal training context.

## Conclusions

The examples of Jane's work with Sarah and of Helena's with Susan illustrate the ways the work of pastoral supervision involves not only helping our supervisees become present to more of themselves and more deeply part of the redemptive story God is telling, but how we ourselves need to be involved in that same process of redemption. This can involve aspects of our life that ostensibly have no bearing on subjects we will explicitly discuss with our supervisees, yet just as for Helena there were resonances for her personal life in the work she was doing with Susan, so for all of us there will be sometimes intimate and personal work we need to do to remain rounded enough characters to be present to those we supervise, and to continue ourselves to be part of the story God is telling.

The reflective exercises that follow here ask you to think about the role of the Christian story and of images and narratives in pastoral supervision. Two tools are offered for working explicitly with biblical texts in supervision. They encourage people to work at the level of images, symbols and emotions and to bring these into dialogue with their explicit and articulate meanings.

# Exercises

## Exercise 7.1 Drawing on the Christian Story

Think about the pastoral supervision you have received.

> What role(s) has the Bible/Christian story played?
> What did you find helpful?
> What have you found unhelpful?

Think about the pastoral supervision you offer/want to offer.

> If you do use the Bible, what effect do you think that has on the supervision relationship?
> If you don't use the Bible, try to articulate why not.
> Is there anything that you have read in this chapter that might change your approach?

## Exercise 7.2 Bringing Artefacts to Pastoral Supervision

Images and symbols are often invested for us with deep meanings. These are often inarticulate and yet contain wisdom others can help us unlock.

**Invite a supervisee to bring to their supervision session an object that matters to them.** This might be something that either speaks about their sense of vocation in general or seems at the moment to be resonant with a piece of work in which they are engaged.

Spend some time with them *eliciting and focusing* why they are bringing this object:

> to supervision
> today
> and what they are hoping for in exploring its significance.

Together, devise a way of exploring the resonance the artefact has for a particular piece of work, bringing the item into dialogue with other objects chosen to symbolize key elements of that work.

Allow time for **bridging and enacting** and **reviewing and closing** in the usual way.

## Exercise 7.3 Co-Supervision with a Biblical Character

*To try in one-to-one supervision*

*(To use this technique in group supervision, invite the group to take note of what strikes them as they listen and to notice and wonder with you at stage 4. Alternatively, ask everyone to do this as a paper exercise and then discuss the outcomes.)*

### Stage 1

### Eliciting and focusing

**Invite your supervisee to name the person they want to bring to supervision.** This should be someone they work with or supervise, where the relationship seems to be stuck or difficult or in which your supervisee wants some help.

**Invite them to name their associations with this person.** How would they describe them? What is their relationship with them? What do they need help to think through?

*Listen carefully to what is said. Note what strikes you and what you wonder.*

### Exploring and imagining

**Invite them to think about who from the Bible or from Christian history they would like some help from in order to work better with this person.** At this stage, it doesn't matter what is known about the character chosen. It is important to assure your supervisee not to be worried prematurely about Christian orthodoxy. What matters is what the character signifies to them and what hidden information about their working relationship there may be in their choice. This should unfold as the session proceeds.

**Invite your supervisee to introduce this character to you as if you had never heard of them.** Ask what they chiefly remember about, admire about, associate with this character. **This character will be their co-supervisor.**

*Listen carefully to what is said. Note what strikes you and what you wonder.*

**Invite your supervisee to introduce themselves to their co-supervisor and state what they need help with.**

*Note anything that strikes you.*


## Stage 2

**Invite your supervisee to imagine introducing their co-supervisor to the person they need help working with/ supervising, and explaining that you are leaving them together for an hour.**

➢ How does the person your supervisee needs help with respond to the fact that they're meeting someone else instead of you?

**Invite your supervisee to imagine that they are going for a walk or for a coffee while the supervision happens.**

➢ What do they think the co-supervisor is doing/saying?
➢ How do they imagine their colleague/supervisee is responding?
➢ How do they feel about not knowing what is going on?

*Listen carefully to what is said. Note what strikes you and what you wonder.*

## Stage 3

**Invite your supervisee to imagine that when they return to the room where they left the co-supervisor and the person they need help with, the latter has gone but has given their permission to talk to the co-supervisor. Invite your supervisee to ask the co-supervisor the following questions and share the responses.**

> What are the co-supervisor's impressions of this person?
> What was the most surprising thing that happened in the encounter?
> What are the co-supervisor's main recommendations?

*Listen carefully to what is said. Note what strikes you and what you wonder.*

## Bridging and enacting

## Stage 4

> Ask your supervisee if there is anything they have realized in this process – or anything they now want to pursue.
> Share what you, as supervisor, have noticed or wondered.
> What do you know about the biblical/historical character chosen? Does any of that resonate with your supervisee?
> What recommendations do you think the co-supervisor might make?
> Invite your supervisee to consider what has struck them about the Christian story, its relevance or power, or about their interpretation of it.
> Finally, invite your supervisee to consider where they will go from here in working with their colleague/supervisee.

Allow time for *reviewing and closing*.

## Exercise 7.4 The Four Elements

This is an exercise that combines some of the drama techniques of the last chapter with the narrative techniques of this chapter. The method was devised by Lia Zografou and was published in 2014.[12] It is a group supervision method, drawn from the world of **playback theatre**.[13]

*To try in a group*

### Hosting and containing

The supervisor acts as 'company director'. The 'stage' is set with two chairs at the left of the stage, one for the director and one for the 'teller'. The group become the audience. Across the back of the stage are set up four 'elements' from which members of the group will volunteer to 'playback' to the 'teller' what they hear: one will draw on a flip chart with marker pens; one will sculpt a scene or short drama using a selection of cloths or objects; one will tell a story or sing a song; one will speak directly from their own experience.

The director invites members of the group to occupy one of the four chairs, to hear the story and to respond from one of the four elements.

### Eliciting and focusing

The director then invites the supervisee to relate a short incident from their work, asking questions as necessary.

### Exploration

Once the basic story is told, the respondents are asked to present what they have heard, in sequence, using the element allocated to them.

## Bridging and Enacting

Having heard and seen their story reflected back to them, the director concludes by asking the teller whether anything has struck them afresh and whether there is anything they see differently or want to do differently as a result.

## Reviewing and Closing

The method is designed to be fast paced and to allow all members of a group to take a turn at being the teller. It is particularly useful for getting a range of issues into the room in a short space of time, and some space should be allowed at the end of the exercise for everyone to reflect on any themes that have emerged.

In a secular context, any songs or stories might be used, but in pastoral contexts, participants may well choose stories and songs from the religious tradition to which they belong.

# Notes

1 Following admission to a psychiatric hospital in the 1920s, Boisen set in motion what would come to be known as **Clinical Pastoral Education** (CPE), a form of seminary education that invited seminarians to interpret their lives as carefully as they interpret the Scriptures.

2 Charles V. Gerkin, 1984, *The Living Human Document: Re-Visioning Pastoral Counseling in a Hermeneutical Model*, Nashville, TN: Abingdon Press, chapter 1.

3 Gerkin, *Living Human Document*, p. 50.

4 Elizabeth O'Connor, 1978, *Letters to Scattered Pilgrims*, San Francisco: Harper & Row, p. 47.

5 Elizabeth O'Connor, 1968, *Journey Outward, Journey Inward*, San Francisco: Harper & Row, p. 5.

6 Rowan Williams, 2007, 'A theology of health for today', in J. Baxter (ed.), *Wounds that Heal: Theology, Imagination and Health*, London: SPCK, pp. 3–14.

7 Mooli Lahad, 2000, *Creative Supervision: The Use of Expressive Arts Methods in Supervision and Self-Supervision*, London and Philadelphia: Jessica Kingsley.

8 See chapter 5 on the Bible and pastoral care in S. J. Pattison, 2000, *A Critique of Pastoral Care*, 3rd edn, London: SCM Press.

9 See the theological account of pastoral supervision in chapter 3 of Frances Ward, 2005, *Lifelong Learning: Theological Education and Supervision*, London: SCM Press.

10 One of Charles Gerkin's criteria for adequate clinical pastoral supervision is that it is focused on the specific; the others are that it is rooted in what he calls the Christian 'fact'; and that it reflects on praxis for the sake of transformed praxis. For a succinct summary of Gerkin's approach, see Thomas St James O'Connor, 1998, *Clinical Pastoral Supervision and the Theology of Charles Gerkin*, Canadian Corporation for Studies in Religion Vol. 22.

11 Richard H. Niebuhr, 1960, *Radical Monotheism and Western Culture*, Lincoln, NE: University of Nebraska Press.

12 Lia Zografou, 2014, 'The four elements', in Anna Chesner and Lia Zografou (eds), *Creative Supervision Across Modalities: Theory and Applications for Therapists, Counsellors and Other Helping Professionals*, London and Philadelphia: Jessica Kingsley, pp. 59–70.

13 For a discussion of playback theatre, see Zografou, 'Four elements', pp. 61–2.

# 8

# Attending to Context

**Summary**

Pastoral supervision needs to pay attention to the context in which the supervisee is working. In its broadest sense this context may be articulated as the body of Christ or the postmodern world, but in a narrower sense as the secure psychiatric hospital or a particular local church. Successful supervision pays attention to context in these senses but also to the context in which the supervision itself is taking place – for example: whether supervisor and supervisee share a working context or not; whether the supervision happens within a management structure or outside it. In this chapter we examine some of the contextual issues to which a supervisor needs to be alert, and offer Farley's **hermeneutical method** and the supervision rhombus as tools for monitoring and responding to these. Attention to context may play a part in the *exploration* of supervision material, and should contribute to what is being *monitored*.

For just as the body is one and has many members, and all the members of the body, though many, are one body, so it is with Christ. If the foot were to say, 'Because I am not a hand, I do not belong to the body', that would not make it any less a part of the body. And if the ear were to say, 'Because I am not an eye, I do not belong to the body', that would not make it any less a part of the body. If the whole body were an eye, where would the hearing be? If the whole body were hearing, where would the sense of smell be? But as it is, God arranged the members in the body, each one of them, as he chose. If all were a single member, where would the body be? As it is, there are many members, yet one body. Now you are the body of Christ and individually members of it.

1 Corinthians 12.12, 15–20, 27

## The Body of Christ as Context

From the outset, the approach to pastoral supervision taken in this book is that it is an exercise of ministry. As such it takes place within the body of Christ. This is its context. In fact the practice of being in supervision is a prime way of locating our ministries within the body of Christ, knit together not simply in a mystical sense, but through disciplined and transparent patterns of relating.

Some of the implications of understanding pastoral supervision in this way were set out in Chapter 1 using Kenneth Pohly's notion of covenant and in Chapter 7 by looking at the ways the supervisor listens for the story God is telling and seeks to help the supervisee embody that story more closely in their ministry. This involves paying attention to the text of the Word made flesh in our own and others' experience. As the first letter of John puts it, 'We declare to you what was from the beginning, what we have heard, what we have seen with our eyes, what we have looked at and touched with our hands, concerning the word of life' (1 John 1.1).

But the ways the Word becomes flesh among particular people in a given place and at a particular time need careful attention, since theological and pastoral practice does not take place in a vacuum, nor can incarnation be reduced to an idea. This requires attention not just to our supervisees – the stories they are telling and the stories behind their stories – but to the contexts in which they are working and supervisee and supervisor are meeting. Another way to put this is to recognize that human beings are bodies and that one of the most fundamental things about human beings is that we are always somewhere.[1] Where we work – in a hospital, a school, a church, an office – shapes us and shapes the way spirit will inhabit flesh among us, and the ways we recognize that life taking shape.

So far in this book we have been concentrating on what happens when a supervisor sits down with a supervisee to accompany them in reflecting on issues arising from their work. We have noted at various points that the context in which this happens is important, but to date have been concentrating on what happens within the time set aside for the supervision session.

To help supervisors pay proper attention to the context in which the supervision is happening, Rudolf Ekstein and Robert Wallerstein devised what we shall call the supervision rhombus (see Figure 8.1).[2]

Figure 8.1 Outline of the supervision rhombus

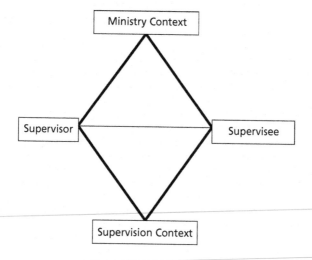

This invites us to paint in some of the contextual issues that affect supervision and helps supervisors to attend to these dimensions of the work.

## Attention to the Ministry Context of the Supervisee

The upper half of the supervision rhombus, depicted in Figure 8.2, invites reflection on the ministry context of the supervisee. This can shape the kind of supervision necessary in a variety of ways.

Figure 8.2 Supervision rhombus: upper half

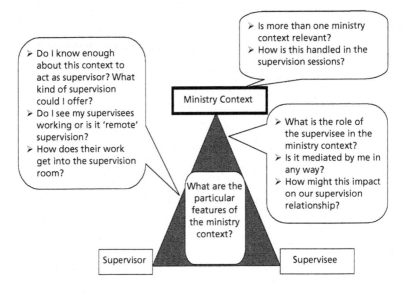

> Is more than one ministry context relevant?
> How is this handled in the supervision sessions?

> Do I know enough about this context to act as supervisor? What kind of supervision could I offer?
> Do I see my supervisees working or is it 'remote' supervision?
> How does their work get into the supervision room?

Ministry Context

> What is the role of the supervisee in the ministry context?
> Is it mediated by me in any way?
> How might this impact on our supervision relationship?

What are the particular features of the ministry context?

Supervisor

Supervisee

## Attention to the Particular Ministry Context

First, the supervision will be shaped by the ministry context of the supervisee: the issues brought to supervision by a mental health nurse will be different from those brought by a youth worker; so also will be the language and conceptualizations with which they work. A good question for a pastoral supervisor to think about when considering taking on a supervisee will be whether or not they themselves know enough about the particular demands of the context concerned. For experienced practitioners, the supervisor being familiar with the particular demands of the context will not be as important as it is for a novice.

## Attention to the Culture of the Organization(s) in which the Supervisee Works

In all supervision relationships the culture of the organization in which the supervisee works needs to be taken seriously. Just as pastoral supervision is attentive to the story behind the stories supervisees tell, and sees them through theological and spiritual lenses, so it will attend to values of the organization or community in which the supervisee is working. This is not a simple matter, partly because culture is a complex thing:

> Culture includes the entire symbolic environment. Culture defines reality: what is, what should be, what can be. It provides focus and meaning. It selects out of the myriad of events and interactions in the world those we pay attention to. Culture tells us what is important; what causes what, how events beyond our lives relate to us. Culture gives us values and standards of value. What we may distinguish analytically (and at our peril) as fact, value and goal is existentially integrated in culture – in identifications, expectations and demands of individual persons.[3]

Listening to the context in which the supervisee works is complex because culture is multi-layered and often implicit. It is embedded not only in mission statements and policy documents, but in the day-to-day, often unconscious, behaviours of ordinary people.

Moreover, if the supervisee works in a secular institution like a chaplaincy, there is likely to be some tension between the values of the supervisee – or their authorizing denomination – and the values of the institution or aspects of the work that seem to ignore key dimensions of the chaplain's identity. As an experienced acute healthcare chaplain asked recently in a group supervision session, 'What difference does it make that I am a chaplain leading the bereavement support group? Does that make it ethical to bring God into it or, as it's a hospital service that the chaplaincy happens to run, should God stay outside the door? Who am I when I'm doing this work?' Where this is the case, pastoral supervisors need to help supervisees articulate the tensions as part of finding a framework for growing in pastoral identity: 'The best supervision is that which brings out the dialogical nature of what occurs – the different voices and perspectives so that any given situation can be explored as a rich encounter.'[4]

Tensions may also arise not from obvious clashes in values, but from practices of the institution that seem to thwart the best attempts of individuals to change their own behaviour. Peter Senge, in his seminal work *The Fifth Discipline*,[5] talks about the importance of identifying implicit system goals. These may well not be the same as the articulated goals. Thus, in helping the supervisee pay attention to the context in which they work, a pastoral supervisor may ask them to think not just about articulated values, but about the implicit theology or ideology at work.

A useful tool for structuring theological reflection in this area is Edward Farley's hermeneutical method, which is set out in Exercise 8.2 at the end of this chapter.[6] This method is exemplified by David Lyall in an article in *Contact* in 1989.[7] Reflecting on his experience of working with both donors and recipients of kidneys in transplant operations, Lyall works through Farley's stages, focusing not just on the interpersonal dynamics, but on the structural dynamics of the hospital context. Having mapped the key features of the situation, considered the implications of the past and framed the experience in wider cultural currents, Lyall looks at the **structures of idolatry** and **structures of redemption** present in the hospital. In pastoral supervision this would not imply asking the more diffuse question, 'Where do you sense God at work?' (perhaps in the kindness of nursing staff or the sacrificial attitude of a donor), but thinking about the *structures* of the NHS governing the spending of money on expensive treatments and the implicit goal of Western medicine to keep patients alive at all costs.

The purpose of using such a method in supervision would be to help the supervisee notice the ways their choices are shaped by the whole ethos of the hospital in which they work, to name tensions and make conscious choices as part of the *exploring and imagining* phase of the work. However, its usefulness is not confined to secular institutions. Although the Church understands itself as a divine society and as such is explicitly structured so as to work towards redemptive outcomes, anyone who is part of it knows that it is also a human institution that needs to pay attention to the ways its structures can form kingdom values.

An example of the relevance of this level of thinking in supervision is provided by Jane's experience of being supervised while working as a tutor in a theological college. Her supervisor pointed out to her that many of the issues cropping up in her supervision of students related to work–life balance and an inability to prioritize taking care of themselves. In the light of this she asked Jane to reflect on the state in which she herself often came to supervision, and Jane acknowledged the irony that she was often too tired to think straight and too busy to find the time to implement any actions that were agreed. By thinking together about the culture of theological training, they were able to realize that this was a systemic problem and not merely recalcitrance on Jane's or her students' part.

Jane found this contextual approach helpful in several ways: she realized why she was finding it so difficult to change her behaviour, when it was part of a much bigger system; she was able to identify the culture of busyness as an essentially faithless belief in human indispensability, which leaves little room for the work of God, in contrast to the practices of Sabbath set out in the Scriptures and embodied in Jesus Christ; and she started to think about how she might divert some energy into identifying levers for change at the systemic level. Further, Jane and her supervisor were able to reflect together – not just on the culture of the Church, but upon the culture of the 24/7 society from which not only religious people are seeking retreat.

## Attention to the Wider Cultural Issues

Reflecting on the ways Western culture affects the embodiment of the body of Christ in our own time and place is one of the ways pastoral supervisors can prepare for the work of supervision and stay alert to these dimensions of the context in which supervisees are working and we ourselves are supervising. Just as empirical studies have demonstrated that in different eras different psychological symptoms have predominated in clients presenting for counselling (in Victorian times, problems associated with sexual repression; in our own, borderline personalities that have suffered from a lack of good enough parenting in infancy),[8] so within pastoral supervision it is likely that those working within the Church now will present with issues different from those our predecessors in ministry did 30 or 50 years ago. The anxieties and pressures caused by the numerical decline of the traditional denominations in the West would be one example. Another might be the fast pace of change within society and the churches and its corollary, an increase in conflict: as Sarah Savage and Eolene Boyd-Macmillan observe, 'In an age of church decline, we should expect more conflict, not less.'[9]

Attention to the contextual issues of the broader culture that shape the ministry contexts in which our supervisees work does not absolve us as pastoral supervisors from proper attention to the particularities of the stories our supervisees are telling us; nor is it always helpful to point out that this is a familiar story. Yet helping a supervisee to attend to the system and structural dimensions of their work can be liberating not only for them, but for their organizations as they seek to use their energies where there is genuine leverage.

For this to happen it is important for the pastoral supervisor to achieve some critical distance from the ministry context of the supervisee, otherwise supervisor and supervisee may unwittingly fall into a collusive pattern by simply accepting the status quo of the latter's working context and failing to see themselves as agents of change. For, as Stanley Hauerwas strikingly points out, 'the most orthodox Christological or Trinitarian affirmations are essentially false when they are embedded in lives and social practices which make it clear that it makes no difference whether Jesus lived, died, or was resurrected.'[10]

Locating pastoral supervision as an exercise of ministry within the body of Christ means that it cannot exempt itself from the gospel imperative to set prisoners free. Being members one of another within the body of Christ denies us the option of turning a blind eye to the injustice expressed in the pay system where our supervisees work, to the discriminatory practices that inhibit their flourishing or to the unequal treatment of male and female employees. While other helping professions like psychotherapy can justify seeing people who present as individuals out of context, the Christian journey is always from 'I' to 'we' in the context of the body. This does not make it appropriate for pastoral supervisors to rush in like the cavalry to 'fix' the problems of the organizations within which our supervisees work, but it does mean we cannot see our role simply as helping our supervisees adapt to whatever working culture they are part of, nor can we expect our own consciences to remain undisturbed about injustices, collusions and avoidances in the organizations in which we have power and influence.

As well as participating in the disciplines of the Christian life – prayer, Bible study and the sacramental life of the Church – attending seriously to context using tools such as the supervision rhombus and Farley's hermeneutical method can help prevent us and our supervisees losing our ability to challenge the organizational structures that shape their lives and the lives of those they seek to serve.

It is already apparent that attending to the ministry context of the supervisee is not a straightforward business. It is an ongoing part of the supervision task, forming part of the *tracking and monitoring* of the supervision relationship. Another dimension to consider is whether or not the supervisor and the supervisee share a ministry context.

## 'Remote' Supervision

Many of the examples of pastoral supervision in this book come from elective supervision sessions where one or more supervisees have covenanted to work with a supervisor who never sees them in their professional environment. As a consequence, the supervisor has no access to the work of the supervisee beyond the latter's presentation of it. As Michael Carroll points out, 'if we, as supervisors, think we are supervising what *actually happens* ... we are deluding ourselves'.[11]

It is very clear in this kind of supervision that the task is to accompany and equip the practitioner and not to fix the problems they bring. What the supervisor pays primary attention to is the congruence between what the supervisee is telling them about the 'there and then' and what they experience of the supervisee in the 'here and now'.

Where supervisors find themselves accompanying supervisees whose working context or culture is unfamiliar to them, they would do well to ask supervisees from the outset to interpret their work settings for them so as to contextualize what is brought to supervision.

Some supervisors do this by asking to be taken and shown round the workplace to get a feel of the atmosphere for themselves. Others will ask supervisees to bring along some literature about the organization or will consult the relevant website; but however this fuller picture is achieved, it will be imperative that it is done with the full awareness of the supervisee. Being perceived to have gone behind someone's back like a private detective will seriously damage the working relationship and hinder trust. Equally, a supervisee who is reluctant at the beginning of the relationship to let a supervisor 'see' or understand their work context is unlikely to receive effective supervision.

## Sharing a Ministry Context

Where the supervisor and the supervisee share a ministry context, the task of supervision is in some ways more complex. The supervisor will have their own impressions of the ministry context to work with but will need to remember that these are their own impressions and interpretations and not an objective description of reality. It can be easy to dismiss the experiences of a supervisee who finds a colleague of yours intimidating, for example, if you relate well to that person. Also, the supervisor may see the supervisee at work and have quite different perceptions of their abilities, strengths and weaknesses than the supervisee does themselves. This will need careful handling if trust in the relationship is to be maintained. An example of the kind of skills needed here was presented by the case of Donna in Chapter 3. Because she and Jane shared a ministry context, as supervisor, Jane needed skills of transparent reporting in order to bring the work into the room: 'I noticed that when we shared the peace in chapel on Thursday, you didn't meet my eye. Can you reflect with me what that is about?'

Beyond the skills needed, however, when both parties share the same working environment, careful attention needs to be paid to the inherent dynamics at play and questions raised as to how this cohabiting of the same culture affects each of the parties.

One of the issues that needs to be addressed is that of collusion and avoidance, since these 'are almost certain to threaten the efficacy of the work where the participants have a vested interest in maintaining a sound working, or social, alliance over and above their joint responsibilities to the supervision relationship'.[12]

When two people who work together in the same team find themselves together in supervision, the key question they have to ask themselves is: 'When push comes to shove, what is non-negotiable in our relationship?' If the answer to that question is 'unswerving loyalty and friendship without critique', then they would be better to look for supervision elsewhere. What Rowan Williams says about vocation is equally true about supervision:

Here at least, whatever the cost, I am *in the truth*. [Anything else] would be playing, messing around with a tame reality I could control; and reality is not like that. Vocation is, you could say, what's left when all the games have stopped. And it's that elusive residue that we are here to discover, and to help one another to discover.[13]

The same question as to where the bottom line lies in the relationship needs also to be asked of peers who covenant to supervise each other in a group. Unless the 'games can stop' and the truth be told, all parties are deluding themselves. Supervision that skirts around the truth – or permits only the supportive dimensions of friendship without the challenges – is a waste of time and energy. When both parties have a vested interested in doing anything other than truth-telling in supervision, inner vision becomes diluted and personal integrity corroded. For this reason, peer supervision is perhaps one of the hardest forms to do well, yet in all supervision relationships the possibility of collusion exists and needs to be faced.

The other important dynamic, which is always present in supervision but perhaps most difficult to handle when supervisor and supervisee work in the same team, is that of power. However much we may want to talk about mutuality within the body of Christ, even within peer supervision there are power dynamics, and these are particularly strong when supervisee and supervisor work together, especially when the supervisor has influence over the future of the supervisee in some way.

## Naming and Handling Power in Pastoral Supervision

Power can often be considered a dirty word in church circles. A proper emphasis on servanthood in ministry can easily be confused with a refusal to name and exercise properly the power that the authorization of the Church confers and with which charismatic gifts are invested. The consequence of a failure to recognize one's power in ministry is that the good one has the power to do may remain undone, and the power one has to damage may go unnoticed except by our casualties along the way.

If this is true generally in the body of Christ, then it is true in pastoral supervision. Simply to be trusted with the story of another is to be given power. The more honest and vulnerable a person is encouraged to be, the more powerful will be the interventions we make and the more important it becomes that we are in touch with what the Holy Spirit is doing and with the dimensions of our own personalities and experiences that are likely to get in the way.

The pastoral supervisor is therefore always a powerful person and needs to be aware of that power and use it for good. Part of the way we ensure that is by being in supervision ourselves and by attending to our own codes of ethics. The APSE code of conduct is included in full at Appendix 3. It is worth looking at it and considering what ethical code you are following if you are currently supervising others, as well as in your own practice.

So far we have drawn attention to the role power of the pastoral supervisor. There are other kinds of power that are also important – particularly the kind of power we embody. The more nearly we embody the most powerful groups in our world – the white, the male, the educated, the heterosexual – the more careful we will need to be to make room for the language, constructs and images of those who are different from us, and the more alert we will need to be in naming what may make our relative sizes as supervisor and supervisee seem disproportionate. Figure 8.3 outlines four kinds of power present in supervision.

The pastoral supervisor is always a powerful person and needs to find ways to help the supervisee claim their own power. The supervision rhombus draws attention to the ways this dynamic is intensified when the supervisor has wider institutional power as well as both the role power that comes with the supervising role and the social power that comes by being a member of a powerful group in society. Examples of this include the relationship of a training incumbent and a curate; a college tutor and an ordinand; a bishop or district chair and a local minister; a senior healthcare chaplain and one of their staff.

Figure 8.3 Four kinds of power

|  | Cultural Power (externally given) | Power of Position (externally given) | Charismatic Power (given by followers) | Personal Power (inner authority) |
|---|---|---|---|---|
| Derived from | Who you are, e.g. race, culture, age – in a social context with particular values | External sources, e.g. promotion, qualifications, reputation, getting published | Intuition, natural empathy; openness to inspiration, personal connection | Lived experience. Reflecting on and making one's own any training, supervision etc. |
| Vulnerable to | Relying too much on valued characteristics or being unable to value yourself | Fear of losing position or being incompetent. Fear of authority | Lack of engagement with rules, systems and organizations | Lack of external backup. Does the buck stop here? |
| Weakness when vulnerable | Dependent on a particular culture; upset by change | Easily influenced or manipulated; overassertive in self-defence. | Running risks without taking responsibility for consequences | Isolation; being unable to access or rely on external authority |

Having both worked with ordinands for several years, we are only too well aware of the fear and trepidation with which both parties – trainee minister and supervising trainers – come to supervision. On the one hand, trainees fear being misunderstood, judged and ultimately deemed unsuitable for licensed ministry or ordination, while on the other hand, training supervisors agonize over the balance between being supportive and, when needed, able to confront; allowing things to be provisional to allow for change and growth and discerning when the time is right to act. Inevitably, what both parties equally fear is the power invested in the reporting process, which results in candidates proceeding towards ecclesially recognized ministries or being stopped in their tracks.[14]

In order to use our power for good, as pastoral supervisors we need first of all to name with our supervisees what our power is and what it is not. This is where attention to the lower half of the supervision rhombus is invaluable.

# Attention to the Context in which the Supervision Takes Place

## Figure 8.4 Supervision rhombus: lower half

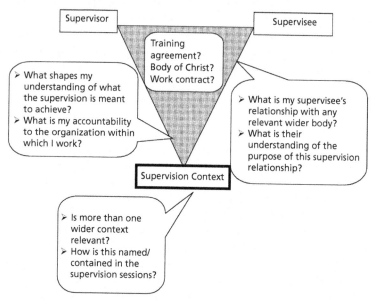

The lower half of the supervision rhombus, set out in Figure 8.4, paints in the context in which the *supervision* – rather than the supervisee's ministry – takes place. When the supervision is elective and 'remote', the context of the supervision will be whatever covenant the supervisor and the supervisee agree to. When the supervision is part of an institutional requirement (for example, to be part of a group supervision arrangement in a prison chaplaincy context, or as an internship student studying for ministry), the supervision will be governed in part by the requirements of the wider body and the relationships of both the supervisor and the supervisee with that body. If the supervision is to be successful, these dimensions need to be clear from the outset, especially if there is any form of reporting involved.

## Attention to Reporting Requirements

There is nothing more damaging than establishing a form of confidentiality and trust in a supervision relationship, which then has to be broken in order for a report to be written. The body that commissioned the supervision in the first place is likely then to be painted as the enemy (persecutor), and supervisor and supervisee are likely to collude in writing a report that says nothing. The supervision rhombus is designed to help supervisors pay attention to the lines of accountability that exist for both themselves and their supervisees and make sure these shape the supervision arrangement from the beginning. If you find that you need to write such a report, the following guidelines should ensure good practice. A reporting exercise is offered at the end of the chapter. Reporting is part of the *tracking and monitoring* process of supervision. It also belongs within Inskipp and Proctor's *normative* dimension of supervision.

1. Make sure that from the outset you and your supervisee have a clear sense of the criteria on which your supervisee's engagement in the supervision or the ministry context will be judged and that your supervision covenant takes them into account.
2. If there is agreed paperwork (such as denominational benchmarks or forms to be completed for an assessment process), make sure you have looked at these together. (Your supervisee assuring you that they have them somewhere will not be sufficient to make sure they understand the process they are engaged in and their responsibilities within it.)
3. Discuss the purpose of the report and think together about this theologically. You might draw on Mark 6; notions of accountability within the body of Christ; the ethic of service and accountability to those we serve.
4. Make it clear whether others will contribute to the reporting process and by what means and on what issues. Think about what kind of reports you want from them and how you will discuss them with your supervisee.
5. Audit the work you do with your supervisee to check that you

are helping them towards these competencies or attitudes and not supervising to another agenda.

6. Keep records of your work together. This should at least be a note of times you have met for supervision and the main issues discussed or decisions taken. This acts as an aide-memoire for you but also as evidence should problems arise later with a supervisee denying having discussed a matter with you. To avoid any confusion, these records should be signed by both of you as a matter of course.

7. Plan ahead so that you write nothing in a report that you have not already discussed with your supervisee.

8. Ask your supervisee for their own observations in relation to the criteria for assessment, as a way of shaping a discussion about them before you draft your report.

9. Be straightforward in your comments and stick to the evidence you have rather than making generalized or personal statements. For example: 'In accordance with the agreed learning objective, Brian has been working on preaching without notes. He has preached four short homilies at the early Eucharist with only a postcard for reference, and has considerably improved his ability to communicate with the congregation.' Rather than: 'Brian is a good preacher, and will make a good priest.'

10. Reports should attempt to state what has improved – in relation to the criteria – and what work still needs to be done. Some comment might also be made in terms of the stage of the process at which the supervisee is: 'Sharon has been working on leading worship in formal situations as part of an objective to extend the contexts in which she is comfortable leading worship. Formal worship was entirely new to her, but Sharon has made progress in her ability to invest herself in written words and inhabit liturgical space with some dignity. Those worshipping at such services have offered the feedback that they appreciate the content of Sharon's sermons but find the colloquialisms overfamiliar and Sharon's movement around the sanctuary distracting. There is still some work for Sharon to do to find a way of preaching at formal services that is

comfortable, both for her and for the congregation. This is not a question of basic competence in worship leading, but of developing repertoire for different contexts, and Sharon has demonstrated a great willingness to learn to operate in an environment she still finds alien.'

11. Reports should be signed by the supervisor and the supervisee before being submitted. This helps the supervisee retain some level of responsibility for their own development. Where you cannot agree a form of words together, there should be room for a supervisee to register their disagreement with the supervisor's judgement.

12. The supervisee should receive a copy of the signed report and have opportunity to discuss it with the body that has commissioned it, such as a training institution or diocesan officer.[15]

For those supervising colleagues who are in training, there are likely to be benchmarks and competencies specified by the sponsoring denominations. In other ministry situations it is true that in general the Church is often not good at spelling out expectations. Most clergy work without job descriptions or clear line management. The introduction of paid lay workers into church life has highlighted the differences between employment and deployment, and often a lack of skills and structures within the life of the church to supervise and manage employees. Despite the fact that plenty of lay people within churches have skills and experience in such areas in their working lives, due to the culture and power structures of the churches it is often difficult for these to be effectively deployed. At one level it is appropriate that secular models of practice should be questioned before being adopted wholesale; at another it is important to note that theological objections to 'management' articulated by individuals may mask a resistance to accountability within the organization itself.

In reality, codes of practice and points of reference for the exercise of ministry within the denominations often do exist but have not reached the conscious awareness of those who exercise those ministries. One consequence for pastoral supervision is that in supervising someone who works within a church context, it may take considerable archaeological skills and persistence to help them identify the codes of practice within which they should be working. These may vary from guidelines on confidentiality and the safeguarding of children and young people, to the declarations made in ordination services. However, being clear about your own code of ethics and helping supervisees identify theirs not only limits your power and helps your supervisees to adopt a mature attitude towards the supervision, but may model for them the importance of clarifying their own code of ethics, so becoming more accountable for the power they exercise themselves.

In summary, the upper half of the supervision rhombus draws the supervisor's attention to the ministry context of the supervisee. It raises questions about the supervisor's understanding of the nature of the supervisee's role and work; it highlights the importance of system and implicit goals in the work culture in which the supervisee is embedded, as well as the influence of the wider culture upon that organization; and it asks the supervisor to name the power dynamics that need attention where they and their supervisee share a ministry context. The lower half of the supervision rhombus draws the pastoral supervisor's attention to the context in which the supervision is taking place. This may be substantially the same as the ministry context or it may be informed by different cultural norms. In either case it is the role of the pastoral supervisor to make sure expectations about the nature and purpose of the supervision sessions are explicitly discussed, and that key relationships with wider expectation-setting bodies are not neglected to the detriment of the effectiveness of the supervision offered.

## The Supervision Rhombus in Practice

An example of what happens when the two poles of the supervision rhombus are neglected is provided by Nick. He and Michael had not met for supervision for about six weeks due to holiday commitments. In that time Nick had been asked by the local theological college to have Marion on placement, which had been underway for three weeks when he and Michael met again for supervision. Nick launched into the story:

About a month ago the local theological college asked me to take on an ordinand (Marion), whose eight-week pastoral placement had fallen through at the last minute. I had never had a student on placement before but felt chuffed and validated to have been asked to help in this way. (Foolishly) I didn't find out much about Marion, except that she was in her twenties and academically very bright. I'd appealed for lodgings, and in due course Marion arrived and moved in with Elsa, one of the café-project volunteers and a church regular. Everything seemed to be OK, but last week I attended the regular management meeting of the care home where I'm chaplain, and the manager wanted to raise some concerns with me about Marion. Apparently she had been 'holding mini evangelistic rallies in the day room urging repentance before death'. The home manager, who had lapsed from church attendance in recent months, was perturbed by this but didn't want to cause waves for Marion, 'who meant well' – but I was horrified.

It then transpired from another member of the management group that this same young woman had been causing quite a stir at the café project, handing out Christian material to some of the young Muslim mums who meet up at the project.

I knew I needed to tackle Marion about this, so I asked her to come and see me after the midweek Bible study yesterday. I know I was nervous, and I'm sure that didn't help. I wasn't really very sure how to approach the subject and as a result probably skirted around the issue too long. But when I did get to the point, Marion was completely affronted that her witness to Christ should be questioned, especially by a minister of the gospel. I tried to explain that my approach was to join people on the road in the hope that they might come to Christ. She told me that 'Jesus is the Way, Truth and Life' and that unless people come to him their souls will be lost. In the end I lost my patience and Marion stormed out.

As supervisor, Michael was immediately aware of feeling pretty cross with the training institution. On the other hand, he was wondering what on earth Nick had been doing in his supervision sessions with Marion, if he hadn't worked out that her theological stance and that of the café project might be at odds and that she would need careful briefing about what was expected. Had he met with her at all? It was easy to see that had Nick sat down before he said 'yes' to the college and mapped out the supervision rhombus, he might have spotted the lack of information from them, the need to check with Marion what she thought the placement was meant to achieve, and the need to think through with Marion what the placement context was like and what her appropriate involvement would be. Michael also wondered what Nick had learnt from his supervisions with him and felt worried that perhaps he had let Nick down in some way – something to take to his own supervisor.

Remembering Inskipp and Proctor's three-legged stool of supervision, Michael wondered what would be most helpful to Nick at this point. Clearly there was some need for restorative supervision. Nick had described feeling validated by the college's faith in him, but how was he feeling now? Perhaps the most important thing to do first would be to help him discharge his emotions or explore why supervising a placement was important enough to take on even without sufficient preparation – was it core to his sense of vocation and therefore too good an opportunity to miss, or had he felt unable to say 'no'?

Other possible avenues are suggested by the other 'legs' of Inskipp and Proctor's stool. If Michael had chosen the formative route he could have helped Nick think about what he needed to learn in order to handle a placement successfully. Perhaps even drawing the supervision rhombus with him would have been a useful formative approach. This would also have had the advantage of bringing up the normative issues: What kind of working agreement did he have with Marion for supervision of her work? What had the college said about the learning outcomes of the placement? What code of ethics did Nick want Marion to observe – had he discussed it with her?

As Michael listened to Nick he ran the possibilities through his mind, but was also aware of the urgency and complexity of the situation. Nick had a situation to go back to with a lot of implications: his relationship with the café project and with the care home, his relationship with Elsa and his reputation with the college were all at stake in his handling of the aftermath of this.

Remembering that this was Nick's supervision, Michael asked him: 'There are lots of directions this supervision could go in. We could explore how you're feeling about it all; we could look at why you agreed to the placement at such short notice; we could look at the implications. What would it be most helpful for us to do today?' Nick said that really he wanted to focus on what to do next with Marion. He said that he was kicking himself for saying 'yes', when he was too busy and hadn't had time to prepare himself or anyone else for Marion coming. He said that he'd always wanted to work with ordinands, so leapt at it, but hadn't given it his full attention and felt very down about it and cross with himself. Michael asked him if all the responsibility was his, and he said that he didn't really think it was Marion's fault – she'd been dumped into the situation too – but that he was cross with the theological college, who'd offered no training or real help to think through the issues.

Bearing in mind that Nick had said he wanted to focus on what to do with Marion now, Michael asked him whether he'd made any plans to see her. He said that his instinct was to try to see her again soon, but he needed to calm down and think about what was salvageable. Michael asked him whether there was anything he needed to think through here or any information he needed in order to meet with Marion. He said that he needed to know what the placement was supposed to achieve – both from the college, but also what Marion thought. Michael asked whether there was some sort of written contract or statement of aims, and Nick agreed that he needed to find out and that it would be a good idea to ring the college to see whether they had any paperwork he could use. Michael asked him how Marion would feel about his contacting the college without her knowledge. Nick said he was worried she had already done that herself and made a complaint about him.

Michael drew the supervision rhombus for Nick (a distancing method), and wrote down what he'd said about the need to pay attention to the wider expectations of the training college and also the issues in the ministry context. They then went on to think about how Nick would approach the meeting with Marion: where it should be held; what he needed to communicate; what he might ask her; what the possible outcomes might be. Michael asked Nick about his sense of his 'size' relative to Marion. He said that when they'd met he'd felt 'small' in relation to her, because she seemed to be rejecting his authority and also because he felt such an idiot generally – particularly in relation to the theological college. On reflection, though, he wondered whether Marion also felt 'small' and was 'puffing herself up to defend herself'. He acknowledged that although Marion had some power to make things difficult for him in the parish in the short term, she might in fact perceive that he had a good deal of power over her future as a priest.

Nick said that he felt pretty small having to bring all this to Michael, but he could see how there were 'pieces of the jigsaw' he hadn't been given and for which he was not solely responsible. He felt that this 'evened up the size thing with the college' at least enough to make him feel he could contact them, adding that he thought it better to talk with Marion first about what the expectations were and then consult the college with her permission. This would avoid getting the college on his side to make him feel bigger and her smaller.

At the end of the hour, Michael asked Nick how he was feeling and what he would take away. He said he was still kicking himself and thought he'd need to think some more about how he got himself into this mess, but he felt a bit more 'grown up' and that he had strategies with which to proceed. He was reconciled to the fact that, although he wanted to try to make the relationship work, that was also up to Marion, the care home and the café. He thought he would begin by apologizing to Marion for not being clear about expectations and seeing what developed from there. He thought that in due course he would need to talk to the training institution about their provision of guidance and training and the management of placements in general.

## Conclusions

This extended example demonstrates some of the pitfalls of neglecting the issues raised by the supervision rhombus. It also demonstrates the ways the various tools offered in this book, such as the three-legged stool of supervision, combine with it to suggest a range of possible avenues of exploration. The following tools for reflection invite you to consider the implications of context for your own ministry and for the pastoral supervision you offer, and suggest some areas for explicit discussion with supervisees to ensure that normative issues are attended to as a matter of course.

# Exercises

## Exercise 8.1 Mapping your Context

*For reflection*

Using an example from your own practice as a supervisor or supervisee, map out the implications of the supervision rhombus (Figure 8.5), answering the questions in the speech bubbles. Is there anything you notice, wonder or realize from doing this exercise? Is there anything you want to change in your practice or any dimension of your work you want to take to supervision yourself?

## Figure 8.5 The supervision rhombus

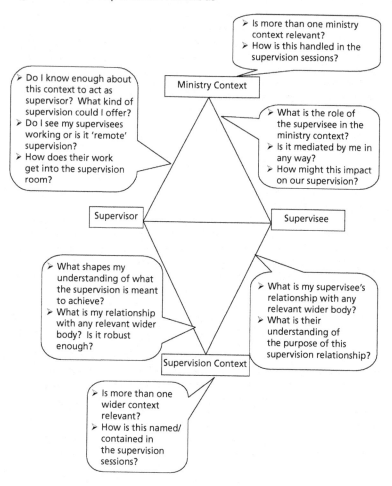

## Exercise 8.2 Attending to Structural Issues

*For reflection*

The situations people in ministry face are shaped by structural and organizational factors. These will include how decisions are made; where power lies; who/what is valued; the implicit goals of an institution – for example, to keep itself in being. It can sometimes be important to attend to these in supervision because they shape the options individuals and groups within the system have and often restrict how they can think and act. Bringing these systemic issues into focus may present a supervisee with new choices and options for strategic action, or help them realize where continued effort may be fruitless without a wider problem being tackled.

Identify a context in which you work. Choose an aspect of your work to think through that you suspect may have structural or systemic dimensions to it. Work through Edward Farley's hermeneutical method, set out here. You will need about an hour to do this. For further guidance, see the examples given in this chapter.

1. Identify the key features of the situation.
2. What is the influence of the past?
3. What are the wider social currents that feed into this situation?
4. What are the structures of idolatry and redemption revealed in this situation?

To use this method in a supervision session with a supervisee, you might ask them to prepare – essentially, focus their own issue before coming and begin to explore it. The supervision might then work through the four questions as a means of exploration, followed by questions about the implications for the supervisee's next steps (***bridging and enacting***). Rather than repeating the work the supervisee has done at home, however, it might be more productive to ask them, in the light of the work they have done in exploring the issue already, what their supervision question is now, and start from there.

## Exercise 8.3 Attending to Power in Pastoral Supervision

Revisit Figure 8.3, which tabulates cultural power, power of position, charismatic power and personal power. Reflect on your own power as a supervisor under each heading.

- Where does your power as a supervisor come from?
- In what ways does having power make you vulnerable?
- To what do you need to attend to ensure your power remains in the service of your supervisees?

## Exercise 8.4 Writing an Evidential Report

*To try*

Try drafting an evidential supervision report. If you are supervising someone within an institutional context for which such a report is necessary, gather together the relevant documents: any published assessment criteria; your supervision covenant; your notes on your supervision sessions. Having drafted your comments, are there any you have not shared with your supervisee? How might you do this? Ask them to complete a self-evaluation according to the same categories and discuss this in supervision together.

If you are not supervising anyone you need to report on, you could consider the codes of ethics and statements about appropriate standards supplied by any bodies relevant to their work, such as ordination vows or church statements on pastoral practice. Do you know where to find these? Does your supervisee? Try asking them to assemble and reflect on these with you.

## Notes

1 This is a philosophical concept particularly elaborated by Martin Heidegger.

2 Rudolf Ekstein and Robert S. Wallerstein, 1972, *The Teaching and Learning of Psychotherapy*, New York: International Universities Press.

They devised the concept, although the term 'supervision rhombus' was first introduced to the pastoral supervision literature in John Foskett and David Lyall, 1988, *Helping the Helpers: Supervision in Pastoral Care*, London: SPCK.

3 Phillip G. Clampitt, 1991, *Communicating for Managerial Effectiveness*, London: Sage, p. 51.

4 Frances Ward, 2005, *Lifelong Learning: Theological Education and Supervision*, London: SCM Press, p. 121.

5 Peter Senge, 1992, *The Fifth Discipline: The Art and Practice of the Learning Organization*, London: Century Business.

6 Edward Farley, 1987, 'Interpreting situations: an inquiry into the nature of practical theology', reprinted in James Woodward and Stephen Pattison (eds), 2000, *The Blackwell Reader in Pastoral and Practical Theology*, Oxford: Blackwell, pp. 118–27.

7 David Lyall, 1989, 'Pastoral action and theological reflection', reprinted in David Willows and John Swinton (eds), 2000, *Spiritual Dimensions of Pastoral Care: Practical Theology in a Multidisciplinary Context*, London and Philadelphia: Jessica Kingsley, pp. 53–8.

8 For a discussion of this, see Charles V. Gerkin, 1984, *The Living Human Document: Re-Visioning Pastoral Counseling in a Hermeneutical Model*, Nashville, TN: Abingdon Press, p. 92, where he explores the relevance of the work of Heinz Kohut for pastoral supervision.

9 Sarah Savage and Eolene Boyd-Macmillan, 2007, *The Human Face of the Church*, Norwich: Canterbury Press, p. 56.

10 Stanley Hauerwas, 1994, *Dispatches from the Front: Theological Engagements with the Secular*, Durham, NC and London: Duke University Press, p. 23; quoted in Duncan Forrester, 2000, *Truthful Action: Explorations in Practical Theology*, Edinburgh: T. & T. Clark, p. 111.

11 Michael Carroll, 1996, *Counselling Supervision: Theory, Skills and Practice*, London: Cassell, p. 6, summarizing a point made by Louis Zinkin; emphasis in original.

12 Steve Page and Val Wosket, 1994, *Supervising the Counsellor and Psychotherapist: A Cyclical Model*, 3rd edn, Hove and New York: Routledge, 2015, p. 57.

13 Rowan Williams, 1994, *Open to Judgement*, London: Darton, Longman & Todd, p. 176, emphasis in original.

14 See Jane Denniston, 'Theory into practice: a challenge for supervisors in formation for ordained ministry', 2014, in Michael Paterson and Jessica Rose (eds), *Enriching Ministry: Pastoral Supervision in Context*, London: SCM Press, pp. 105–18.

15 A set of ten conditions that need to be present in any supervisory relationship that includes an evaluative or reporting dimension are offered in J. M. Bernard and R. Goodyear, 2009, *Fundamentals of Clinical Supervision*, 4th edn, New Jersey: Pearson-Merill, pp. 25–7.

# 9

# Attending to Group Matters

**Summary**

Until now, the tools and models of pastoral supervision in this book have been offered without particular regard for whether the supervision is offered to individuals or groups. This has been partly because in either context the tasks of supervision and the ethos one is seeking to create are the same. Group supervision, however, introduces an additional level of issues and dynamics of which the pastoral supervisor needs to be aware. For this reason we have left this chapter until almost the end. Here we look at some of the advantages and disadvantages of working in groups. We draw attention to some of the complex processes that happen in groups and teams and offer a range of tools to help the pastoral supervisor work creatively with these processes. Theologically, we take up the narrative of Mark 6 to see how the disciples' private supervision session is interrupted by the hungry crowds, in order to explore the importance of Christian ministers belonging to and being fed in community.

The apostles gathered around Jesus, and told him all that they had done and taught. He said to them, 'Come away to a deserted place all by yourselves and rest a while.' For many were coming and going, and they had no leisure even to eat. And they went away in the boat to a deserted place by themselves. Now many saw them going and recognized them, and they hurried there on foot from all the towns and arrived ahead of them. As he went ashore, he saw a great crowd; and he had compassion for them, because they were like sheep without a shepherd; and he began to teach them many things. When it grew late, his disciples came to him and said, 'This is a deserted place, and the hour is now very late; send them away so that they may go into the surrounding country and villages and buy something for themselves to eat.' But he answered them, 'You give them something to eat.'

Mark 6.30–37a

## Being Met and Fed in Community

At the outset of this book we began by reflecting on the first few verses of this passage from Mark's Gospel. We pointed to the importance of rest and reflection upon ministry with others as part of our accountability within the body of Christ. We observed that when this passage is read with ministers of various kinds who have struggled to get away for a few days for some training in pastoral supervision, the words about not having enough leisure even to eat elicit the laughter of recognition. So too does the fact that no sooner have the disciples escaped the demands of ministry than the crowds work out where they are going to be. Any minister who has been enjoying a quiet coffee in a café or even pushing the trolley around the supermarket as a break from responding to others' needs will know the sinking feeling of needing to find resources of compassion and concentration when they were the one needing to recuperate.

In Mark's account, Jesus sees the crowds arriving on the shore and has compassion on them. Doubtless this was not the disciples' reaction – their private time with Jesus had come to an abrupt end. All day until nightfall the disciples had to share Jesus with the crowds, until finally they suggested that he send the people away to get something to eat. Jesus' dumbfounding reply was to tell the disciples: 'You find them something to eat.'

For tired ministers hearing this, Jesus' words can sound harsh, even cruel. Surely Jesus knows that in order to feed others the disciples need to be fed themselves? Surely he knows that they are running on empty – what else do they have to give? Yet the surprise is that the food that will feed both the disciples and the crowd does not have to come from the depths of the disciples' own resources; they are not required to spend what they do not have in buying food for thousands. Instead, to their great surprise they find that the resources come from the community itself – and not just bread but fish; and not just enough but twelve baskets left over. Somehow, when food is offered to Jesus to be blessed and broken, there is enough for all to be fed and more.

The implication we draw from this passage for pastoral supervision is not that time apart in prayer and reflection and with a supervisor is unimportant; rather, although our instincts may be to escape the Christian community for our own feeding when we minister within it all the time, we should not neglect Christian fellowship as a means of grace. Although we may well need to get away from the hospice or local church for a while, it is often those we work with in those very contexts who have what we need for our healing. Certainly our experience of group supervision suggests that the opportunity to be part of a group for those who spend their working lives seeking to be a resource for others can be an important reminder that it is not necessarily expert advice we need, but the restorative experience of genuine community in which the members receive from and give to one another.

An example is provided by a group supervision weekend in which Jane took part. The group was very mixed: some were working as supervisors and wanted to improve their skills; some were simply seeking supervision for their work. The weekend was designed to be experiential, during which participants would take it in turn to present their work using the creative method of psychodrama. Jane went on the weekend hoping for the space to present a particular dilemma, yet as the weekend progressed, she realized she was receiving so much through the presentations of others that she didn't in the end choose to present her own work. What this underlined for Jane was the truth of the saying that when one person is supervised, everyone benefits. Indeed, one of the advantages of group supervision is that, although there may not be time for everyone in the group to present their work, each member can benefit from the presentation of the work of others. This is why as a facilitator of a group it is important in the *bridging and enacting* stage of the session to allow each person to speak and think about the impact of each piece of supervision work on them. There can be a real depth of reflection stimulated by situations that have echoes for us, and a real sense of solidarity in voicing them to others with similar experience.

What Jane found on this weekend was that as each person presented their work, she was receiving back parts of her personality she had lost over the preceding few months: as one person presented, she found herself getting murderously angry on their behalf; the next day as someone else presented, she found herself feeling a deep compassion and tenderness, and realized that this too had been missing from her own emotional range recently. By the end of the weekend, Jane was marvelling that, without having any private or dedicated time with the supervisor, she had been met and fed and was going home with renewed understanding (third level of seeing) and focus for her work (enactment).

It may or may not be our experience that day-to-day church life offers a community in which we are invited to be fully present and so be met and fed, and yet this is what the body of Christ is called to and what it celebrates in holy communion: through Christ's real presence we are invited to be fully present to him and to one another and so be fed in the community. Our struggle as Christians is to live the eucharistic life for longer than the duration of the Sunday service – to be open to Christ's real presence in our daily lives and so have the courage to be fully present ourselves and invite others to take that risk and so be met and fed.

Pastoral supervision is a way of embodying this eucharistic life, and it belongs to the supervisor of such a group to be fully and yet eccentrically present in order to make room for others to communicate and find Christ in their midst. In this sense, to be a pastoral supervisor is to exercise a priestly – though not exclusively clerical – ministry; an incarnational ministry of full presence that others may be met and fed in the body of Christ.

# The Role of the Group Supervisor

Practising this kind of presence, the supervisor of a group needs to pay attention to all the dimensions of supervision we have so far explored, and in addition to think about how to structure the group so that everyone benefits from the time; how to get the best out of the group experience by facilitating group responses; the management of group dynamics; the monitoring of the group's covenant (see Figure 9.1).

Figure 9.1 The tasks of group supervision

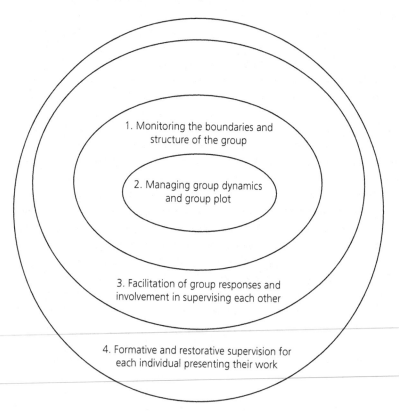

1. Monitoring the boundaries and structure of the group

2. Managing group dynamics and group plot

3. Facilitation of group responses and involvement in supervising each other

4. Formative and restorative supervision for each individual presenting their work

Adapted from Peter Hawkins and Robin Shohet, 2006, *Supervision in the Helping Professions*, 3rd edition, Buckingham: Open University Press, p. 155.

Inskipp and Proctor list four kinds of group supervision:[1]

1. authoritative, where the group supervisor does one-to-one supervision in the group with members looking on;
2. participative, where participants are invited to contribute to the supervision;
3. co-operative, where the facilitator manages the group boundaries but leaves the supervision to the group;
4. peer-group supervision, where all the members take joint responsibility for everything.

The relative roles of the supervisor and the group will depend on the developmental stage of those in the group. In training contexts, groups often begin as authoritative groups; yet even here the supervisor needs to pay attention not just to the learning of the individual who is presenting, but to the whole group's. Part of the learning will be how to contribute to a supervision group. Therefore as in one-to-one supervision, the supervisor needs to focus on helping the supervisees make good use of the advantages of a group supervision context:

- being able to draw on a range of experience;
- being able to check out the supervisor's insights with others and avoid treating them as the expert;
- the supportive atmosphere of peers;
- the ability to use action methods, such as bibliodrama, sculpting, role work;
- the opportunity in working with a group to address issues that arise in teams and with colleagues – given that much of ministry involves team work, this can be particularly useful.


## 1 Monitoring the Boundaries and Structure of the Group

The *hosting and containing* guidelines for establishing a supervision covenant, outlined in Chapter 2, are equally as relevant for a group as for one-to-one supervision: aims; timings; venue; arrangement of the furniture; any preparation needed; session format; the boundaries of the session and the kind of confidentiality needed; arrangements for review. To do this in a group you will need a flip chart and pens and a means of displaying or recording what is agreed for distribution to the group. It is important to have a record so that review can take place effectively.

If you are working in a team, establishing the purpose of **team supervision** is particularly important. If, for example, a team member felt that their appraisal had not been well handled by the team leader, would it be appropriate for this to be raised in team supervision? Reflecting on an example like this helps the team refine what the group is for.

In addition to establishing what it is for and what kind of issues people might bring, the group also needs to think about how those issues are going to be explored. The kinds of methods particularly suitable for group use are those that draw on the reactions of group members, such as picturing, verbatim, sculpting. A stable pattern of group supervision helps to develop confidence and safety. A common framework for group supervision is as follows.

## Suggested Format for Group Supervision

It is usual for a regular group supervision session to last about two hours. The structure of a session broadly follows that of an individual supervision session, but with some additional dynamics for the supervisor to attend to. Some things – such as giving everyone a chance to name how they are or what they notice – take time, which needs to be factored.

## Figure 9.2 Structuring a group supervision

| | | *Tracking and monitoring* | *Hosting and containing* |
|---|---|---|---|
| Before the session | **Hosting and containing**<br>getting room and self ready<br><br>**Tracking and monitoring**<br>reading notes; thinking about the shape of the session; identifying any deadlines; thinking about group dynamics | being alert to what the context, the developmental stage of the group and the focus of the session require; making interventions to facilitate the best use of the time; keeping an overview of the usefulness of the supervision space for the group and the individuals within it; taking notes | being alert to the relational dimensions of the group; being alert to one's own ability to be present; being alert to the hosting and containing that God is doing |
| First 15 minutes | **Hosting and containing**<br>welcome; check-in; prayer | | |
| 10–15 minutes | **Focusing and eliciting**<br>identifying the focus for the session and deciding who will present | | |
| Bulk of the session | **Exploring and imagining**<br>involving the group in exploring the material presented using words, images, stories, communication by impact; objects; body work to shed light on it as appropriate | | |
| | **Bridging and enacting**<br>identifying possible ways forward with the presenter(s)<br><br>opportunity for group members to name resonances and ways forward for their own work | | |
| Last 5–10 minutes | **Reviewing and closing**<br>commenting on any group covenant issues<br><br>checking arrangements for next session and any other administration | | |
| After the session | **Tracking and monitoring**<br>making notes; identifying any issues that might need taking to own supervision; reflecting on group dynamics | | |

## Hosting and containing

- Tea/coffee and informal conversation as people arrive;
- Brief opportunity for the group to name where they are – this is sometimes aided by a short exercise to help people distil what they want to say rather than speaking for a long time (six-minute exercise; timeline – see Chapter 4);
- Prayer/reading of Scripture – for example, the day's lectionary reading.

## Eliciting and focusing

- Deciding on the group or team issue that needs addressing;
- Agreeing who will present their work today if individuals are to offer their work, and focusing that issue. As one of the potential disadvantages of group supervision is that not everyone gets the chance to present each time the group meets, suggestions for how to determine who should present are in the exercises at the end of the chapter;
- Naming of work issue to be explored by one or more group members;
- Clarifying the issue being brought to supervision.

## Exploring and imagining

- According to the ground rules of the group, members articulate what they notice and wonder from the presentation. The exploration may be verbal, embodied or creative, using art materials, objects or role work.

## Tracking and monitoring

- Particularly in group supervision, where the supervisee is likely to be offered a variety of 'takes' from group members, it is important that the supervisor pause regularly to monitor the usefulness for the presenter of what is being offered. This also allows the group to refocus and get back on track.

## Bridging and enacting

- *Tracking and monitoring* come to a natural stop when it becomes clear that the presenter has found some insight for the situation they brought to the group for supervision.
- At this point the supervisor's task is twofold: first, to encourage the presenter to say how they will carry that insight back into their work (name the bridge) and put it into place (enactment); second, to invite each member of the group to name any learning or resonances evoked by the presentation for their own practice. It is crucial that the supervisor does not invite multiple storytelling here but simple statements, such as 'I am reminded of the importance of boundaries in my own work'; 'I want to think further about working with people with whom I have multiple roles'.

## Reviewing and closing

- Attention to group process – anything that needs naming or reviewing in relation to the group's covenant;
- Administration – attention to venues, dates and who is presenting next time;
- Closing prayer.

## 2 Managing Group Dynamics and Group Plot

'Groups do not happen. They are created and nurtured.'[2] Part of the role of the supervisor is to set this process in motion and to track and monitor the development of the group and the way it relates. In particular this involves attention to power dynamics and group plot.

## Power in groups

One of the advantages of working in a group is that some of the **projections** around authority figures can be diluted. Rather than feeling intimidated or infantilized by going to an individual who is cast as the 'expert', group members can derive a good deal of support and learn a lot from one another. The role of the facilitator of group supervision is to establish and maintain a group that is run *for* and largely *by* its members. As Gillie Bolton suggests, 'Participants are encouraged to consider and express what they want and need from the start, to meet their own learning needs. The facilitator is there to orchestrate and support the group (to meet their needs), or collaboratively to create appropriate objectives.'[3] Although some power dynamics may be diluted in group supervision, there are plenty of other power issues to attend to. Considering the potential dynamics before meeting a group for the first time is important preparation for a facilitator, but equally important is helping the group name the dynamics in the room. Examples of how to tackle this sensitively are offered in the exercises at the end of the chapter.

In a team context, all these dynamics may be present, and yet naming them will be a significant act because the group already has a history together. Exposing alliances and sub-groups – based on attitudes to new measures being introduced or theological preferences – may be difficult for the team to bear if normally these are unnamed, yet there is little point in having supervision as a team if you do not want to look at these dynamics.

It is also important to note here that if a team leader attempts team supervision rather than bringing in an outside facilitator, the dynamics of institutional power combined with role power are likely to be problematic. While it is hoped that staff teams might use some of the exercises in this book to create a culture of reflective practice, the team leader needs to be alert to the complexity of the dynamics of their own power and should certainly seek supervision themselves for this kind of work.

An outside supervisor has more chance of being, and of being seen as, a neutral presence who can contain the dynamics of a team. This also has the advantage of allowing the team leader to participate. An example of this process at work is Michael's experience of being asked to lead a team day for a group of healthcare chaplains, looking at their sense of shared vision. He began by asking them each to explore their own sense of vocation through the MAP exercise shared in Chapter 1 (Exercise 1.4). Having done this in the spirit of getting to know one another at a deeper level, they were then invited to explore the similarities between the visions and the gaps between them – what was complementary and what seemed contradictory. Because Michael was coming from outside he had no investment in endorsing the team leader's vision as the one to be followed, nor in resisting his vision because he was the boss. The team were able to name differences and explore resonances and come to a deeper understanding of the way they related, even if they were not able immediately to articulate a common vision.

The use of such an exercise would be possible in a staff team without a facilitator but the participants would need to be very clear about the purpose of the activity. If a supervision space is going to fulfil the functions of supervision set out in Chapter 1 (to be ourselves; to dream dreams and reconnect with our calling; to admit tiredness, weakness, failure, disillusion, ambition, hope, confusion; to be heard and have our work valued; to be challenged; to examine the gap between our conscious intentions and our practice; to allow God to work with us through honest interaction with another), it needs to be clear that it is not a decision-making body, nor a consultation process that might lead to a decision. Whatever style of decision-making the team leader normally adopts is therefore not an appropriate mode of leadership for team supervision. The team leader needs to decide what type of group is appropriate (using Inskipp and Proctor's four categories above), and then facilitate the group so that the functions of a pastoral supervision space can be fulfilled – or delegate the facilitation of the group to an appropriately skilled member of the team.

## Following the group plot

In Chapter 7 we outlined Charles Gerkin's approach to listening for the story behind the stories supervisees are telling. In groups there are not only stories behind the individual stories participants tell, there is a also group story. A closed group that meets on successive occasions – a supervision group or a team meeting for supervision – will feel different at the various stages of its life. Various attempts have been made to outline the plot of a group's development. Gillie Bolton describes the stages as: meeting, falling in love, lovers' tiff, kiss and make up, mission, end and mourning.[4] Rather less romantically, Bruce Tuckman named the stages: forming, storming, norming, performing – and, later, adjourning.[5]

i. *Beginning a new group*

The early stages of a group are about forming relationships. Few personal risks are taken as the group prioritizes forming a tentative bond. In this stage, people are likely to conform to expectations and to co-operate with the process – at least at a superficial level. The hope is that people will fall in love with the process and express that commitment in a covenant to work together. The supervisor needs to encourage everyone in the group to share (especially those who are naturally reticent); help the group make a realistic covenant that will be robust enough to withstand the testing of the next stage; and model the kind of communication that is agreed upon.

ii. *Managing early conflicts*

In the next stage conflicts start to emerge. The boundaries will be tested and the group leader will be challenged as people try to work out at a deeper level what they are doing here and how much they really want to commit to the group. At this stage people are often defensive, assertive, distrustful, suspicious and do not listen to each other. The supervisor needs to keep modelling the ground rules of the group; respond rather than react; stay open; encourage exploration of differences rather than becoming defensive; draw attention to the group's covenant in order to help them remember what it is about and move into a more productive mode of working.

In some groups the conflict will be open and direct, in others it will be suppressed and then bubble up – the culture of the group in this respect is likely to reflect the culture of the organization in which the supervision is happening. Because of the moral imperative to be 'nice' in most church contexts, conflict is likely to be suppressed but leak out in barbed humour and become attached to superficially trivial issues. It is also worth noting here what was said about context in the last chapter. If Sarah Savage and Eolene Boyd-Macmillan are right that churches today should expect more conflict, not less,[6] this is likely to appear in supervision groups not just in the work that people present, but in the dynamics of the group as parallel process.

Recognizing conflict for what it is – and its relationship to anxiety – and that it is a necessary stage of group development allows the group supervisor to stay focused on their role and help the group move to the next stage, thus modelling and rehearsing the kind of leadership that many of their contexts need.

One strategy we have found helpful in encouraging groups to get beyond suspicion is to frame the supervision as an act of discernment, reminding the group that we meet as the body of Christ, seeking to allow the Holy Spirit to work in and among us in the confidence that God is for us (Romans 8.31). Exposing our vulnerability to each other is daunting and anxiety-provoking, and yet if we are in Christ we need to be Christ for each other.

It is no accident that in the New Testament it is not hate but fear that is opposed to love. Often in the Gospels, when Jesus appears his first words are 'It is I, do not be afraid.' God is not another human being in competition with us. He is the ground of being to whom we may be open without fear of being swamped with another's agenda. In pastoral supervision it can help to be reminded that this is the God who meets us in one another. Helping groups to name their fears – fear of being found out; of being too much for others to cope with; of being thought a terrible minister; of being competed with – can help a group move through this stage.

It may also be the case that work brought at this stage of a supervision group will unconsciously reflect the group dynamics. In one group of local ministers Michael supervised there was a member of the group who was very vocal, defensive and disruptive; Michael was worrying about how to help him integrate. Another group member presented a case from his own context in which he was struggling to manage the behaviour of a difficult member of a Bible study group. Seizing courage, Michael asked the group if there was any resonance between the case being presented and the experience of the group.

Routinely asking a group to reflect on its process can help prevent the escalation of such dynamics and help the group to do its own work. Peter Hawkins and Robin Shohet recommend a regular feedback slot in which each member says what they appreciate and find difficult in each other's contributions. A further suggestion of theirs is to ask participants to write in response to prompts and then to share what they have written: 'What I can't bring to this group is …'; 'What I'd like to say to other members of the group is …'; 'The hidden agenda of this group is …'.

### iii. *Supervising the mid stages*

Working through the conflict stage honestly means that a group can settle into a good level of functioning with a high degree of trust and commitment to one another and to the tested aims and ground rules. The task of the supervisor becomes less visible as the group takes more responsibility for its functioning. Individuals have come to value the group; they take care to listen and make careful interventions; they can take risks; they can agree to stick to original aims or change direction if needed, paying attention to context and the needs of individuals.

It should be noted, however, that the supervisor's role is

not over! There will be tasks and individual needs to attend to and any disruption to the group's dynamic will change the plot of the group. It is particularly important to note that if a new member joins a supervision group, the whole plot will be recapitulated – not in order to bring the new person up to speed, but because a new member means a new group. The covenant needs to be revisited with this person's contribution taken seriously; the potential danger of their being an 'outsider' needs to be named; there will be more jostling for position as the group moves through the storming stage again.

### iv. *Making an ending*

Ending is the final stage, which will be explored in detail in the next chapter. Here it need only be said that the quality of an ending depends largely on the supervisor's attention to the needs of the group and to individuals within it, who may need to mourn its passing, find alternative means of supervision or say thank you to the group for what they have learnt. Various strategies that groups have for avoiding the work of ending will be discussed in Chapter 10.

## 3 Facilitating Group Responses

In one-to-one supervision, teaching the supervisee how to make good use of supervision is part of the task; in group supervision each person needs to learn not just how to make their own good use of the space, but how to be a helpful member of the group for others. Some of the tools already introduced can help to establish an exploratory ethos in a group. We have found that reading John 20 together and reflecting on the verbs of seeing, as suggested in Chapter 3, helps to prevent closed questions and counters the temptation of group members to give each other advice. It can be useful to think together with a group about what they are listening for when they listen to someone else's presentation; it is important to encourage 'I' statements from group members so that they don't impute motives and emotions to others when they speak, and take responsibility for what they say. Establishing the ground rules is part of the supervisor's responsibility; so also is modelling them and maintaining them when the group strays into other modes of communication.

Simple exercises that practise basic skills are very useful early in a group's life. An example is asking each member to choose a picture postcard – as suggested in Exercise 5.3 – that says something to them about their working life. In pairs, people might take it in turns to say what they notice and what they wonder about each other's choice of postcard. Group members might then reflect together on what was helpful in the exercise, giving the facilitator a chance to reinforce the kind of communication appropriate to supervision.

Once basic ground rules have been established, unhelpful interventions still need to be gently challenged. Often the effect of an unhelpful comment by a group member can be checked quite simply by the supervisor's use of *tracking and monitoring*. This leaves the group free to offer a range of random as well as highly attuned interventions, knowing that the supervisor will at key moments in the *exploring and imagining* stage of the session ask the presenter whether anything of what they have been offered resonates with them. This invitation to identify insight (third level of seeing) enables the group to go with the flow, while at the same time protecting the presenter from being either overwhelmed by what is offered or steamrollered off track. Another tactic is to ask a group member to rephrase what they have said: 'Are you asking an *open* question there?' 'Is that something you are *wondering*?' 'Is that about *your own* experience?' 'Did you hear the presenter actually say that?'

# 4 Providing Supervision for the Individual

It is perhaps too obvious to say that in all this the supervisor needs to pay attention to each member of the group as an individual. In all groups there are characters who are noisy or demand attention; in all groups there are characters one instinctively warms to and finds wise; in all groups there are people whose needs are in danger of being overlooked. One of the ways of preparing for a group we have found helpful is to pray for each member before a supervision, thinking about their needs and ministries. Keeping notes about each member as well as about the group plot is also helpful in remaining focused on the whole group and not being distracted either by those you warm to or those you find difficult. Being in supervision yourself also helps with this dynamic, and with the demanding task of dealing with resistance.

## Dealing with Resistance

There are several reasons why particular individuals may be resistant to supervision beyond the testing phase of the group's plot. Resistance can manifest itself in a variety of ways:

- in the person who attends only to the needs of others but is never prepared to open up about their own work;
- in the person who appears confident and gives out authoritative advice – often citing an external authority such as the Bible or a particular guru;
- in the person who is critical of every aspect of the supervision, from the venue to the format to the refreshments;
- in the person who intellectualizes everything and will discuss theory but never their own responses;
- in the person who agrees with everything that is said but never seems really engaged.

Sometimes resistance is expressed because people are afraid of being known or of exposing their work to others, but there are other reasons for resistance. For example, a supervisee may feel silenced in the group because of beliefs they hold or because their experience makes them seem 'incredible' to the supervisor and the group.[7] An example might be a supervisee who feels that the culture of the group does not respect the Bible sufficiently, who is dismissive of 'non-Christians' or who assumes there are no gay people in the room. Gender and race dynamics may also contribute to this. It is desirable, if at all possible, to handle resistances in the group so that the group can handle and learn from the process. However, if a member is unable to respond to the ethos of the group and to the encouragement of the supervisor to take part, it may be necessary for the supervisor to tackle this individually with the person concerned. In some cases, telling the supervisor their experience may be sufficient to enable the person to 'join' the group, or it may be a first step towards their being able to name the issues in the group itself. Making regular opportunities to review group process makes it more likely that a group member can raise something about the nature of the group that makes them feel excluded.

Alternatively, even after a conversation with the supervisor an individual may feel that they need to leave the group. If at all possible they should be encouraged to explain to the group why they feel this is the best course. This will enable them to leave without shame and the group to process how they have behaved or been perceived, or simply to understand that there are different perspectives from theirs. Like other endings, one member leaving can be traumatic for a group and needs careful handling. This will be explored further in Chapter 10.

The unsuitability of a particular supervision group for an individual does not necessarily suggest their unfitness to practise in whatever field of ministry they are working, but it may raise serious questions. In a situation in which the pastoral supervisor needs to report on the group members' participation, such as in a training context, such a report is likely to have serious consequences for the supervisee. In an elective group the consequences are not apparent in the same way, but a serious question arises about the context of the group supervision. If group supervision is being offered as part of the body of Christ and as an exercise of accountability, what happens when a supervisor feels that a supervisee is resistant to the work they need to do in order to be fit to practise? Is elective supervision a private arrangement or, by virtue of being part of the body of Christ, does it bring with it corporate responsibilities?

The answer must depend on the covenant established with the group from the outset. Because pastoral supervision is also about the safety of those among whom we minister and not just about our own support or development, any supervision relationship we enter into needs to include a discussion about what happens if we are concerned about a supervisee's fitness to practise. In the case of having to ask an individual to leave a group because of their resistance, our procedure would to be to:

- discuss our concerns about their practice with them;
- invite them to share these with their line manager or team leader;
- share with them the contents of any letter we might write to their line manager or team leader;
- seek their permission to make such a contact;
- make it clear if our concerns were such that we would make the contact even without their permission.[8]

It is never an easy decision to take someone aside from a group, suggest that they are resisting important work or to contact their line manager. All of these steps risk undermining any trust that has developed. Nevertheless, it needs to be remembered that pastoral supervision includes two purposes: the development of the practice of the practitioner but also the safety of those among whom they minister. The pastoral supervisor's responsibility when they are concerned about their supervisee's fitness to practise is to present what evidence they have to an appropriate person.

To do this well, pastoral supervisors need good supervision themselves. It is advisable to have discussed the possible courses open to you with your own supervisor beforehand; to have ascertained whether or not they agree with your interpretations; and to have worked through any feelings of anger or frustration you may have at this person's behaviour or impact on the group, so that you can approach them eccentrically – with their interests and the interests of those they work among at heart. Above all, it is important as a supervisor handling complex dynamics and strong emotions to have supervision yourself in a context that can contain your anxieties and worst-case scenarios so that you can withstand whatever comes at you.

## Conclusions

Despite the complexities of group supervision and the courage needed by the supervisor to exert appropriate authority, it is our experience that group supervision as a form of theology-in-action has a power, quite unlike that of one-to-one work, of grounding participants in their primary identity as 'members one of another in the body of Christ'. This recalls us to our understanding of the pastoral supervisor as witness to the identity of the supervisee in Christ. In our experience, when people meet in a group to share their inner vision and to account for themselves in community, the gospel unfolds before our very eyes in a unique way and, in the reciprocity of grace, each person's commitment and practice is touched and reshaped by the person with whom the group is working at any given time. In a highly individualized world where even Christian leadership has become tainted with the private language of 'my ministry', 'my priesthood', 'my church', it can be salutary to meet in supervision and experience the truth that we are saved in community, for community and by community, and to be surprised that even a little bread and fish, when offered in faith, can feed a multitude.

# Exercises

## Exercise 9.1 Mapping the Tasks of Group Supervision

*For reflection*

Using the tasks of supervision outlined below, review any supervision group of which you have been part or which you have led, reflecting on which dimensions have been attended to well and which less well.

### 1 Monitoring group boundaries and covenant
➤ What attention was paid to *hosting and containing*?
➤ Was the covenant clear and appropriate?
➤ Was it reviewed?
➤ Were challenges to it handled appropriately?

### 2 Managing the group dynamic
➤ Did the group culture foster an atmosphere conducive to *exploring and imagining*?
➤ Were inhibiting factors and dynamics named?
➤ Was it a group with hidden agendas? If so, were there opportunities to explore these?
➤ Was there resistance in the group? If so, how was this handled?

### 3 Facilitating group responses
➤ What type of group was this?
  i. Authoritative, where the group supervisor does one-to-one supervision in the group with members looking on.
  ii. Participative, where participants are invited to contribute to the supervision.
  iii. Co-operative, where the facilitator manages the group boundaries but leaves the supervision to the group.
  iv. Peer-group supervision, where all the members take joint responsibility for everything.
➤ Was this appropriate to the developmental stages of the participants?

➤ How was the group inducted into what was expected?

➤ Did the group change over time?

➤ How was the ending of the group handled?

## 4 Providing Supervision

➤ How was the time divided between participants (*tracking and monitoring*)?

➤ What was the balance between normative, formative and restorative approaches?

➤ What methods were used for presenting material and eliciting a focus?

➤ What were the advantages/disadvantages of being supervised in a group?

What strike you as the main challenges for group supervisors? Is there anything in particular you feel you need to learn?

## Exercise 9.2 Dealing with Resistance

*For reflection*

Dealing with resistance in pastoral supervision is a demanding aspect of both group and one-to-one supervision. Spend a few minutes thinking about situations in which you have experienced resistance in supervision contexts. To explore your own responses to this dimension of the work further, write for six minutes on the subject, 'If I'd had the courage …', as detailed in Chapter 4.

When you have done this, read back what you have written. What issues are emerging for your own practice as a pastoral supervisor?

## Exercise 9.3 Naming Dynamics in Group Supervision

*To try*

Ask your group to space themselves out, standing in a circle. Depending on the culture and stage of your group's development, try out some of these exercises:

1 **Who's who?** This game is about name reinforcement and forming relationships through eye contact and laughter. It also illustrates the complexity of attention in group supervision. These purposes might be explained beforehand or drawn out from the group's experience of the game afterwards. You will need several large, soft balls. Begin with a single ball, explaining that to throw it you need to gain eye contact with another person and then say their name aloud. Once the group can reliably name each other, introduce a second, third, and fourth ball until the game falls apart.

2 **Who are we?** The purpose of this game is the naming of dynamics in the room and considering together the consequences of these for the life of the group and its covenant.

    Ask the group to take it in turns to stand in the middle of the circle and name something about themselves. Others who share this interest or characteristic will join them in the centre. Lead by example: 'I hate Mondays'; 'I can juggle'; 'I work in healthcare'; 'I've never been part of a supervision group before.' Some dynamics will be named early in a group's life; many will not emerge by this method, though the game can be played at different stages in the group's life. Members should become more courageous in naming significant dynamics as the group develops. It is useful to ask the group to reflect on which dynamics that were named seem significant, which dynamics have not been named (such as race, age or gender balance), and any that point to areas in which to be mindful.

3  **Who knows who?** The purpose of this game is to name the relationships that already exist in the room and consider the implications of those relationships for group dynamics and for the group covenant, for instance issues of confidentiality and boundaries.

Ask those who already know each other to step into the circle and name the nature of their connection. As each sub-group 'outs' itself, ask if there are any consequences of the relationship for the work about to be done – for example, if two people are friends and know each other's spouses, what are the confidentiality issues? If the supervisor teaches or supervises some of the group as individuals, what can be referenced here or in other contexts? Don't forget to ask those who don't know anyone else to step into the circle. Ask them how that feels.

4  **How are we feeling?** The purpose of this exercise is to name anxieties as a legitimate response and so to lower their level.

Ask everyone to step into the centre of the circle and shout out at random things that make them anxious. This can be anything from 'going to the dentist' to 'expressing my feelings in a group'.

A new group might leave it there or reflect on what would make them feel safe enough to do some work together as part of forming a covenant. In an established group in which resistances are happening, the supervisor might invite the group to name defence mechanisms in a similar vein and then to reflect on the anxieties and defences operating in the group.

## Exercise 9.4  Deciding Who Will Present their Work Today

*To try*

In group supervision one of the dynamics is that it is not always possible for everyone to present their work. There are a variety of ways to decide how to handle this dynamic:

1   Make sure there is always time for some paired or small-group work or mini exercises in which everyone can reflect on something of their own. Strict timekeeping is necessary if there is to be room for more extended pieces of work.

    a.   Invite everyone to do a six-minute journaling exercise (see Exercise 4.1) on a given topic or a topic of their choice, and share what they notice and wonder or realize with another person (allow 12 minutes).

    b.   Invite everyone to complete a timeline (see Exercise 4.2) and share in threes.

2   The group take it in turns to prepare and present. The advantage of this method is that it fairly allocates the time available. It works well in training settings and when the method of supervision is fixed, for example a verbatim group. The disadvantage is that there may be no opportunity for urgent work to be explored or for the dynamics of the group to shape the work organically.

3   The group decides when they meet who will present. This method is responsive to the members' needs in the present and trusts that everyone will benefit through reflection on the presenter's work. It can mean that little preparation goes on before the group and that some members routinely will not think about what they are bringing to supervision. Group dynamics will operate in the selection process and this may produce material for group reflection.

    ➤   Ask the group to walk around in the space and think about what they would bring to supervision today if they were to present (*eliciting a focus*).

    ➤   Ask the group to space out in a circle and invite each person to name in a sentence what they are bringing (naming the focus using the **tools of distillation**).

    ➤   Ask those who are willing to present work today to come into the centre.

If there are more people than time allows (30–45 minutes per person is a good rule of thumb), invite those still in the outer circle to put their hand on the shoulder of someone in the centre whose work has resonance for them and from whom they might learn something that would be helpful for their own situation.

Invite each person with their hand on someone's shoulder to name the resonance they feel that person's work might have with their own. If there are any people who have not placed their hand on someone's shoulder, invite them to comment on what is happening for them. Similarly, if anyone's work has no resonance for others, they should be invited to comment on their experience.

Invite the person with the most hands on their shoulder to present.

Do not forget at the end of the session to invite everyone to name the resonances for their own practice that have arisen from the presented work (***bridging and enacting***).

# Notes

1 Cited in Peter Hawkins and Robin Shohet, 2006, *Supervision in the Helping Professions*, 3rd edn, Buckingham: Open University Press, p. 156.

2 Gillie Bolton, 2005, *Reflective Practice: Writing and Professional Development*, 2nd edn, London: Sage, p. 204.

3 Bolton, *Reflective Practice*, pp. 194–5.

4 Bolton, *Reflective Practice*, pp. 200–1.

5 Bruce W. Tuckman, 1965, 'Developmental sequence in small groups', *Psychological Bulletin* 63.6, pp. 384–99.

6 Sarah Savage and Eolene Boyd-Macmillan, 2007, *The Human Face of the Church*, Norwich: Canterbury Press, p. 56.

7 Frances Ward, 2005, *Lifelong Learning: Theological Education and Supervision*, London: SCM Press, p. 167.

8 See Mary Creaner, 2014, *Getting the Most out of Supervision: A Guide for the Supervisee*, London: Sage, pp. 100–8 for a helpful chapter on feedback, reporting and evaluation in supervision.

# IO

# Attending to Endings

## Summary

Although stable supervision relationships are good places in which to develop sufficient trust for work to be done, supervision arrangements have a limited life. Managing a good ending in the 'here and now' of supervision is an important part of the work. Supervisors can also usefully help supervisees attend to endings in the 'there and then' of their pastoral contexts. By firmly locating the containment supervision provides within the covenant love of God, and by facing the difficult issues and opportunities for truth-telling raised by endings, supervision offers an important rehearsal space for the handling of endings in ministry and in our personal lives.

> Master, now you are dismissing your servant in peace, according to your word; for my eyes have seen your salvation, which you have prepared in the presence of all peoples, a light for revelation to the Gentiles and for glory to your people Israel.
>
> Luke 2.29–32

The presentation of Jesus in the Temple (Luke 2.22–38) presents a bridge between things old and things new. Not only does it hold together the wisdom of old age (exemplified by Simeon and Anna) and the innocence of new life (in the infant Jesus), it also marries the future longings of the Jewish community (who await the messenger who will cleanse the Temple) with the gratitude of the Christian community (who remember Christ's sacrifice made once and for all). The story presents Simeon as the last of the Old Testament prophets, ready to let go of his life, and Anna as the first New Testament evangelist who simply cannot stop herself from telling everyone what she has seen and heard. In one moment a birth and a death are wrapped together. Whereas Simeon's words take us to the foot of the cross, Anna's propel us to Easter Sunday morning when, finding the tomb empty, the holy women run to announce to the disciples that the one they thought dead is risen. Anna, at the great age of 84, teaches us that things seen and heard are for sharing and giving away and that the Christian journey is missionary, while Simeon underscores the importance of letting go rather than of clinging to the gifts (and relationships) God places temporarily in our hands.

## Endings

Endings are built into the very nature of human life. Some, like leaving home to get married and start a family, can be long awaited and joyfully anticipated, while others, such as the breakdown of a relationship or the death of a loved one, come into our lives unbidden, unwelcome and unprepared for, bringing pain and loss in their wake.

Often, with the healing of the years, pastoral carers can look back and point to a particular uninvited ending in their life that triggered the journey that led them into ministry in the first place. Thus experiences such as miscarriage, bereavement, broken relationships, loss of meaning or purpose, crisis of identity, psychological breakdown, unemployment, disability or life-threatening illness, which once seemed like endings, no longer jar like shards of broken glass in the person's life but have been transformed into 'gifts wrapped in thorns'[1] equipping the saints for ministry (Ephesians 4.12). This is not to say that being familiar with endings through one's life experience makes them cleaner or easier to handle. In fact those of us who know only too well the pain and darkness of such endings need to be extra vigilant in our management of endings in pastoral ministry and supervision.

## Ending Supervision Relationships

Parker Palmer writes:

> The openness of a space is created by the firmness of its boundaries. A learning space cannot go on forever; if it did, it would not be a structure for learning but an invitation to confusion and chaos. A space has edges, perimeters, limits.[2]

One of the key things, then, that supervisors can do as they approach the ending of a supervisory relationship is to offer people a chance to experience the 'edges, perimeters [and] limits'[3] of life. This offers the possibility of endings that are negotiated and planned for rather than experiences resulting in confusion and chaos.

A supervisory relationship that 'begins with the end in mind'[4] will have kept the ending continuously on the horizon and been a place where supervisees will have learnt a language and found a map for the future that will hold them in good stead. But it will also have been a place in which supervisors have seen – sometimes unwittingly – how their supervisees handle endings, through:

1. their responses to those with whom they work (such as colleagues retiring, patients dying, people moving away);
2. the manner in which they handle the micro endings (the *reviewing and closing* stages) of each supervision session (lingering, suddenly dashing off);
3. their reactions to interruptions in the normal pattern of supervision (supervisor's absence due to holidays or cancellations due to sickness).

The converse is also true, that supervisors will have been modelling from the very outset of the relationship their own default manner of dealing with endings (such as overrunning the allotted time; 'forgetting' to bring a diary to fix the next appointment).

## Reasons for Ending

Supervisory relationships can be terminated for a whole range of reasons, not all of which allow of a neat and tidy ending.

### 1. *Ending before the work ever really started*

A number of reasons could be behind such premature or early endings. A supervisee, not sure what to expect, might have been overwhelmed by the experience or found the supervisor's perception too accurate to bear. Conversely, they may have experienced the supervisor as too distant and unapproachable or did not feel they 'clicked' due to a difference of personality, gender, social class or what is often termed 'churchmanship'. Given how few pastoral supervisors there currently are in the UK, we should not be surprised how common 'ending before the work ever really started' is likely to be. Even if the supervisee is willing to work through those differences, the work might never get started because the supervisor feels that he or she is not the right person for this supervisee or does not have expertise in the particular field of ministry for which supervision is being sought, and encourages them to seek supervision elsewhere. Sometimes, at the first meeting, supervisors come to the opinion that the person sitting before them is not really looking for work-based supervision but is in need of another supportive relationship, such as personal counselling or spiritual direction, and so the work never begins. Most complex of all is the situation in which, after a session or two, a supervisor plucks up the courage to inform the supervisee that, in their judgement, they are not fit to practise and that the supervisor therefore refuses to supervise them. (For dealing with fitness to practise issues, see Chapter 9.)

## 2. Ending due to a move

Supervisees can find themselves having to leave behind a valued supportive supervision relationship simply by moving job or area, whether or not they have chosen this. Such endings need careful handling, since geographical moves often mean that we lose our ministry relationships, colleagues, support structures and social networks all in one go. This may result in feelings about the ending of the supervision relationship (here and now) becoming entangled with feelings about the ending of other relationships affected by the move (there and then). This may play out in supervision in a number of ways – for example, a supervisee may find it restorative to name their feelings about leaving their work, but be reluctant to engage with their feelings about ending the supervision relationship. Helping such a supervisee to notice this and name feelings in the moment can be formative in supporting them to end well in real time with their colleagues and those in their pastoral care.

Where a supervisee moves because their training has come to an end, the ending is likely to be overladen with anxieties about managing 'on my own' and a reluctance to have to start to 'get to know someone like you all over again'. For their part, the supervisor may well wish they could continue to work together or, on the contrary, be relieved to have an acceptable reason to bring the work to an end.

Endings can also be occasioned by the supervisor moving on. As well as dealing with their own feelings about this, supervisors might have to manage a level of questioning and even anger on the part of their supervisees. Keeping the space supervisee-centred rather than supervisor-centred will require careful attention, and again the supervisor being in supervision themselves will be a good place to monitor this.

## 3. Ending due to dissatisfaction or breakdown in the relationship

Sometimes supervisees call for the relationship to end because they are not having their needs met or because they feel pigeonholed, restricted or not understood. This could indicate that the supervisor has misjudged the developmental level of the supervisee and is pitching their interventions at the wrong level, either boring them with a rudimentary line of questioning that undermines them or devoting such an inordinate amount of time and energy to parallel process that the supervisee never feels they have the opportunity to work through what they came with. Careful attention to the *tracking and monitoring* stage in each session will go a long way towards minimizing such surprises.

The supervisory relationship can also break down due to an actual or perceived violation of boundaries. Whereas those who supervise counsellors and psychotherapists are not usually in contact with their supervisees outwith the contracted sessions, the life of ministry often means that we have multi-levelled overlapping relationships with those we supervise – all the more reason for extra vigilance in maintaining confidentiality in speech and safeguarding privileged information. In our experience, most breakdowns in pastoral relationships – supervision included – can be traced to insufficient attention to the normative dimensions of contracting and review (see Chapter 1).

The multi-layered nature of many pastoral roles also means that when a supervision relationship ends, other strands of the relationship may continue. Ending a supervision relationship in such cases means defining what is ending, what needs renegotiating and what can fruitfully continue. For example, on ordination a curate or probationer minister will continue to be a colleague and to be overseen in some ways by their supervising minister. Negotiating what should remain and what should change in the relationship can facilitate an appropriate transition.

## 4. Other reasons for ending

Sometimes involuntary endings occur due to the actions of an external party. Perhaps funding is withdrawn or the powers that be issue a directive that supervision must now be in-house. At a local church level, supervision may cease because the new person in charge (of the parish, youth group, care team) has no experience of supervision, is not willing to give it a try or is not willing to have an outsider (the supervisor) interfere with how things are done on their patch. And, of course, endings can be brought about by the death or serious illness of one of the parties.

## Different Types of Endings

Most human beings shy away from loss by not acknowledging or dealing with it, and so our range of messy ways of ending is quite extensive.

### 1. Sticky endings

Sometimes referred to as 'Velcro endings', these are the situations in which one or both parties find it hard to let go. The reasons behind this may be deeply unconscious. Where the ending is prolonged by the supervisor it may be a result of:

- their need for more practice (typical of a supervisor in training who needs to clock up more hours of experience);
- a sense of buzz in this area of ministry not experienced elsewhere, forcing the supervisor to confront the issues in other areas of their work;
- an overinflated sense of the supervisor's importance to the ministerial well-being of the supervisee.

In all cases supervisors need to look in their own supervision at whose needs are being met in the relationship.

Of course, the overdependency can be the other way round, a supervisee clinging to you and telling you that you are the first person who has ever allowed them to bring their faith and work into the same conversation and they just don't know how they will cope without you ... Even if not verbally stated, this dependency can be expressed by supervisees coming up with some big issue or crisis each time you have agreed to end. Those who contract a fixed number of sessions in the initial working agreement report 'sticky' supervisees failing to keep one or more appointments (especially at times when they do not feel the need for supervision), only to claim at the end that they have not had the allotted number of sessions they had been promised and therefore cannot end. One way of minimizing the possibility of a sticky ending is for the supervisor to ask the supervisee in the very first session what support structures or people they have in place, and to monitor their effectiveness throughout the duration of the relationship so that the supervisee has less need to end up clinging to the supervisor.

## 2. Cut and run endings

Cut and run endings are those in which the ending is avoided by one or other party. Where a supervisor senses that this might be the preferred option for a supervisee they can counter it by naming the impending end in the sessions running up to it, and by beginning the final session by making the implicit explicit and asking for a good chunk of time to be set aside in the session to deal with feelings and reactions to the ending. Sometimes supervisees who cannot face ending come to the final meeting armed with a whole catalogue of new and significant issues that they use to fill the space so that there will be no room for anything more than a quick goodbye at the door. Worse still, in the case of a planned ending a supervisee may simply not turn up for the last meeting at all. A not infrequent variation on that is that a supervisee who is prone to anticipatory grief – the kind of person who misses their partner for days before they go away on business – might surprise a supervisor by turning up one day and announcing that they have decided to close down the supervision relationship – today! This news may be accompanied by a range of supposedly explanatory factors: childcare responsibilities, time constraints or a decision to try spiritual direction instead.

## 3. Bin-bag endings

This term refers to endings in which one or other party devalues the work that has taken place in supervision and treats it as disposable. This usually happens as a mechanism for avoiding the pain of loss: 'If it didn't mean anything, I don't have to grieve it.'

Strategies that might help a supervisee who is reluctant to name what has been good in a relationship include various review activities, such as a timeline identifying key moments in the supervision (see Exercise 4.4) or a request asking them to review their learning journal for the relevant period. Even if a supervisee is unable to name what has been formative for them, this does not prevent the supervisor from stating what they have found valuable and naming the learning they feel has taken place. Supervisors need to deal with their feelings of rejection or hurt in their own supervision.

## 4. Loose endings

Loose or uncertain endings occur when neither party is really sure whether they are still working together or have finished. They are often caused by a failure to turn up for an appointment or by repeated failure to bring their diary to fix up the next session – the last words from supervisees prone to loose endings are often 'I'll be in touch'. Once again the attentive supervisor will probably have seen this approach played out in miniature form in the working relationship. When all else fails, the supervisor retains the right and professional duty to inform a supervisee who has not been in touch that they have a set period of time to fix an appointment, otherwise the supervisory relationship will be deemed over.

The way a supervisor goes about managing the ending of supervision relationships will be shaped by their own life experiences. It is important that supervisors are reflexive about what they themselves may be carrying into endings. An exercise is provided at the end of the chapter to help you think about this.

## Healthy Endings in Supervision

Managing a good ending in supervision is an important part of the work and may provide a lasting corrective to earlier less helpful endings in the supervisee's past. Modelling a good ending can bring about a positive rearrangement of a supervisee's own interior psychological furniture and broaden their repertoire of pastoral responses to people in their care. What follows are some of the characteristics that contribute to healthy endings in pastoral supervision.

### 1. The ending is negotiated

Just as *hosting and containing* enables people to be welcomed into a space conducive to trust and well-being, so too does it imply the ability to enable people to leave the supervisory relationship able to trust the good work that has been achieved and to maintain confidence in the person or persons involved (the supervisor, the supervision group). Nothing undermines the good work that has been done or dilutes the trust that has been established more than a sudden, unexpected end to a relationship that has been valued by at least one of the parties involved. Negotiated endings – wherever possible – allow supervisees a degree of control over the timing of the ending and allow them time for appropriate adjustment. In addition to ensuring good endings to supervision relationships, a pastoral supervisor can also help a supervisee plan for endings in their own work. One colleague of Jane's commented how helpful he had found it, when moving from one ministry appointment to another (with more than a year's notice), to plan how he would make good endings with his churches and with particular groups and individuals.

## 2. *Opportunity for review is provided*

Just as *tracking and monitoring* within a supervision session ensures that the supervisee is able to do the exploratory work they came to supervision to do, so too at a macro level, healthy endings provide an opportunity to take stock of the relationship: what the expectations were at the beginning; whether they have been met; what has been accomplished together; how insight and capacity to enact change in the workplace have developed through the practice of supervision; what has been the character of the relationship. This should be an extension of a regular review process.

## 3. *Appreciation is expressed*

Where it is true, and only then, it can come as a surprise to a supervisee to find their supervisor naming what they have learnt and how they have grown through the work they have done together. Especially when the relationship has been experienced as supportive and constructive, supervisees can be blind to their own giftedness as channels of grace for their supervisors. Being able to show appreciation and bring out into the open the mutual character of the relationship further relocates the parties as disciples and fellow members in the body of Christ and reinforces the missiological task of supervision, which is to 'release power in the supervisee to enable those they work with'.[5]

## 4. *The unspoken is named*

Because of the very real or perceived power differential in the supervision relationship, supervisees may be reluctant – or feel it is illegitimate – to tell their supervisors what they really make of them and how they experience their ways of working. A less experienced supervisor might be lulled into a sense of complacency and interpret this silence as evidence that all is well when the reality is otherwise. The supervisor who has avoided attending to the here and now dimensions of the supervisory relationship, especially at times of review, might therefore be in for a surprise in asking if there is anything left unsaid – but better late than never.

## 5. Closure is achieved

Supervisors who have the opportunity to move through the four stages above are well on their way to achieving a sense of closure both for themselves and for those with whom they work. However, as we indicated earlier, not all supervisees will permit such closure to take place, in which case it remains incumbent on the supervisor to find a way of bringing the relationship to an end in their own way. Some tried and tested ways include: writing a letter that is never sent and later burned; keeping an hour's appointment in which you imagine telling the person in the empty chair what you have learnt from them and in which you thank them for the part they have played in your life; expressing your feelings about the lack of a chance to end as you would wish, either in a six-minute journaling exercise or with paint or crayons; finding, interacting with and then laying down something that symbolizes that person or that relationship. Whether closure is achieved alone or together, there is always the possibility of praying for your supervisee and blessing them on their way.

## 6. Practice is reviewed

The ending of a supervisory relationship presents an invaluable opportunity for supervisors to review their own practice, since 'to stay a good supervisor is to return regularly to question not only the work of the supervisees, but also what you yourself do as a supervisor and how you do it'.[6] What worked well? What would you do differently? What do you now understand about supervision that you did not know before? How has working with this supervisee – or group of supervisees – shaped your practice? This is a good subject for your own supervision sessions.

## Developmental Levels, Gender and Endings

In Chapter 5 we discussed the importance of identifying the developmental level at which supervisees are working, to ensure a fit between need and approach. Cal Stoltenberg and Ursula

Delworth correlated those developmental levels with the ways supervisees handle endings.[7] Stage 1 supervisees experience the end in terms of the loss of a trusted mentor but generally bond easily with the next supervisor who comes along; stage 2 supervisees are warier about starting up again with a new supervisor, often putting them to the test to see if they are up to scratch; stage 3 supervisees 'experience termination in supervision as a parting of friends'.[8] The same authors differentiated further between the ending patterns of male and female supervisees. According to their findings, male supervisees generally struggle more to say hello in the early stages of the relationship and, not surprisingly, therefore downplay the importance of endings; female supervisees tend to say hello easily but are then reluctant to say goodbye.[9]

## The Last Word

In the UK in the first years of the twenty-first century, the churches are beginning to grasp the rewards a culture of pastoral supervision might deliver:

> The rewards of good supervision are rich. They include growing self-awareness and self-confidence, the freedom genuinely to 'learn from experience' and, in theological terms, having experienced grace in the supervisory relationship to be able to mediate that grace in the pastoral relationship. All of these gains, rooted in a good supervisory experience, are fundamental … to pastoral care as a creative art form … a care rooted in the personal and pastoral identity of the carer: an identity shaped by supervision.[10]

If the leadership and care those in ministry offer is to be rooted, courageous and visionary enough 'to serve the present age',[11] it is our belief that those who minister will need to be part of supervision relationships that model and teach a prophetic ministry of real presence. For the quality of attentiveness – to the detail of individual situations and contexts; to the horizon of God's coming kingdom; to the presence and leading of the Holy Spirit in the here and now – is essential to the authentic incarnation of the body of Christ in our own cultures and time.

# Exercises

## Exercise 10.1 Reflecting on Endings

*For reflection*

The experience people have had of endings in their lives will influence how they manage endings as supervisors.

Review the types of endings listed in the chapter:

- Sticky endings
- Cut and run endings
- Bin-bag endings
- Loose endings

Think back over the way you have handled endings – such as moving jobs, moving house, saying goodbye to colleagues, bereavements, the break-up of relationships.

- ➤ How have you managed the pain of ending?
- ➤ If you are finding it difficult to get in touch with your experience, try a six-minute exercise entitled 'A difficult ending'.
- ➤ What might you be prone to in handling the ending of supervision relationships?

Now think of an example of a good ending you have been party to. Again, you might access this through a six-minute exercise.

- ➤ How do you want to handle endings as a supervisor?

## Exercise 10.2 Dealing with Unfinished Business

*For reflection*

If, despite your best efforts, a supervisee does a cut and run ending, this may leave you with unfinished business you need to deal with.

Think of someone – not necessarily a supervisee – who has cut and run from a relationship with you. Try one of the following:

1. Book an appointment with them; set a chair for them near to yours and spend an hour saying what you need to say:

   • What you valued in the relationship.
   • What you will miss.
   • How you feel.
   • How you want to proceed from here.

2. Try writing a letter to this person, covering the same themes. This is not a letter to be sent, so before you begin you might think about what you will do with it once written. Will you burn it? Share it with your supervisor?


## Exercise 10.3 Ending a Supervision Relationship

*To try*

The importance of negotiating the timing and manner of the ending of a relationship has already been discussed. Is it important to allow people to prepare for an ending several sessions in advance and to have the chance to think about what they want to say or do. Having agreed what needs to happen, it can be useful to have some ideas about how to help people articulate what they need to say to each other. Some examples include:

1. **Reviewing the work:** Spread picture postcards around the room and ask people to choose one that speaks to them of the work they have done in this relationship/group. Invite people to share what the card means to them.

2. **Naming feelings:** Invest in a set of drama therapy cards.[12] These are specifically designed to represent and evoke feelings. Participants – including the supervisor – might choose a handful of cards that represent the range of emotions they are feeling. These can then be laid like dominos as people talk about the cards they have chosen.

3. **Moving on:** Give each person a blank postcard, an envelope and a stamp. Ask them to self-address the envelope, attach the stamp and then write a postcard to themselves naming:

   a. one thing I have learnt in this context that I don't want to forget;

   b. one thing I will do as a result of this supervision.

In a group situation the completed cards might be placed in their envelopes in the centre of the room and form part of an ending with prayer or other act of worship. Participants might be invited to take someone else's card to post to them on an agreed date.

## Exercise 10.4  Review

*For reflection*

Think back over your journey through this book. If you have kept a journal this might be done by reviewing what you have written and drawn. Address and stamp an envelope and write yourself a postcard naming:

- one thing I have realized in working with this book that I don't want to forget;
- one thing I will do as a result of reading this book.

On the front of the envelope write the date on which you want it posted and ask a friend to keep it for you until then.

# Notes

1 The words of a man living with AIDS, reflecting on his diagnosis and the welcome changes it had brought to his life.

2 Parker J. Palmer, 1983, *To Know as We Are Known: A Spirituality of Education*, San Francisco: Harper & Row, p. 72.

3 Palmer, *To Know as We Are Known*, p. 72.

4 Stephen R. Covey, 2004, *The 7 Habits of Highly Effective People*, London: Simon & Schuster, p. 95.

5 Mary Creaner, 'Reflections on learning and transformation in supervision: a crucible of my experience', 2011, in Robin Shohet (ed.), *Supervision as Transformation: A Passion for Learning*, London: Jessica Kingsley, pp. 146–59.

6 Peter Hawkins and Robin Shohet, 2006, *Supervision in the Helping Professions*, 3rd edn, Buckingham: Open University Press, p. 55.

7 Cal D. Stoltenberg and Ursula Delworth, 1987, *Supervision Counsellors and Therapists: A Developmental Approach*, San Francisco and London: Jossey-Bass.

8 Cited in Michael Carroll, *Counselling Supervision: Theory, Skills and Practice*, London: Cassell, p. 115.

9 Cited in Carroll, *Counselling Supervision*, p. 115.

10 David Lyall, 2000, 'Pastoral care as performance', in James Woodward and Stephen Pattison, *The Blackwell Reader in Pastoral and Practical Theology*, Oxford: Blackwell, pp. 317–18.

11 Charles Wesley, 1762, 'A charge to keep I have'.

12 These are available under various names, including 'oh-cards', and are available to order online from www.evokecards.com.

# Glossary

**action methods**: deployed in group work and *creative supervision*. Involve showing as a form of telling.

**APSE**: The (UK) Association of Pastoral Supervisors and Educators, founded in 2008 to bring together pastoral supervisors working in various healthcare, educational and local ministry settings, both from *Clinical Pastoral Education* and other supervision backgrounds.

**bibliodrama**: an embodied way of exploring the meaning of a scriptural text. Involves the close reading of a text and the adoption of roles by participants, who imagine themselves into the characters of people, objects and places with the aim of better relating to the biblical material and understanding themselves in relation to it.

**Christian practices**: those corporately recognized practices of the Church that sustain the life of the body of Christ in the world, such as prayer, worship, baptism, Eucharist, hospitality etc.; a developing field of study in *pastoral theology*.

**Clinical Pastoral Education (CPE)**: developed from 1920s in the USA. A key figure was Anton Boisen, who studied himself as a 'living human document' when a patient in a psychiatric hospital. Developed as a general method of seminary education by Seward Hiltner in the 1960s, it involves placement hours in a clinical setting (usually healthcare, although prisons, parishes and other settings have also been used), theory seminars and clinical *pastoral supervision*, both one-to-one and in groups. A well-established movement in the USA, Canada, continental Europe, Ireland, Scotland and elsewhere, but not in England and Wales.

**clinical pastoral supervision:** developed from a combination of *clinical supervision* and Christian theology into a key element of the *Clinical Pastoral Education* movement (CPE). Usually takes place in a clinical setting and focuses on development in pastoral identity, skills and theological framework in reflecting on live work.

**clinical supervision:** a method employed in the training and development of professionals in healthcare settings, social work, counselling etc. Focuses on the practitioner's identity, skills and theoretical framework by reporting, and shared reflection, on their live work.

**communication by impact:** an unconscious process whereby one person seeks to communicate what they are experiencing to another through their impact on the hearer, making the other person feel what they are feeling. A laicization of a collection of psychoanalytic terms including *transference, countertransference* and *parallel process*.

**concretization:** the act of converting a concept (e.g. a role, a metaphor or a scene) into a concrete image (using an object, cloth, paint on page etc.).

**countertransference:** a psychoanalytic term describing an unconscious process by which feelings, thoughts and behaviour originating in another context or relationship are stimulated in a care-giver by the person or group with whom they are working.

**creative supervision:** a method of supervision that focuses on non-verbal means of communication, using art, music and drama, and draws on the imagination to reveal what is unconsciously known and bring that into dialogue with the level of consciousness. For examples of creative techniques see Exercises 3.4; 7.2; 7.3; 9.3 and Chapter 6.

**doubling:** within creative supervision, the ability/opportunity to tune in to a character and hold that role with or for the supervisee.

**dramatherapy:** the intentional use of drama and/or theatre processes to achieve therapeutic goals.

**eccentric:** literally, 'outside the centre'. In this context a practice in which the practitioner intentionally allows another, or God's activity, to be at the centre of what is happening.

**embodiment:** one of the three key techniques of *dramatherapy* whereby clients are helped to develop their body awareness, preparatory to work with *projection* and *role*.

**episcope:** the Greek word for oversight; often used in theological literature to indicate the governance of the Church, whether personal *episcope* (exercised by bishops, superintendent ministers or other representative persons); collegial *episcope* (exercised by groups within the same order of ministry, such as a House of Bishops or elders' meeting) or communal *episcope* (exercised by a mix of various orders of ministry, e.g. a Parochial Church Council or General Assembly/Synod).

**formative function of supervision:** a term deriving from Inskipp and Proctor's *functional model of supervision*. Here the focus of the supervisor is on helping the supervisee grow and develop as a practitioner.

**functional model of supervision:** an approach to supervision that seeks to outline the main tasks of the discipline, e.g. Inskipp and Proctor's normative, formative, restorative model, or Michael Carroll's seven tasks of supervision.

**group supervision:** usually refers to facilitated supervision that takes place remotely from any of the ministry contexts of the participants, as opposed to *team supervision*.

**hermeneutical method:** a means of *theological reflection* that concentrates attention on *the way we interpret the situations in which our pastoral actions take place.* Becoming conscious of the way we are viewing a situation makes it possible to view it differently and choose to act differently in the future. The most notable hermeneutical method of theological reflection is that of Edward Farley (see Chapter 8).

**impact:** see *communication by impact.*

**incarnation:** literally, 'enfleshment'; used of the Word of God made flesh in Jesus Christ, and also of approaches to Christian living, ministry and mission that stress the embodiment of the gospel in human lives.

**mirroring:** within creative supervision, the ability and opportunity to stand back from a sculpt and view it as from the outside.

**narrative supervision:** an approach to supervision that focuses on the storied nature of human experience, seeing human beings primarily as interpreters of those stories. The role of the supervisor is to be a co-interpreter, working with the supervisee's images and stories and seeking to help them re-frame their experience – in Christian contexts – in the light of the gospel.

**normative function of supervision:** a term deriving from Inskipp and Proctor's *functional model of supervision.* Here the focus of the supervisor is on the managerial aspects of supervision and on the boundary-setting capacities of the practitioner in their work.

**parallel process:** a dimension of *countertransference* in which aspects of the relationship between a care-seeker and the care-giver may be unconsciously played out between the care-giver and their supervisor. The supervisee is unaware of having identified with the care-seeker's situation, cannot see it clearly from their own viewpoint and unconsciously communicates in ways that are different from their normal style, appearing distracted or inappropriately emotional or incoherent. It is a form of *communication by impact.*

**pastoral counselling:** the practice of a counsellor meeting with individuals, groups or couples in need of help within an explicitly Christian context.

**pastoral supervision:** a discipline of the Church by which ministries are ordered and ministers supervised. Latterly it has come to be defined, by associations such as *APSE*, as 'a regular, planned, intentional and boundaried space in which a practitioner skilled in supervision (the supervisor) meets with one or more other practitioners (the supervisees) to reflect together on the supervisees' practice'. Although the practitioner may be accountable to their bishop or senior minister for being in pastoral supervision, this ministry may be exercised by someone outside the formal ecclesial structure.

**pastoral theology:** variously defined by theologians, it can be used synonymously with *practical theology* though it tends to imply a more Church-focused approach than the broader term. Older uses indicate theology from the perspective of the pastor and would include such disciplines as Christian education, liturgy, preaching, pastoral skills etc.

**playback theatre:** a form of spontaneous theatre that relies on the enactment of the audience's stories. Often used therapeutically among traumatized communities to help them process their experiences in solidarity with one another.

**praxis:** a term originating in liberation theology to indicate the awareness of theory – and social theory in relation to power structures – present in practice. Now used more generally to indicate awareness of the theologies present in practice.

**process model of supervision:** an approach to supervision that seeks to identify the processes happening in supervision as different modes of operating within it, e.g. Hawkins and Shohet's seven modes; the model presented in Chapters 4 and 5.

**projection:** in psychoanalytic theory the unconscious process whereby painful or other difficult feelings such as rage or vulnerability are disowned by an individual and ascribed to another as a way of avoiding the pain entailed in feeling them or acknowledging them as one's own. In *dramatherapy* also the method by which clients are invited to 'show' the therapist what is happening in their world, by projecting their thoughts and feelings and associations onto objects, paper or members of a therapy group who agree to hold roles for them for the duration of the session.

**psychodrama:** an *action method* predominantly used in group work in which each person can become a therapeutic agent for each other member of the group. Developed by Jacob Moreno, psychodrama has strong elements of theatre and is often conducted on a stage, where props can be used to explore whatever an individual brings to the group. A technique used in therapeutic and supervision groups.

**reflective:** *(of a tool)* an exercise to facilitate deep thought about the situations in which one is engaged; *(of a person)* the capacity to think deeply about the situations in which one is engaged, involving taking responsibility for one's own actions, motivations and influence, questioning norms and structures, and being willing to stay with uncertainty and provisionality. Involves a high degree of *reflexivity*.

**reflective practice:** a term originating in secular professional practice though it has come to dominate the current model of pastoral (or practical) theological education, indicating the importance of placement work and reflection on it in the development of individual practitioners (ministers), and drawing on theological and other relevant disciplines. Involves developing *reflexive* and *reflective* capacities.

**reflexivity:** the capacity to reflect on one's own approaches, feelings, pre-judgements, responses and identity. Goes beyond problem solving and seeks to come as close as possible to understanding how others experience oneself. Requires a willingness to be open to feedback and new ways of thinking and doing things. Goes beyond protocols and procedures to develop wisdom in handling complexity and ambiguity.

**restorative function of supervision:** a term deriving from Inskipp and Proctor's *functional model of supervision.* Here the focus of the supervisor is on helping supervisees discharge emotion and reconnect with aspects of themselves with which they have lost touch.

**role:** a way of being. Within supervision the supervisor and the supervisee adopt a variety of roles, such as facilitator/explorer; teacher/learner. Within creative supervision, inviting a supervisee to work with various roles – social, somatic and psychological – is a key way of working, involving *doubling, mirroring* and *role-reversal.*

**role-reversal:** within creative supervision, involves the supervisee inhabiting the world of someone they are bringing to supervision, e.g. by allocating that person a chair and sitting in the chair to imagine the world from their perspective.

**role repertoire:** the ability to move between one role and another, adopting an appropriate role for the supervisee/situation while maintaining a high degree of congruence.

**script:** a psychological term referring to the way human beings unconsciously develop sequences of expected behaviours for a given situation. Making unconscious scripts explicit in therapy or supervision can yield options for developing new and healthier scripts.

**sculpt:** a term from *psychodrama* meaning a tableau or static presentation of an incident or situation achieved by positioning group members' bodies and props to represent characters, emotional states etc. Can also be used as a verb, 'to sculpt'.

**somatization:** literally, 'becoming bodily or embodied'. In psycho-analytical usage denotes a process whereby a person's unconscious thoughts or feelings come to be expressed in their body, e.g. as a bodily sensation or 'psychosomatic' illness. In supervision such feelings may, via *communication by impact*, mean that the supervisor picks up bodily the stiffness, pain or exhaustion of the supervisee.

**spiritual direction:** a relationship in which one or more people are accompanied by a guide or companion who helps them focus on their lives as disciples and their relationships with God.

**structures of idolatry:** from idolatry, a biblical term used primarily to refer to the worship of other gods than Yahweh. 'Structures of idolatry' was coined by Edward Farley to draw attention to the ways the priorities and values of institutions or societies can centre on money, productivity or status and draw individuals away from the priorities of the kingdom and the valuing of all human beings as those made in the image of God. See Appendix 4.

**structures of redemption:** from redemption, a biblical term referring primarily in the New Testament to the saving work of Jesus Christ. 'Structures of redemption' refers in Edward Farley's work to the way institutions and societies can put the well-being of all creation and all God's creatures at the heart of their policies and priorities.

**symbolization:** process of selecting an object to represent a role, concept, situation or state. By its nature the symbol is multivocal and allows exploration of different aspects of what it has been chosen to signify.

**team supervision:** group supervision in which all members of the group routinely work together and the objectives and dynamics of the team are explored as well as or instead of focusing on the work of individuals. Usually facilitated by a supervisor who is not part of the team.

**theological reflection:** a broad term used to describe a range of theological processes. In the last 30 years has become associated with a number of models that provide a series of questions or stages to work through. Their purpose is to help practitioners connect theology and action. Increasingly, theological reflection is seen as an aim of *pastoral supervision.*

**tools of distillation:** techniques used for getting the work of the supervisee into the room or helping them narrow their focus or get to the heart of the matter; see e.g. Exercises 3.4; 4.1; 4.2; 4.3; 4.4.

**transference:** strictly, a form of *projection* in which feelings and interactions originating in one relationship/setting are transferred to another, such as the projection of feelings about authority figures onto care-givers or supervisors.

**verbatim:** developed by the **CPE** movement as a way of bringing live work into clinical *pastoral supervision.* Involves the practitioner writing as accurate a word-for-word account as they can remember of a live encounter from which they want to learn, and discussing this individually with their supervisor or with others in a supervised group.

# Appendix 1

# APSE Definition of Pastoral Supervision[1]

*Agreed by members on 17 October 2008*

## Pastoral Supervision is ...

- *a regular, planned, intentional and boundaried space* in which a practitioner skilled in supervision (the supervisor) meets with one or more other practitioners (the supervisees) to look together at the supervisees' practice;
- *a relationship* characterised by trust, confidentiality, support and openness that gives the supervisee freedom and safety to explore the issues arising in their work;
- *spiritually/theologically rich* – works within a framework of spiritual/theological understanding in dialogue with the supervisee's world view and work;
- *psychologically informed* – draws on relevant psychological theory and insight to illuminate intra-personal and inter-personal dynamics;
- *contextually sensitive* – pays attention to the particularities of setting, culture and world view;
- *praxis based* – focuses on a report of work and /or issues that arise in and from the supervisee's pastoral practice;
- *a way of growing in*
  - vocational identity
  - pastoral competence
  - self awareness
  - spiritual/theological reflection
  - pastoral interpretation
  - quality of presence
  - accountability
  - response to challenge
  - mutual learning

- *attentive to* issues of fitness to practice, skill development, management of boundaries, professional identity and the impact of the work upon all concerned parties.

## Pastoral Supervision is not ...

- *Spiritual accompaniment* – for the sole or primary purpose of exploring the spiritual life and development of the supervisee(s). Aspects of this may arise in Pastoral Supervision but are not the main focus.
- *Counselling* – for the purpose of helping the supervisee(s) gain insight into their personal dynamics, or helping the supervisee(s) to resolve or live more positively with their psycho-social limitations. Aspects of this may arise in Pastoral Supervision and, if necessary, the supervisee(s) may be encouraged to seek counselling support.
- *Line management* – for the purpose of addressing professional practice and development issues in relationship to the supervisee(s)'s performance and accountability (whether paid or voluntary) to her/his employer. Aspects of this may arise in Pastoral Supervision but are not the main focus.

## Note

1 Included with the kind permission of the APSE executive committee.

# Appendix 2

# Supervision Covenant Proforma

| Aims | • What is my understanding of the purpose of supervision?<br>• What experience of supervision does my supervisee have?<br>• What hopes and fears does s/he bring?<br>• What is s/he looking for?<br>• Is this something I can offer? |
|---|---|
| Practicalities | • How often will we meet?<br>• How long will the sessions last?<br>• Where will we meet?<br>• Is there a fee involved? |
| Structure | • What will the pattern of the sessions be?<br>• What tools for supervision has your supervisee encountered?<br>• What might s/he like to try?<br>• What preparation will your supervisee need to do before s/he comes to each session? |
| Boundaries | • Are there any external requirements?<br>• Is a report required?<br>• What is the process for compiling the report?<br>• What are the criteria for assessment?<br>• To whom is this confidential?<br>• What records will be kept?<br>• Might there be any conflicts of interest because of other roles either of us hold?<br>• If I am worried about your fitness to practise for any reason, how will we proceed?<br>• Can we handle these? If so, how?<br>• If either of us needs to cancel a session, how is this done? |
| Arrangements for Review | • Is this an open-ended or fixed-term commitment?<br>• Do we need a trial period?<br>• How often shall we review our work together?<br>• If either of us needs/wants to end the supervision arrangement, how is this done? |

# Appendix 3

# APSE Code of Conduct[1]

The conduct of an accredited supervisor will be examined at accreditation and again at five yearly reviews. Each Member and Accredited Member accepts that it is at all times imperative to conduct oneself in a manner which is a credit to their profession and in accordance with the following general principles.

**Any accredited member is required to:**

1. only accept supervisees who are aware of the role and relationship provided by supervision, making that clear through a contracting-in process either in writing, or by verbal agreement, or ideally both.
2. contract the terms of confidentiality and maintain clear professional boundaries.
3. explain and agree the role of supervision in fostering and developing a supervisee's professional development and monitoring their fitness to practice; and the action the supervisor will take when fitness to practice has been compromised.
4. act immediately, and in accordance with the law, if a supervisee discloses information relating to risk of harm to self or others.
5. act with due respect for integrity and difference, including sexual orientation, ethnicity, religion, disability, or gender.
6. in matters relating to the well-being of a supervisee, act solely in the interests of the supervisee.
7. use their professional judgment to encourage supervisees who require further support to seek that support for themselves,

whether through spiritual guidance, counselling, medical attention, or some other source of support.

8. maintain regular and sufficient supervision for the supervisor or educator's own practice and workload.[2]
9. be appropriately insured for any supervision work undertaken.
10. engage in regular professional development activities.

## Resolving Differences

Where another party, whether colleague, fellow supervisor, or supervisee, has experienced the supervisor as contravening this Code of Conduct, the following steps will be taken:

1. **Informal approach:** an informal approach is to be made by the complainant to the supervisor outlining, in person and in private, what the issues are and seeking to find a mutual solution to those difficulties. If a solution can be found and maintained, this is the best option.
2. **Formal approach:** following an unsuccessful informal approach the complainant must put in writing their grievance to the supervisor and ask for a formal resolution of the problem. The supervisor or the complainant may choose to involve a third party or mediator at this stage. If a solution can be found and maintained (including termination of the supervisor-supervisee relationship), this should be implemented. The complainant must receive a written notification of the agreed solution.
3. **Second Formal Approach:** If the formal approach does not produce a satisfactory solution or if breaches of the Code of Conduct are perceived to persist, the complainant may make an approach in writing to the Secretary of APSE, outlining the Informal and Formal stages which they have taken and providing any relevant written material. This will then be dealt with under the APSE Complaints Procedure.

## Complaints Procedure

A complaint is defined as a grievance presented in writing involving an alleged violation of ethical, and/or professional conduct as defined by the APSE Code of Conduct.[3] Complaints should be resolved as close to the event as possible, in a spirit of face-to-face mutual respect and consideration (see Resolving Differences above).

Where this process has not led to a satisfactory resolution, either party to the complaint may lodge a written appeal with the Secretary. The Secretary will arrange an appeal panel of at least three Members who have not previously been involved in the case.

The appeal panel will investigate the case and decide upon one of the following outcomes:

i.   the complaint is not upheld;
ii.  the complaint is found to have some grounds and remedial action may be recommended;
iii. the complaint is upheld and remedial action may be recommended, or the supervisor may have their Accredited Status removed.

The decision of the appeal panel shall be final. All parties will be informed in writing of the outcome.

## Notes

1 Included with the kind permission of the APSE executive committee.
2 It is expected that Accredited Supervisors would receive a minimum of one hour of supervision for every eight hours of providing supervision.
3 Where the issue relates to a criminal or civil offence, or where information is disclosed pertaining to the safety of children, the legal process supersedes the stages outlined above and parties should go directly to the relevant authorities. Any disciplinary action taken by APSE will be suspended until the outcome of a criminal investigation is known.

# Appendix 4

# Values-based Reflective Practice

If ministry is to reach beyond the confines of church life and practice, it needs to be multilingual and able to converse in a manner that is both comprehensible and meaningful to the rest of the world.

Values-based Reflective Practice is one such attempt to place spiritual values at the heart of supervision for people with no explicit faith allegiance. It aims to foster professional actions that are aligned with personal beliefs and values. While its origins lie in liberation theology and feminist theology, its application is much wider. It is currently being promoted by the Scottish government as a model for reflective practice across NHS Scotland.[1]

It owes its inspiration to David Lyall, who writes:

a situation is not neutral. It demands a response. It is a concentration of powers which impinges upon us as individual agents or as communities. Situations may offer promise and possibility or situations may require obligation. But neither the promise nor the obligation are straightforward.[2]

Lyall continues, quoting Edward Farley, 'human beings shape the demands of the situation according to their idolatries, their absolutized self-interests and their participations in the structures of power. Situations pose to human beings occasions for idolatry and redemption.'[3]

Values-based Reflective Practice asks five questions of every situation brought to supervision:

1. **N** Whose needs were met by doing what was done?
   Whose needs were left unmet?

2. **A** What does the situation say about our abilities or capabilities?
   Competence, physical and human resources, training etc.?

3. **V** Who had a voice in the situation?
   Who was silent or silenced?

4. **V** What was valued in the situation?
   What was undervalued or overvalued?

5. **Y** What does the situation say about you?
   You the practitioner, you the team, you the organization?

## Notes

1 See Michael Paterson and Ewan Kelly, 2013, 'Values-based reflective practice: a method developed in Scotland for spiritual care practitioners', *Practical Theology* 6.1, pp. 51–68. The VBRP website offers tools and resources – www.vbrp.scot.nhs.uk.

2 David Lyall, 1989, 'Pastoral action and theological reflection', reprinted in David Willows and John Swinton (eds), 2003, *Spiritual Dimensions of Pastoral Care: Practical Theology in a Multidisciplinary Context*, London and Philadelphia: Jessica Kingsley, pp. 53–8.

3 Cited in Lyall, 'Pastoral action and theological reflection', p. 56.

# Appendix 5

# Learning Needs Analysis

There are a variety of courses now offering training for pastoral supervisors in the UK but as yet there are no standard routes. Those who have become pastoral supervisors have largely learnt the craft in situ through the experience of leading teams in churches or chaplaincies, through training and as supervisors in other disciplines (psychotherapy, pastoral counselling), or through the experience of Clinical Pastoral Education. While those familiar with supervision from other disciplines may need to concentrate on the distinctiveness of pastoral supervision and on thinking theologically, others with theological training may need to focus more on developing psychological fluency in handling unconscious dynamics impacting upon the work.

In an attempt to ensure 'theologically rich', 'psychologically informed', 'contextually sensitive', 'praxis based'[1] supervision (see the APSE definition in Appendix 1), the Institute of Pastoral Supervision and Reflective Practice[2] has drawn up certificate and diploma courses in pastoral supervision based around the APSE eight competencies, which are grouped around the four headings tabled below:

## Setting the Foundation

### 1. Meeting ethical guidelines and professional standards

The competent pastoral supervisor:

- understands and exhibits an ethical framework for supervisory practice;

- clearly communicates the distinctions between pastoral supervision, counselling, psychotherapy and other support structures;
- knows when to refer clients to other support structures;
- knows the limits of their own competence;
- shows commitment to the well-being of those they supervise through engaging in regular and appropriate supervision themselves;
- can assess and manage issues related to fitness to practise in the supervisee.

## 2. Establishing the supervision covenant/contract

The competent pastoral supervisor:

- understands the supervisory process and relationship;
- co-creates a contract for engaging in supervision with the supervisee;
- demonstrates clarity about the responsibilities of all parties in the supervisory relationship (supervisee, supervisor, agency);
- understands and can effectively work with the supervisee concerning the boundaries and practicalities of the supervisory relationship (including logistics, fees, scheduling etc.);
- is able to elicit a focus for each session;
- is able to work with supervisees at differing developmental stages;
- is able to conduct an effective review of the supervisory relationship after an agreed number of meetings;
- is able to bring the supervisory relationship to a satisfactory ending for both supervisor and supervisee (and agency where applicable).

## Co-creating the Relationship

### 3. Establishing a safe and supportive environment conducive to learning

The competent pastoral supervisor:

- demonstrates personal integrity, honesty and sincerity;
- demonstrates respect for supervisees' perceptions, learning style, personal being;
- demonstrates cultural sensitivity to the supervisee's world view, spirituality, practice and context;
- is able to create a safe and supportive environment that produces ongoing mutual respect and trust;
- can establish trust and intimacy in the supervisory relationship;
- can build a relationship conducive to learning;
- provides ongoing support for and champions new behaviours and actions;
- shows genuine concern for the supervisee's welfare.

## Facilitating Learning and Insight

### 4. Ability to shape supervision to enhance the supervisee's learning, development and practice

The competent pastoral supervisor:

- can identify the shape of a supervision session;
- can enable the supervisee to get work into the room;
- can elicit a focus for the session;
- can explore and track the focus;
- can identify appropriate methods for working that will serve the focus and the supervisee;
- can coach the supervisee where appropriate;
- can build up the supervisee's confidence and professional skill;
- can build a bridge from reflection back to the supervisee's practice;

- can enable the supervisee to articulate what they have learnt from supervision.

## 5. Ability to draw on a range of skills for supervision

The competent pastoral supervisor:

- demonstrates a wide range of skills to enable supervisees to work in ways that are helpful and appropriate for them;
- is able to ask open, reflective questions;
- is able to listen at a deep empathetic level for meaning beyond words and actions;
- is able to summarize, understand the essence of and reflect back what the supervisee is saying.

## 6. Ability to reflect theologically

The competent pastoral supervisor:

- is able to articulate a theological understanding of supervision that includes the values and vision underpinning their own work as a practitioner;
- can give a critical account of the values – perceived and real – within the supervisory relationship;
- can articulate their own values-based approach to supervision and reflective practice;
- is attentive to issues of power and voice in the supervisory relationship;
- is able to elicit the value base of supervisees;
- is able to help supervisees reflect on issues of value that lie within the work they bring.

## 7. Ability to bring psychological insight into dialogue with work and context

The competent pastoral supervisor:

- is able to use psychological frameworks, concepts and models to facilitate deeper understanding and insight in the supervisee;
- is able to work within the supervisee's own level of competence in using psychological insights;
- is able to help supervisees integrate psychological awareness into their work;
- is able to work with feelings – their own and the supervisee's;
- is able to work with the supervisee's underlying concerns and default ways of perceiving and identify disparities between thought, feelings and actions;
- is able to recognize and constructively engage with transference, countertransference and parallel process within the supervisory relationship;
- is able to recognize the boundary between pastoral supervision, spiritual accompaniment, personal therapy or counselling.

## Capturing Learning and Insight

## 8. Professional development and reflexivity

The competent pastoral supervisor:

- is able to reflect on their own journey as a practitioner and as a supervisor;
- is able to name what supervisees have taught them;
- is able to show how supervision on supervision has contributed to their learning and formation as a supervisor;
- is able to seek out and constructively engage with peers and their feedback;
- can demonstrate awareness of strengths and growth areas as a practitioner;
- can demonstrate awareness of what they model as a supervisor;

- can demonstrate awareness of the impact their stance and style as a supervisor may have on prospective supervisees;
- can demonstrate an ability to monitor and review learning throughout the course.

## Notes

1 The Association of Pastoral Supervisors and Educators – www.pastoralsupervision.org.uk.

2 The Institute of Pastoral Supervision and Reflective Practice runs courses in pastoral supervision in Belfast, Cambridge, Edinburgh, Glasgow, Nottingham and Salisbury – www.ipsrp.org.uk.

# Appendix 6

# Pastoral Supervision
# Professional Bodies

## Association of Pastoral Supervisors and Educators (UK)

The Association of Pastoral Supervisors and Educators (APSE) exists to promote high standards of pastoral supervision by: providing a system of accreditation for pastoral supervisors and educators in pastoral supervision; supporting initiatives in the training of pastoral supervisors; fostering groups for the support, accountability and continuing development of pastoral supervisors; encouraging conversation among the various traditions and contexts of pastoral supervision and pastoral supervision education.

See www.pastoralsupervision.org.uk.

## Institute of Pastoral Supervision and Reflective Practice (UK)

The Institute of Pastoral Supervision and Reflective Practice is a community of advanced practitioners committed to training, research and publishing. Members of the institute offer training across the UK ranging from taster events and skills workshops to professional diploma-level courses in pastoral supervision and reflective practice.

See www.ipsrp.org.uk.

## Supervisors Association of Ireland

The Supervisors Association of Ireland (SAI) is a learning community that seeks to promote cross-professional supervision. SAI's commitments are to promote a code of ethics and discipline among its members; to develop high standards of practice in supervision and training for supervision; to respond to ongoing developmental needs and research within the area of supervisory practice through support, networking, workshops, conferences and publications.

See www.saivision.ie.

## Transforming Practices (Australia)

Transforming Practices is a group of autonomous practitioners who foster personal and social transformation through skilled practices in adult education, mediation, spiritual direction, counselling and professional and pastoral supervision. Practitioners are recognized Supervisors with the Australasian Association of Supervision (AAOS) as well as other relevant Professional Associations. Transforming Practices offers training in supervision.

See www.transformingpractices.com.au.

## College of Pastoral Supervision and Psychotherapy (USA)

The College of Pastoral Supervision and Psychotherapy is a theologically based covenant community dedicated to 'Recovery of Soul'. CPSP offers accredited training in pastoral psychotherapy, pastoral supervision, pastoral counselling and clinical chaplaincy.

See www.pastoralreport.com.

# List of Referenced Works

Bazely, M. and R. Layzell, 2014, 'Pithead time for pastors: training in pastoral supervision', in Michael Paterson and Jessica Rose (eds), *Enriching Ministry: Pastoral Supervision in Practice*, London: SCM Press, pp. 119–37.

Bernard, J. M. and R. Goodyear, 2009, *Fundamentals of Clinical Supervision*, 4th edn. New Jersey: Pearson-Merill.

Berne, E., 1964, *Games People Play: The Psychology of Human Relationships*, New York: Grove Press.

Boff, C., 1987, *Theology and Praxis: Epistemological Foundations*, Maryknoll, NY: Orbis, ch. 8, 'Hermeneutics: constitution of theological pertinency', pp. 132–53.

Bolton, G., 2005, *Reflective Practice: Writing and Professional Development*, 2nd edn, London: Sage.

Boud, D., R. Keogh and D. Walker (eds), 1985, *Reflection: Turning Experience into Learning*, Abingdon: Routledge.

Campbell, A., (1979) 2000, 'The politics of pastoral care', in D. Willows and J. Swinton (eds), *Spiritual Dimensions of Pastoral Care: Practical Theology in a Multidisciplinary Context*, London and Philadelphia: Jessica Kingsley, pp. 158–69.

Carroll, M., 2001, 'The spirituality of supervision', in M. Carroll and M. Tholstrup, *Integrative Approaches to Supervision*, London and Philadelphia: Jessica Kingsley, pp. 76–90.

Carroll, M., 1996, *Counselling Supervision: Theory, Skills and Practice*, London: Cassell.

Chesner, A., 2014, 'Role as a concept in creative supervision', in A. Chesner and L. Zografou (eds), *Creative Supervision Across Modalities: Theory and Applications for Therapists, Counsellors and Other Helping Professionals*, London and Philadelphia: Jessica Kingsley, pp. 43–58.

Chesner, A., 2014, 'The six-shape supervision structure', in A. Chesner and L. Zografou (eds), *Creative Supervision Across Modalities: Theory and Applications for Therapists, Counsellors and Other Helping Professionals*, London and Philadelphia: Jessica Kingsley, pp. 71–87.

Clampitt, P. G., 1991, *Communicating for Managerial Effectiveness*, London: Sage.

Coombe, N., 2011, 'Fear and stepping forward anyway', in R. Shohet (ed.), 2011, *Supervision as Transformation: A Passion for Learning*, London and Philadelphia: Jessica Kingsley, pp. 192–8.

Couroucli-Robertson, K., 'Supervisory triangles and helicopter ability', in E. Tselikas-Portmann (ed.), 1999, *Supervision and Dramatherapy*, London and Philadelphia, Jessica Kingsley, pp. 95–113.

Covey, S. R., 2004, *The 7 Habits of Highly Effective People*, London: Simon & Schuster.

Creaner, M., 2011, 'Reflections on learning and transformation in supervision: a crucible of my experience', in R. Shohet (ed.), 2011, *Supervision as Transformation: A Passion for Learning*, London and Philadelphia: Jessica Kingsley, pp. 146–59.

Davys, A. and L. Beddoe, 2010, *Best Practice in Professional Supervision: A Guide for the Helping Professions*, London: Jessica Kingsley.

Denniston, J., 2014, 'Theory into practice: a challenge for supervisors in formation for ordained ministry', in Michael Paterson and Jessica Rose (eds), *Enriching Ministry: Pastoral Supervision in Context*, London: SCM Press, pp. 105–18.

Dykstra, C. and Dorothy C. Bass, 2002, 'A theological understanding of Christian Practices', in Miroslav Volf and Dorothy Bass (eds), *Practicing Theology: Beliefs and Practices in Christian Life*, Grand Rapids: Eerdmans, pp. 13–52.

Ekstein, R. and R. S. Wallerstein (1958) 1972, *The Teaching and Learning of Psychotherapy*, New York: International Universities Press.

Farley, E., 1987, 'Interpreting situations: an inquiry into the nature of practical theology', reprinted in J. Woodward and S. Pattison (eds), 2000, *The Blackwell Reader in Pastoral and Practical Theology*, Oxford: Blackwell, pp. 118–27.

Farley, E., 1979, *Ecclesial Man: A Social Phenomenology of Faith and Reality*, Philadelphia, PA: Fortress Press.

Ford, D., 2009, 'Are you able to drink the cup that I drink?', *Practical Theology* 2.3, pp. 343–54.

Forrester, Duncan, 2000, *Truthful Action: Explorations in Practical Theology*, Edinburgh: T. & T. Clark.

Foskett, J. and D. Lyall, 1988, *Helping the Helpers: Supervision in Pastoral Care*, London: SPCK.

Fowler, J. W., 1981, *Stages of Faith*, San Francisco: Harper & Row.

Gerkin, C. V., 1984, *The Living Human Document: Re-Visioning Pastoral Counseling in a Hermeneutical Model*, Nashville, TN: Abingdon Press.

Graham, E., H. Walton and F. Ward, 2005, *Theological Reflection: Methods*, London: SCM Press.

Hawkins, P. and R. Shohet, 2012, *Supervision in the Helping Professions*, 4th edn, Buckingham: Open University Press.

Hughes, L. and P. Pengelly, 1997, *Staff Supervision in a Turbulent Environment: Managing Process and Task in Front-Line Services*, London and Philadelphia: Jessica Kingsley.

Inskipp, F. and B. Proctor, (1993) 1995, *Making the Most of Supervision Part 1: The Art, Craft and Tasks of Counselling Supervision*, Bend, OR: Cascade Publications.

Jennings, S., 1999, 'Theatre-based supervision', in Elektra Tselikas-Portmann (ed.), *Supervision and Dramatherapy*, London and Philadelphia: Jessica Kingsley, pp. 62–7.

Karl, J. C., 1998, 'Discovering spiritual patterns: including spirituality in staff development and the delivery of psychotherapy services', *American Journal of Pastoral Counseling* 1.4, pp. 1–23.

Lahad, M., 2000, *Creative Supervision: The Use of Expressive Arts Methods in Supervision and Self-Supervision*, London and Philadelphia: Jessica Kingsley.

Leach, J., 2006, 'Pastoral theology as attention', *Contact: Practical Theology and Pastoral Care* 153, pp. 19–32.

Lyall, D., 1989, 'Pastoral action and theological reflection', reprinted in D. Willows and J. Swinton (eds), 2000, *Spiritual Dimensions of Pastoral Care: Practical Theology in a Multidisciplinary Context*, London and Philadelphia: Jessica Kingsley, pp. 53–8.

Lyall, D., 2000, 'Pastoral care as performance', in J. Woodward and S. Pattison, *The Blackwell Reader in Pastoral and Practical Theology*, Oxford: Blackwell, pp. 311–18.

Lynch, G., 2001, *Pastoral Care and Counselling*, London: Sage.

Neafsey, J., 2005, 'Seeing beyond: a contemplative approach to supervision', in M. R. Bumpus and R. B. Langer (eds), *Supervision of Spiritual Directors: Engaging in Holy Mystery*, New York: CPI Morehouse, pp. 17–31.

Niebuhr, H. R., 1960, *Radical Monotheism and Western Culture*, Lincoln, NE: University of Nebraska Press.

O'Connor, E., 1968, *Journey Outward, Journey Inward*, San Francisco: Harper & Row.

O'Connor, E., 1978, *Letters to Scattered Pilgrims*, San Francisco: Harper & Row.

Page, S. and V. Wosket, 2015, *Supervising the Counsellor and Psychotherapist: A Cyclical Model*, 3rd edn, Hove and New York: Routledge.

Palmer, P. J., 1983, *To Know as We Are Known: A Spirituality of Education*, San Francisco: Harper & Row.

Paterson, M. S. and J. Rose, 2014, *Enriching Ministry: Pastoral Supervision in Context*, London: SCM Press.

Pattison, S., 1989, 'Some straw for the bricks: a basic introduction to theological reflection', in J. Woodward and S. Pattison (eds), 2000, *The Blackwell Reader in Pastoral and Practical Theology*, Oxford: Blackwell, pp. 135–45.

Pattison, S. J., 2000, *A Critique of Pastoral Care*, 3rd edn, London: SCM Press.

Pitzele, Peter A., 1991, 'Psychodrama and the Bible: mirror and window of soul', *The Journal of Religious Education* 86.4.

Pohly, K., 1988, 'The purpose and function of supervision in ministry', *Journal of Supervision and Training in Ministry* 10, p. 8.

Pohly, K., 2001, *Transforming the Rough Places: The Ministry of Supervision*, 2nd edn, Franklin, TN: Providence House.

Proctor, B., 2008, *Group Supervision: A Guide to Creative Practice*, 2nd edn, Thousand Oaks, CA: Sage.

Robinson, M., 2005, *Gilead*, London: Virago.

Ryan, S., 2004, *Vital Practice: Stories from the Healing Arts, the Homeopathic and Supervisory Way*, Portland, OR: Sea Change.

Savage, S. and E. Boyd-Macmillan, 2007, *The Human Face of the Church*, Norwich: Canterbury Press.

Schön, D., 1983, *The Reflective Practitioner: How Professionals Think in Action*, New York: Basic Books.

Searles, H. F., 1966, 'Feelings of guilt in the psychoanalyst', reprinted in H. F. Searles, 1979, *Countertransference and Related Subjects: Selected Papers*, New York: International Universities Press.

Senge, P., 1992, *The Fifth Discipline: The Art and Practice of the Learning Organization*, London: Century Business.

Shohet, R. (ed.), 2008, *Passionate Supervision*, London and Philadelphia: Jessica Kingsley.

Shohet, R. (ed.), 2011, *Supervision as Transformation: A Passion for Learning*, London and Philadelphia: Jessica Kingsley.

St James O'Connor, T., 1998, *Clinical Pastoral Supervision and the Theology of Charles Gerkin*, Waterloo, Ont.: Published for the Canadian Corporation for Studies in Religion.

Stoltenberg, C. D. and U. Delworth, 1987, *Supervision Counsellors and Therapists: A Developmental Approach*, San Francisco and London: Jossey-Bass.

Tuckman, B. W., 1965, 'Developmental sequence in small groups', *Psychological Bulletin* 63.6, pp. 384–99.

Vest, N. (ed.), 2003, *Still Listening*, New York: CPI Morehouse.

Ward, F., 2005, *Lifelong Learning: Theological Education and Supervision*, London: SCM Press.

Weld, N., 2012, *A Practical Guide to Transformative Supervision for the Helping Professions: Amplifying Insight*, London: Jessica Kingsley.

Wells, S., 2013, *Learning to Dream Again: Rediscovering the Heart of God*, Norwich: Canterbury Press.

William, A., 1995, *Visual and Active Supervision*, New York and London: W. W. Norton.

Williams, R., 1994, *Open to Judgement*, London: Darton, Longman & Todd.

Williams, R., 2007, 'A theology of health for today', in J. Baxter (ed.), *Wounds that Heal: Theology, Imagination and Health*, London: SPCK, pp. 3–14.

# Suggestions for Reading

The suggestions for reading offered here are arranged, in the first instance, thematically and include some further texts not referenced in the alphabetical List of Referenced Works above.

## Supervisory Frameworks

A. Davys and L. Beddoe, 2010, *Best Practice in Professional Supervision: A Guide for the Helping Professions*, London: Jessica Kingsley.

P. Hawkins and R. Shohet, 2012, 4th edn, *Supervising in the Helping Professions*, Buckingham: Open University Press.

F. Inskipp and B. Proctor, (1993) 1995, *Making the Most of Supervision Part 1: The Art, Craft and Tasks of Counselling Supervision*, Bend, OR: Cascade Publications.

S. Page and V. Wosket, 2015, *Supervising the Counsellor and Psychotherapist: A Cyclical Model*, 3rd edn, Hove and New York: Routledge.

S. Ryan, 2004, *Vital Practice: Stories from the Healing Arts – the Homeopathic and Supervisory Way*, Portland, OR: Sea Change.

## Supervision, Spirituality and Ministry

M. R. Bumpus and R. B. Langer, 2005, *Supervision of Spiritual Directors: Engaging in Holy Mystery*, New York: CPI Morehouse.

M. Carroll, 2001, 'The spirituality of supervision', in M. Carroll and M. Tholstrup, *Integrative Approaches to Supervision*, London and Philadelphia: Jessica Kingsley.

R. Coll, CSJ, 1992, *Supervision of Ministry Students*, Collegeville, MN: Liturgical Press.

W. R. DeLong, 2010, *Courageous Conversations: The Teaching and Learning of Pastoral Supervision*, Lanham, ML: University Press of America.

# SUGGESTIONS FOR READING

J. Foskett and D. Lyall, 1988, *Helping the Helpers: Supervision in Pastoral Care*, London: SPCK.

C. Hunter, 2003, *Supervised Theological Field Education: A Phenomenological Inquiry*, Doctor of Ministry Studies thesis, Melbourne: Melbourne College of Divinity.

C. Hunter, 2006, One small step: creative art and the art of supervision for ministry', *Reflective Practice: Formation and Supervision in Ministry* 26, pp. 133–48.

J. Leach, 2006, 'Pastoral supervision: a review of the literature', *Contact: Practical Theology and Pastoral Care* 151, pp. 37–45.

J. Leach, 2009, 'Pastoral supervision: an annotated bibliography', *Practical Theology* 2.3, pp. 387–93.

J. Leach and M. Paterson, 2010, *Pastoral Supervision: A Handbook*, 1st edn, London: SCM Press.

J. Neafsey, 2005, 'Seeing beyond: a contemplative approach to supervision', in M. R. Bumpus and R. B. Langer (eds), *Supervision of Spiritual Directors: Engaging in Holy Mystery*, New York: CPI Morehouse, pp. 17–31.

S. Miller, 2007, *Keeping it Together: A Reflective Practice Tool for Faith-Based Community Development Practitioners*, London: Faith Based Regeneration Network Publishers.

M. Paterson, 2013, 'Mirror mirror on the wall: from reflective to transformative practice', *Journal of Health and Social Care Chaplaincy* 1.1, pp. 67–74.

M. Paterson and E. Kelly, 2013, 'Values-based reflective practice: a method developed in Scotland for spiritual care practitioners', *Practical Theology* 6.1, pp. 51–68.

K. Pohly, 2001, *Transforming the Rough Places: The Ministry of Supervision*, 2nd edn, Franklin, TN: Providence House.

H. Richardson, 2009, 'A musical metaphor for pastoral supervision', *Practical Theology* 2.3, pp. 373–86.

J. Rose, 2013, *Psychology for Pastoral Contexts: A Handbook*, London: SCM Press.

H. Smith and M. K. Smith, 2008, *The Art of Helping Others: Being Around, Being There, Being Wise*, London: Jessica Kingsley.

D. A. Steere, 2002, *The Supervision of Pastoral Care*, Edinburgh: John Knox Press.

Frances Ward, 2005, *Lifelong Learning: Theological Education and Supervision*, London: SCM Press.

B. Whorton, 2011, *Reflective Caring: Imaginative Listening to Pastoral Experience*, London: SPCK.

## Supervision as Transformative Learning

M. Carroll, 2009, 'Supervision: critical reflection for transformational learning, Part 1', *The Clinical Supervisor* 28.2, pp. 210–20.

M. Carroll, 2010, 'Levels of reflection: on learning reflection', *Psychotherapy in Australia*, 16.2, pp. 28–35.

M. Carroll and M. Gilbert, 2011, *On Being a Supervisee: Creating Learning Partnerships*, 2nd edn, London: Vukani Publishing.

J. Leach, 2014, 'Power and vulnerability: creative supervision and theological education', in A. Chesner and L. Zografou (eds), *Creative Supervision Across Modalities: Theory and Applications for Therapists, Counsellors and Other Helping Professionals*, London and Philadelphia: Jessica Kingsley.

J. Mezirow, 1991, *Transformative Dimensions of Adult Learning*, San Francisco: Jossey-Bass.

R. Shohet, 2008, *Passionate Supervision*, London: Jessica Kingsley.

R. Shohet, 2011 *Supervision as Transformation: A Passion for Learning*, London and Philadelphia: Jessica Kingsley.

N. Weld, 2012, *A Practical Guide to Transformative Supervision for the Helping Professions: Amplifying Insight*, London: Jessica Kingsley.

## Group Supervision

A. Chesner and H. Hahn (eds), 2002, *Creative Advances in Groupwork*, London: Jessica Kingsley.

E. Hillerbrand, 1989, 'Cognitive differences between experts and novices: implications for group supervision', *Journal of Counseling and Development* 67.5, pp. 293–6.

E. L. Holloway and R. Johnston, 1985, 'Group supervision: widely practiced but poorly understood', *Counselor Education and Supervision* 24.4, pp. 332–40.

F. McDermott, 2003, *Inside Group Work: A Guide to Reflective Practice*, Melbourne: Allen & Unwin.

S. Page and V. Wosket, 2015, *Supervising the Counsellor and Psychotherapist: A Cyclical Model*, 3rd edn, Hove and New York: Routledge, pp. 136–55.

B. Proctor, 2008 *Group Supervision: A Guide to Creative Practice*, 2nd edn, London: Sage.

## Organizational Supervision

M. Carroll, 2001, 'Supervision in and for organizations', in M. Carroll and M. Tholstrup, 2001, *Integrative Approaches to Supervision*, London: Jessica Kingsley, pp. 50–64.

A. Davys and L. Beddoe, 2010, *Best Practice in Professional Supervision: A Guide for the Helping Professions*, London: Jessica Kingsley, pp. 69–87.

L. Hughes and P. Pengelly, 1997, *Staff Supervision in a Turbulent Environment*, London: Jessica Kingsley.

J. Pritchard, 1995, *Good Practice in Supervision: Statutory and Voluntary Organisations*, London: Jessica Kingsley.

N. Weld, 2012, *A Practical Guide to Transformative Supervision for the Helping Professions: Amplifying Insight*, London: Jessica Kingsley, pp. 81–98.

## Journalling and Creative Writing

G. Bolton, 2005, *Reflective Practice: Writing and Professional Development*, Thousand Oaks, CA: Sage.

J. Moon, 2004, *A Handbook of Reflective and Experiential Practice*, Abingdon: Routledge.

J. Moon and J. Fowler, 2008, 'There is a story to be told: a framework for the conception for story in higher education and professional development', *Nurse Education Today* 28.2, pp. 232–9.

## Creative Approaches

A. Chesner and L. Zografou (eds), 2014, *Creative Supervision Across Modalities: Theory and Applications for Therapists, Counsellors and Other Helping Professionals*, London and Philadelphia: Jessica Kingsley.

N. Hartley and M. Payne, 2008, *The Creative Arts in Palliative Care*, London: Jessica Kingsley.

M. Lahad, 2000, *Creative Supervision: The Use of Expressive Arts in Supervision and Self-Supervision*, London: Jessica Kingsley.

C. Schuck and J. Wood, 2011, *Inspiring Creative Supervision*, London: Jessica Kingsley.

R. Verney and G. Ansdell, 2010, *Conversations on Nordorff-Robbins Music Therapy*, Gilsum, NH: Barcelona Publishers; see 'Conversation 8: on teaching and supervising music therapists', pp. 71–84.

A. Williams, 1995, *Visual and Active Supervision: Roles, Focus, Technique*, New York and London: W. W. Norton.

## Ethical Issues

BACP, 2010, *Ethical Framework for Good Practice in Counselling and Psychotherapy*, Lutterworth: BACP – www.bacp.co.uk.

UKCP Ethical Principles and Code of Conduct – www.psychotherapy.org.uk.

J. Dewane, 2007, 'Supervisor, beware: ethical dangers in supervision', *Social Work Today* 7.4, p. 34 – www.socialworktoday.com/archive/july-aug2007p34.shtml.

J. E. Falvey and C. R. Cohen, 2004, 'The buck stops here', *The Clinical Supervisor* 22.2, pp. 63–80.

G. Leonard and J. Beazley Richards, 2001, 'How supervisors can protect themselves from complaints and litigation', in M. Carroll and M. Tholstrup, *Integrative Approaches to Supervision*, London: Jessica Kingsley.

S. Page and V. Wosket, 2015, *Supervising the Counsellor and Psychotherapist: A Cyclical Model*, 3rd edn, Hove and New York: Routledge, pp. 156–74.

## Power in Supervision

C. Barstow, 2008, *Right Use of Power: The Heart of Ethics: A Resource for the Helping Professional*, Boulder, CO: Many Realms Publishing.

H. Dhillon-Stevens, 2001, 'Anti-oppressive practice in the supervisory relationship', in M. Carroll and M. Tholstrup, *Integrative Approaches to Supervision*, London: Jessica Kingsley.

A. Guggenbuhl-Craig, 1971, *Power in the Helping Professions*, Woodstock: Spring Publications.

E. Holloway, 1998, *Power in the Supervisory Relationship*, Keynote Address, British Association of Supervision Practice and Research Conference, London.

M. J. Murphy and D. W. Wright, 2005, 'Supervisees' perspectives of power use in supervision', *Journal of Marital and Family Therapy* 31.3, pp. 283–95.

S. Page and V. Wosket, 2015, *Supervising the Counsellor and Psychotherapist: A Cyclical Model*, 3rd edn, Hove and New York: Routledge, pp. 175–93.

N. Sims, 2008, 'Power and supervision in the context of the Church and its ministry', *Practical Theology* 1.2, pp. 203–17.

## Professional Identity

C. Clegg, 2011, 'Pastoral supervision: ministry, spirit and regulation', in L. Bondi, D. Carr, C. Clark and C. Clegg, *Towards Professional Wisdom: Practical Deliberation in the People Professions*, Farnham: Ashgate, pp. 219–31.

E. Kelly, 2012, *Personhood and Presence: Self as a Resource for Spiritual and Pastoral Care*, London: Continuum.

## The Self of the Supervisor

I. Renzenbrink, 2011, *Caregiver Stress and Staff Support in Illness, Dying and Bereavement*, Oxford: Oxford University Press.

T. M. Skovholt and M. H. Ronnestad, 1995, *The Evolving Professional Self*, Chichester: Wiley.

L. van Dernoot Lipsky, 2009, *Trauma Stewardship: An Everyday Guide to Caring for Self while Caring for Others*, San Francisco, Berrett-Koehler Publishers.

V. Wosket, 1999, *The Therapeutic Use of Self: Counselling Practice, Research, and Supervision*, London: Routledge.

## Values-based Practice

K. W. M. Fulford and K. Woodbridge, 2007, 'Values-based practice: help and healing within a shared theology of diversity', in M. E. Coyte, P. Gilbert and V. Nicholls (eds), *Spirituality, Values and Mental Health: Jewels for the Journey*, London: Jessica Kingsley.

S. Kahan, 2008, 'Creating value-based competition in health care', *Essays on Issues. The Federal Reserve Bank of Chicago*, September, No. 254a.

E. Kelly, 2013, 'Translating theological reflective practice into values based reflection: a report from Scotland', *Reflective Practice: Formation and Supervision in Ministry* 33, pp. 245–56.

P. M. Lencioni, 2002, 'Make your values mean something', *Harvard Business Review*, July, pp. 113–17.

J. M. Little, 2002, 'Humanistic medicine or values-based medicine. What's in a name?', *Medical Journal of Australia* 177.6, pp. 319–21.

M. Petrova, J. Dale and B. Fulford, 2006, 'Values-based practice in primary care: easing the tensions between individual values, ethical principles and best evidence', *British Journal of General Practice* 56, pp. 703–9.

M. Paterson and E. Kelly, 2013, 'Values-based reflective practice: a method developed in Scotland for spiritual care practitioners', *Practical Theology* 6.1, pp. 51–68.

J. Rose, 2002, *Sharing Spaces? Prayer and the Counselling Relationship*, London: Darton, Longman & Todd.

B. Thorne, 1998, 'Values and spirituality at work', *Counselling at Work* 21, pp. 3–4.

## Developmental Stages in Supervision

T. M. Bear and D. M. Kivlighan, 1994, 'Single subject examination of the process of supervision of beginning and advanced supervisees', *Professional Psychology: Research and Practice* 25.4, pp. 450–7.

J. Chagnon and R. K. Russell, 1995, 'Assessment of supervisee developmental level and supervision environment across supervisor experience', *Journal of Counseling and Development* 73.5, pp. 553–8.

# Index of Biblical Texts

# Index of Names

# Index of Subjects

abuse of children and
  vulnerable adults xv, 23
action methods 4, 49,
  146–56, 221, 260; Exercises
  5.3: 139, 6.2: 160, 6.3:
  161, 6.4: 162, 7.2:
  181, 7.4: 185, 9.4:
  240, 10.3: 257
accountability
 as purpose of pastoral
  supervision 1–2, 4, 7–8,
  24, 203, 205, 217, 234, 283;
  Exercise 1.1: 24
 of supervisee 7, 8, 92, 203–4,
  216–17, 233, 269–70
 of supervisor 199–200,
  201–2
 see also report writing
anger 15–16, 20, 69, 76, 98,
  99–103, 119, 128, 147,
  169–70, 219, 235, 247
anxiety, fear 43, 63, 93, 126,
  131–2, 201, 229–30
APSE: The (UK) Association
  of Pastoral Supervisors and
  Educators xiii, 5, 10, 19,
  200, 260, 269, 272, 283

art, use of in supervision
  148; Exercises 2.4: 59, 3.4:
  83, 4.4: 113, 7.4: 185
assessment, see report writing
  and roles of a supervisor,
  evaluator

beginning
 a supervision relationship 22,
  29–30, 197, 203, 228;
  Exercises 1.3: 26, 5.2: 137
 a supervision session 39–40,
  90
Bible, use of in pastoral
  supervision 14, 19, 45, 76,
  82, 112, 165, 174, 176,
  233, 224;     Exercises
  1.4, 7.1; see also Index of
  Biblical Texts
Bibliodrama 221, 260;
  Exercise 6.4: 162
body of Christ 1–2, 7, 9,
  17–18, 26, 145, 188–9,
  195, 199–200, 203, 217,
  219, 229, 234, 253
boundaries
 of ministry 22–3, 269

CPSIA information can be obtained
at www.ICGtesting.com
Printed in the USA
BVOW06s1748080118
504753BV00007B/74/P

9 780334 053446